Experiential learning

This book explores in detail the ways in which the assessment and accreditation of prior and current experiential learning (APEL) is being practised in higher education, further education, community and voluntary provision, training organisations and employment, in provision for the unemployed, youth training schemes, and for updating and retraining. In the context of the current debate on improving access and raising participation rates in all forms of post-secondary education it offers a way forward, showing that individuals can be encouraged and motivated to learn if they are enabled to develop a due sense of their own capacity to learn. Systematic assessment of prior and experiential learning can give credit for all the knowledge and skills that people have acquired through life, work experience and study which have not been formally attested through any educational or professional certification.

The book looks at the background to the introduction of APEL in Britain, showing how it has progressed over ten years into a day-to-day concern for policy-makers and providers of formal courses and training and development programmes in many sectors. Norman Evans also gives an insight into how APEL can be used alongside other economic and social developments to improve the organisation and provision of opportunities for learning at the post-secondary stage.

The book will be valuable to academic staff in higher and further education, in open college networks, in community and voluntary organisations, and staff in organisations, in both public and private sectors.

Norman Evans is Director of the Learning from Experience Trust, and has been working to promote the theory and practice of APEL in Britain since 1980. Throughout this time he has been a Regional Manager for the Council for Adult and Experiential Learning in the USA, visiting the country regularly with small groups of academics, policy-makers and employers on study tours of universities and colleges.

Experiential learning

Its assessment and accreditation

Norman Evans

London and New York

First published 1992
by Routledge
11 New Fetter Lane, London EC4P 4EE

Simultaneously published in the USA and Canada
by Routledge
a division of Routledge, Chapman and Hall, Inc.
29 West 35th Street, New York, NY 10001

© 1992 Norman Evans
Typeset by GilCoM Ltd, Mitcham, Surrey.
Printed and bound in Great Britain by Biddles Ltd,
Guildford and King's Lynn

British Library Cataloguing in Publication Data
Evans, Norman 1923–
Experiential learning: its assessment and accreditation.
1. Learning
I. Title
371.3I

ISBN 0–415–03823–5

Library of Congress Cataloging-in-Publication Data
Evans, Norman, 1923–
Experiential learning: assessment and accreditation / by Norman Evans.
Includes bibliographical references and index.
ISBN 0–415–03823–5
1. Non-formal education–Evaluation. 2. Experiential learning–Evaluation. 3. College credits–Outside work. 4. Degrees, Academic. I. Title.
LC45.3.E93 1991
378.1'68–dc20   91–2788 CIP

For the friends who licensed American explorations
and the early developers of APEL in Great Britain

Contents

Foreword   ix
List of abbreviations   xiii

Part I   **Beginnings: a personal story**

1   The American dimension   3
2   The British dimension   9
3   APEL in action begins   15
4   Reflections   46

Part II   **A decade of APEL**

5   Introduction   59
6   The assessment and accreditation of experiential learning   66
7   APEL and higher education   72
8   APEL and further education   103

Part III   **APEL in the future: a two-way street to opportunity**

9   Introduction   119
10   Some tensions   122
11   Post-industrial learning   143
12   Access: a two-way street   162
13   Restructuring, reorganising, redeploying   197
14   Endpiece   205
         Postscript   208
Appendix Study tour participants   213

Notes and references   220
Selected reading list   222
Index   225

Foreword

Experiential Learning: its assessment and accreditation is an attempt to combine strands of personal experience with an unfolding understanding of what the assessment and accreditation of experiential learning can mean for individuals, educational institutions, employers and, in the last resort, which perhaps should be the first, government policy, all based on experiential learning and its assessment.

It is offered as a contribution to the urgent debate about access and higher participation rates in all forms of post-secondary education, not to argue the principle which at long last is generally accepted, but to look for ways of turning rhetoric into action. As such it tries to tackle some of the issues which for deplorable, if understandable, reasons were not addressed in the Education Reform Act of 1988; how to encourage, motivate and entice into the business of learning, men and women, young, middle-aged and old from the 50 per cent of the population which at present rejects education beyond school. That is talking about a fundamental cultural shift in society. To make any headway towards it in the 1990s requires commitment from employers and government as well as educational institutions to work towards that end.

The general argument here is that one high road towards that cultural change is to provide opportunities for individuals to get a due sense of their own capacity to learn, especially for those who think they are hopeless as learners. In a word, to exploit the possibilities of experiential learning. Experiential learning here is taken to mean all the knowledge and skills people have acquired through life and work experience and study which have not been formally tested through any educational or professional certification. It follows that it can include instruction-based learning, provided by an institution which has not been examined in any of the public examination systems. It can include those undervalued elements of formally provided education which are not encompassed by current examinations.[1] Clearly it includes all informally acquired learning. There is of course nothing new in taking experiential learning seriously. What is relatively new is discussing ways of assessing it systematically.

The book is arranged in three parts. Part I is personal; an account of my involvement in the development of the overall field of the assessment of prior experiential learning (APEL) in Britain during the 1980s. Many people have urged me to to do this on the grounds that some attempt to plot the story could be of interest and that it should be set down before some of the details become overlaid with subsequent events. As I have tried to emphasise in the text, the work has given me a sense of personal and professional fulfilment beyond anything I had ever anticipated, none of which would have happened without a series of coincidental factors, most of which were not of my making. Those factors make it clear beyond peradventure that a similar story would have been written by someone else. APEL's time had arrived, irrespective of individuals.

Part II stands as an attempt to produce an account of the developments in APEL at the end of the decade. It makes no claim to be comprehensively inclusive. The speed of change and development in every aspect of education, vocational preparation and extended training makes it impossible to take a reliable snapshot picture which catches all action on the wing. Scores of institutions are busy with APEL in one way or another. This section is not the result of systematic research; it is not an academic study. That is for somebody else to do.

Part III is speculative, trying to use what has been learned experientially – on the job learning concerned with APEL – as a launching pad for ideas about future developments. It is here that the two-way street of opportunity seems a common and integrating theme.

Much of the stimulus for the interest in the assessment of experiential learning came from the American experience during the 1970s and onwards. There it was fuelled by an anxiety that by awarding academic credit for life experience, some institutions were endangering the integrity of higher institutions. Developments in this country have been helped by a critical appraisal of US practices leading to adaptations and trials rather than adoptions.

Formal personal acknowledgements in a book of this kind pose baffling problems. There are so many to make if names are named. Part I stands as a tribute to those many people mentioned there, one offered with deep gratitude. Part II could not have been written but for the scores of academic staff who collaborated in the projects. Moreover it is important to mention the great benefits I have had from accompanying those 100 people on study tours. They fed my professional development as well as their own.

But there is one set of formal acknowledgements which needs to be made and usually is not: that is to the Further Education Unit[2], the Council for National Academic Awards, the Training (Enterprise and Education Directorate (TEED)[3] and more recently the National Council for Vocational Qualifications and the awarding bodies, all as national institutions. American friends and colleagues often comment with surprise and some envy at the speed and extent of development in APEL in Britain. When Morris Keeton reflected on his fifteen years of promoting activities of APEL in the USA, he noted that despite the extensive applications of APEL, there is little or no sense that it has become mainstream activity within the system as a whole. There are many reasons for that, but pre-eminent among them is the lack of national institutions capable of exercising pervading influence. So it is that due recognition should be given to the present and former chief officers, senior staff and civil servants of our national bodies, for the way in which they have evolved key roles for their institutions to play in the development and practice of APEL as an attempt to provide a better service to the national community. Without them, their vision, their willingness to take risks, this APEL story would yet wait to be written.

List of abbreviations

APEL	Assessment of prior experiential learning
APL	Assessment of prior learning
BACS	Banks Automatic Crediting System
BTEC	Business and Technician Education Council
CAEL	Council for Adult and Experiential Learning
CATS	Credit Accumulation and Transfer Scheme
CCETSW	Central Council for Education and Training in Social Work
CMED	Council for Management Education and Development
CNAA	Council for National Academic Awards
CPCS	College of Public and Community Service
CPD	Continuing Personal Development
CPVE	Certificate of Pre-Vocational Education
CRE	Commission for Racial Equality
CUOP	Colleges and Universities Option Programme
DES	Department of Education and Science
ECCTIS	Educational Counselling, Credit Transfer and Information Service
EDAP	Employee Development and Assistance Programme
EEPTU	Electrical, Electronic and Plumbing Trades Union
FEU	Further Education Unit
GCSE	General Certificate of Secondary Education
HND	Higher National Diploma
ILEA	Inner London Education Authority
LET	The Learning from Experience Trust
MARIS	Materials and Resources Information Service
MBA	Master of Business Administration
MEC	Making Experience Count
MOCF	Manchester Open College Federation
MRCGP	Member of the Royal College of General Practitioners
NAFMED	National Forum for Management Education and Development
NCB	National Coal Board
NCVQ	National Council for Vocational Qualifications
NELP	North East London Polytechnic
NIACE	National Institute of Adult Continuing Education
NVQ	National Vocational Qualifications

PCFC	Polytechnics and Colleges Funding Council
PICKUP	Professional Industrial and Commercial Updating Programme
PSI	Policy Studies Institute
RIBA	Royal Institute of British Architects
TAP	Training Access Points
TEED	Training Enterprise and Education Directorate
TVEI	Technical and Vocational Education Initiative
UDACE	Unit for the Development of Adult Continuing Education
UGC	University Grants Committee
WEA	Workers' Educational Association
YTS	Youth Training Scheme

Part I

Beginnings: a personal story

1 The American dimension

It all began in 1977 – or so it seemed. On reflection it all began in 1948. That year as an ex-service new graduate at Cambridge, I attended a tutor's training course for the Workers' Educational Association and then began a regular part-time teaching stint in the WEA Eastern Region which lasted until 1956. Although no-one then talked about experiential learning, the methodology propounded by John Hampden Jackson, Tutor at the Board of Extra Mural Studies in Cambridge and Frank Jacques, District Secretary to the WEA's Eastern Region, was based on the self-evident truth that adults attending extra-mural or WEA classes brought with them knowledge, experience and insights which were different from and just as important as those of the visiting tutor whatever the discipline or topic. Again although no-one referred to things in psychological terms, the message was that adult education is based on respect of persons. Nor did they refer to a negotiated curriculum, which was clearly the way in which syllabuses were drawn up. That tutor's training course proved to be a profoundly significant beginning to a professional career, an induction into the liberal tradition of adult education and with it the affective aspects of what came to be called later experiential learning. But most certainly there was no thought of experiential learning and academic credit.

But in 1977 the explicit interest in experiential learning with direct connections with the notion of academic credit did begin. And it began with the American dimension. It can read like a chapter of accidents. Retrospectively it seems that the American dimension was an integrating tool for a whole series of interests, hopes and frustrations, and as it has turned out, satisfactions.

In April 1977 a tutor in the college where I was principal, was due to accompany a group of students on exchange with Keene State College, New Hampshire. He fell sick. This exchange programme had been running for several years and frequently Keene State College had pressed me to go. I had never been able to because of complicated and protracted negotiations concerning the future of the college in the post-James reorganisation period of teacher education. By April 1977 the reorganisation plans were secured and agreed; the tutor fell sick; I took his place.

So it was that waiting for a faculty member of Keene State College I noticed a series of buff coloured A4 size publications without any name on the spines. I took one or two off the shelf and idly thumbing the papers, realised that I was reading some of the results of a research project funded by the Carnegie Foundation, entitled 'The Cooperative Assessment of Experiential Learning". As the words and ideas fell into place, I understood that I was reading about ways in which adult learners could have their informally acquired knowledge and skills assessed and used for academic credit towards a baccalaureate degree. A little later that week I was in another American institution and discovered an external degree which was an individually negotiated learning programme based on the assessment of the prior experiential learning which the adult students brought with them.

All this happened at the same time as I was beginning to try to think out what I had let myself in for by agreeing to conduct what came to be known as 'The Preliminary Evaluation of the In-Service Bachelor of Education Degree' for serving teachers, a project funded by the Department of Education and Science (DES) which was due to start in October 1977 and went on until May 1980. The coincidence of reading these CAEL documents and my early musings about the research project on the in-service B.Ed. brought me up sharp. Throughout all the exhaustive and exhausting consultative meetings in the college with serving teachers to try to work out what was the best content for the in-service B.Ed. degree, and the negotiations with the University of Nottingham which validated it, and during all those validation meetings of in-service degree proposals from other institutions, at no time had I or anyone else thought to include provision in the degree regulations for giving academic recognition to the knowledge and skills which teachers have acquired through their professional experience.

That was a shattering realisation. As I thought about it whilst visiting other American universities during that month of April 1977, it began to dawn on me that there is an axiom for all post-experience courses, whether or not they lead to qualifications. It is that any post-experience course for experienced practitioners will be successful to the extent that it begins where practitioners actually are. The point of the axiom is that it is no good course designers making assumptions about where the experienced practitioners actually are at the beginning of any course, no matter how thorough and extensive have been their consultations beforehand with representative groups of experienced practitioners, and thinking they have arrived at a satisfactory course. At one leap this led me to realise that what the CAEL project on the assessment of experiential learning was about when applied to the in-service B.Ed. degree for experienced teachers was that the very first thing that ought to be happening at the beginning of any such course was an assessment of the experiential learning of the teachers enrolled on the course. The only way to know where they were as learners was to find out. Interest was fired. Now the shaming thing about this realisation was that during all the time I was doing the preliminary evaluation project it was clear that there was no possibility of any regulations either of the Council for National Academic Awards or of universities accommodating such a provision for the assessment of experiential learning. This frustration over the potential significance of the assessment of experiential learning for adult learners went spinning on in my mind as an idea which needed working out in practice somewhere somehow in Britain.

In part this firing of interest came from what happened to teacher education. One educational justification for creating a third group of institutions out of the reorganisation of teacher education following the James report (in 1972, on the education and training of teachers), was to extend the curriculum available to students beyond what was already on offer in universities and polytechnics. In other words there was little point in offering more of the same. It would be far better to try to offer something different. It was and is relatively easy to find young men and women who are completing their second year as undergraduates who think they have had enough of the courses they are currently following. Frequently they will complain that there is so much desk and book study of abstractions whatever the subject and not enough practical action. One way of providing a curriculum which would incorporate both theory and practice and meet that criticism would be to offer periods of fieldwork experience as learning opportunities so arranged as to result in assessable knowledge and skill within degree programmes but not necessarily related to a particular occupation.

The head of the teachers branch in the DES said it was an interesting idea. He rejected it out of hand, it was much too difficult a proposition to see developed. What I had suggested was that a pilot project or two along those lines could be a very valuable means of extending the overall offering of higher education. Instead he presented me with the in-service B.Ed. preliminary evaluation project, hence the continuing interest.

This interest in the assessment of experiential learning had been further fuelled by demography. In 1977 the figures were already demonstrating that in the 1980s and 1990s whether it liked it or not, higher education would have to be taking account of adult learners in a way which it hadn't been required to up to that date. During the month in the United States in 1977, quite by chance I happened to attend a conference which was addressed by Peter Smith, President of Vermont Community College. (Later he became deputy governor.) With almost evangelical fervour his theme was that because of demography and changes in the patterns of employment in a technological age, academic institutions had to come to terms with their need to provide adequate service for adult learners if they were not going to find themselves in acute recruitment difficulties. He used the analogy of the tide going out, saying that institutions would be left high and dry if they didn't look at the demographic tidal tables very carefully.

The curricular development idea for higher education seemed equally appropriate to a considerable proportion of the 18+ as well as some older learners. It appealed so strongly that I found ways and means of returning to the United States in 1978. Peter Smith suggested people I could call on. One of them was Dr John Strange, Founding Dean of the College of Public and Community Service in the University of Massachusetts at Boston. Sometime in July 1978 I found myself talking to Dr Strange, almost totally bemused by his description of the competence-based curriculum which was the basis for degrees being awarded to older learners through his institution. What I did understand was the significance of the assessment of prior experiential learning within his programme.

Months later on the same trail I presented myself again at the Dean's office and found myself facing a similar beard but a different face. This was the Acting Dean, John Strange having been seconded as the Vice-President of CAEL.[1] Clark Taylor surprised me by saying that John Strange had been trying to get in contact with me. I phoned him in Columbia, Maryland; we met the next morning in Boston when he returned. From that meeting the American dimension strengthened.

It strengthened the American dimension for particular reasons. There was a warm steady encouragement of friends who gave a home base for explorations, and John Strange's entrepreneurial spirit. As Vice-President of CAEL, John Strange's particular task was to develop a network of regional managers in the US. These regional managers were to be frontline developers of the theory and practice of APEL in an attempt to encourage universities and colleges to adopt it as part of their provision for adult learners. This work was being undertaken by CAEL under a W.K.Kellogg Foundation Institutional Development Program. As our Saturday morning conversation went on, eyes gleamed as we began to discuss the various possibilities of opening up a transatlantic strand to this regional manager notion, as a means of pursuing the possibilities for APEL development in Britain. I did not know it at the time but retrospectively it is clear that John Strange's entrepreneurial spirit was working overtime.

All that was in April 1979. As a first shot at the transatlantic connection, in the summer of 1979 he arranged an individual study tour for me taking in Peter Smith's institution, Vermont Community College, his own College of Community and Public Service, Delaware Community College, Thomas Edison State College, and La Guardia Community College in New York City. The object of the exercise was to enable me to examine the assessment procedures being used in each of these institutions so that I might come to some conclusions about the possibilities of developing procedures for APEL in Britain.

The next strengthening of the American dimension was that I was invited to lead a seminar for the New England Regional Meeting of CAEL in December 1979. My brief was to give a foreigner's view of the assessment procedures in institutions as I had observed them during the previous summer. It aroused some interest, the room was crowded. What I did not know was that sitting in the front row was Morris Keeton, the President of CAEL. As I realised subsequently, he had come to look me over.

In February 1980 I found myself summoned to a regional managers' meeting in Florida. It was being held in Florida because at that time of the year the climate is warmly inviting. In fact it was so cold that Morris Keeton put on more and more clothing. The air conditioning, for some reason best known to the hotel management, refused to take note of the temperature and insisted on treating us to summertime air conditioning. The point of this regional managers' meeting was to take the first steps towards putting APEL on to an interactive computer program, which subsequently emerged as 'Encore'. That meeting was attended by Dr Arlon Elser, who was the W.K.Kellogg Foundation Project Officer who had funded the institutional development project for CAEL. Morris Keeton invited Arlon Elser and me to a private dinner at which the possibilities of a transatlantic connection were explored. Arlon Elser was enthusiastic and invited me to prepare a grant proposal for submission through CAEL. All seemed to be going swimmingly.

Subsequently Morris Keeton gave me a grilling at Logan Airport, Boston with John Strange in attendance, really trying to work out whether the gleam in our respective eyes was just an excited enthusiasm, or whether it looked like a gleam green for action. Apparently he decided the latter.

Whilst all these stimulating possibilities about a Kellogg grant were emerging, there was the problem of finding an appropriate base in Britain for mounting exploratory stages for activities based on APEL for higher education. The Cambridge Institute of Education which was my base for the in-Service B.Ed. study would not do. One or two universities and polytechnics were interested. It seemed however that there were two compelling objections to being based in an existing educational institution. Either the institution would in effect be underwriting the general proposition about the desirability of developing the assessment of prior experiential learning, giving it in effect an institutional imprimatur. Or the notion of the assessment of prior experiential learning would take on the colour of the public reputation of the institution that provided the working base, and therefore serve general notice on the academic community of its provenance. Where then were other possibilities?

2 The British dimension

At this point in the story the British cast of actors appear: the Right Honourable Shirley Williams, the Secretary of State for Education and Science in the 1974–79 Labour Government; Sir Charles Carter, first Vice-Chancellor of the University of Lancaster 1963–79; and Dr Edwin Kerr, Chief Officer of the Council for National Academic Awards 1974–87.

I had noticed that Sir Charles Carter had taken early retirement and was Chairman of the Research Committee for the Policy Studies Institute (PSI). I had never met him. I had admired his writings about teacher education during the post-James Report period. People told me he was approachable, so with nothing to lose I made an appointment to see him. Simultaneously I telephoned Shirley Williams, who was at that time a senior fellow at PSI, and simply tried out the idea. Did she think that it made sense to attempt to introduce the ideas of the assessment of prior experiential learning to higher education? Yes, she did. Boosted with that response I found myself talking to Sir Charles Carter and F.C.R. Ruffitt who had recently joined PSI, having retired from being the Divisional Her Majesty's Inspector for the London Region. I put the case. They listened. Sir Charles was interested. The interview ended with him saying something to the effect, 'Well what are we going to do about it?'

What PSI did about it was to offer me a four-month appointment as a senior fellow during which time I would have to arrange for funding to enable the appointment to continue. That was all in April 1980.

By that time I was already in close contact with CAEL and the next move was to attempt to convince Dr Arlon Elser of the Kellogg Foundation that funding a project through CAEL for Britain made sense. To this end we set up a meeting in Washington to be attended by Sir Charles Carter, Morris Keeton, Pamela Tate, an editorial associate of CAEL and now its President, Dr Edwin Kerr and myself.

Edwin Kerr had taken a close interest in these possibilities when I had discussed them with him earlier in 1980. It so happened that at Easter time in 1980 both he and I attended the first International Meeting for Co-operative Education, in Boston. He agreed to travel to Washington after that meeting and that gave me the opportunity to take him to American University outside Washington as well as a meeting set up with Arlon Elser, Charles Carter, Morris Keeton and Pamela Tate. Our visit to American University produced a most remarkable result. Having had a thorough briefing on the APEL project there where we had learned how the portfolio preparation for the assessment of prior experiential learning was based on two taught classes for older learners, we found ourselves reading specimen portfolios. By good chance the portfolios that Edwin read included sections on computer studies. He was a computer studies man. Sitting on the grass afterwards in the sun, he said quite simply, 'This university is awarding academic credit in computer studies for years 1, 2, 3 and 4 on the basis of portfolios. If they can do it why can't we?'

At this point disaster struck. A strike at Heathrow Airport meant that Sir Charles Carter was unable to fly to Washington. As the Chairman of the Northern Ireland Economic Development Committee he had a meeting which he could not risk missing. Delayed flights would make that tricky. So at the round-table conversation with Arlon Elser a vital component was missing. Nevertheless it all resulted in a small grant being awarded to Morris Keeton as President of CAEL to enable me to undertake a twelve-month exploration as a first effort at developments in Britain.

This meant that from October 1980 until December 1981 I was able to spend half my time in the United States visiting scores of universities and colleges. The central purpose was to try to find assessment procedures which were sufficiently rigorous to suggest ways in which assessment procedures could be developed in Britain which would be consistent with the requirements of examining boards and external examiners. That proved difficult. Many American procedures were not sufficiently rigorous. The second half of the time was spent taking soundings in this country to work out where developments might fit in.

At this point it is important to say that the Americans divide the assessment of experiential learning into two categories. There is prior experiential learning, which means taking a dipstick reading of the uncertificated learning and skills that the men and women bring with them at the point when they are assessed. The Americans tended to call that unsponsored experiential learning. They used the phrase sponsored experiential learning to refer to the assessment of learning acquired experientially from fieldwork components of a degree programme. Unsponsored then because no institution had any control or influence over what was learned. Sponsored because the institution was responsible for providing those opportunities for learning.

It will be immediately obvious that sponsored learning translated across the Atlantic refers to the field-work components of sandwich courses. It is also obvious that it refers to the fieldwork and practical experience component of the curriculum development I had proposed to the DES for higher education in the third group of institutions which were being created. Sponsored programmes of experiential learning were generally referred to as co-operative education in the US, though in some cases internships got included. An internship is simply a period of work experience underwritten for the purposes of academic credit towards a baccalaureate degree. But the internships are not necessarily related to professional preparation. Co-operative education usually applies to the same range of degree programmes as applied to sandwich courses in Britain – engineering, business studies and the like. Now co-operative programmes had existed in the United States for a long time just as had sandwich courses in Britain. The assessment of prior learning in the US was a newcomer. There was a great debate about whether the principles on which the assessment of prior experiential learning were based, were the same as or different from the principles on which the assessment of experiential learning on sponsored programmes was conducted.

One of the most interesting features of the visits to American universities and colleges (during what turned out to be nearly an eighteen-month period) was the contrast between assessment of prior unsponsored and sponsored experiential learning. It became quite evident that the procedures for the assessment of prior experiential learning were generally speaking far more rigorous than the procedures for the assessment of sponsored experiential learning. There were exceptions of course. One or two examples of the assessment of sponsored experiential learning were and remain models of their kind. Indeed sandwich course designers have a great deal to learn from these degrees. But generally speaking the unsponsored experiential learning assessment was more rigorous, more consistent, more professionally conducted than the assessment of sponsored experiential learning. CAEL's first remit, to find valid and reliable ways of assessing experiential learning seemed to have been met.

Having discovered this interesting feature it became a staple topic of conversation as I went round these various institutions. Without the least expecting it I found myself operating more or less with half the function of a Her Majesty's Inspector in Britain; a kind of messenger boy with good news from one institution to another, with warning noises about bad news that one had heard, and perhaps most important a shoulder to lean on, a sympathetic handkerchief for tears, a safe listener to whom burdensome matters could be unburdened.

All of this suggested that there were two prongs for potential action in

Britain. One was the assessment of prior experiential learning which seemed relevant to the overall question of access to higher education. The other was to tackle the field-work component of sandwich courses. Both seemed worth trying.

The launch for the possibilities in Britain was an invitation meeting in May 1980 at PSI, chaired by Sir Charles Carter and addressed by Morris Keeton who came across especially, and Richard Hoggart, Warden of Goldsmiths' College of the University of London. One of the most persistent and perceptive questioners at that meeting was Janet Cockerell, Principal of Hillcroft College (a small residential college for women in Surbiton offering two-year non-graduate courses). Another was Dr George Tolley, still then Principal of Sheffield City Polytechnic.

While all this was going on I was learning fast about the ways and vagaries of foundations. Having been encouraged in that Florida meeting to think out a major proposal, all went cool. The twelve-month period to be covered by the President's grant gave time and space to negotiate the successful award of a major grant. Time passed. Letters went to and not often from. Telephone calls were made. Encouragement continued. No cheque arrived. Anxiety mounted. Not only for me but for PSI. At this point the cast of British actors lengthened. Jack Mansell, Chief Officer of the Further Education Unit joined in. George Tolley became an invisible encouraging cheer leader.

The follow-up to the launch was to identify two groups of supporters, one at senior institutional level and the other at the practitioner level of doing things with real live students. This seemed a sensible way of proceeding. It offered both strategy and tactics for dealing with what was anticipated as a major Kellogg grant for institutional development. In the event things did not work out like that at all. The senior institutional group never met. The members who had agreed to serve did not seem to mind. They were Charles Carter, Edwin Kerr, George Tolley, Janet Cockerell and Richard Hoggart. But the doers did meet and went on meeting. This group was a mixture of people I knew well who were likely to share this interest and those recommended. The doers group emerged as Colin Griffin, a lecturer in Hillcroft College (recommended by Janet Cockerell); Edwin Cox from Goldsmiths' College, who was subsequently replaced by Colin Titmus, Dean of Adult and Community Education there (recommended by Richard Hoggart); Malcolm Brewer, Principal Lecturer and Sandwich Placement Officer in Sheffield City Polytechnic, (recommended by George Tolley); Sinclair Goodlad from Imperial College whom I had known in conection with his peer tutoring work with undergraduates collaborating with teachers in schools; and Ned Binks, in charge of careers, (and formerly chaplain), at the College of Ripon and York St John which had attempted to pioneer the curriculum idea of fieldwork experience within degree programmes.

That group explored ideas but could not readily envisage action. That is all except Hillcroft. Now at that time Hillcroft College recruited older and not necessarily conventionally qualified women to a two-year full-time course, so it was not in the slightest interested in the assessment of prior experiential learning as a contribution to its policy for access. What Janet Cockerell and Colin Griffin spotted very quickly was that the assessment of prior learning could be used as a curriculum development tool. To this end they designed what was in effect a supplementary application form and invited all those who had been accepted for a place at Hillcroft for the coming September to complete it. This supplementary form had three parts. It invited the women students to describe the work experience they had had. It asked them to comment on what they had learned from that experience. And last, to make a guess as to how that learning from experience would compare in level with the anticipated learning at Hillcroft. So here was a piece of unanticipated action which proved to be of great significance to Hillcroft.

Things were more frustrating for the rest of the group. Malcolm Brewer could see no easy way of subjecting the field-work component of sandwich courses to any formal assessment of knowledge and skills acquired without first going through a systematic research exercise. Ned Binks had developed an interesting college requirement whereby all students had to do a six-week placement of practical work as a degree requirement, but the University of Leeds which validated degree courses for the College of Ripon and York St John would not countenance the assessment of learning from that fieldwork as contributing to the award of a degree. So it was that this was a college requirement but was not integral to the degree. Nevertheless we talked and did not give up.

These meetings went on fairly regularly during this first eighteen months at PSI. My own experience of visiting so many universities and colleges in the US gave me the idea that one of the best ways of instigating developments in this country was to attempt to provide enthusiasts with similar opportunities. After some persuasion the DES agreed to grant me £2,000 to send as many people as I could squeeze in for the money on study tours to the US. The first two were Colin Griffin and Ned Binks in Spring 1982. Subsequently Colin Titmus went from Goldsmiths' College, and Malcolm Brewer from Sheffield City Polytechnic.

The autumn of 1981 was a nerve-wracking period. No answer had come from the Kellogg Foundation. Morris Keeton had no means of supporting further activity. Without further funding the PSI arrangement would lapse. It began to look as if the initial exploration could well be the end of the story. Then a remarkable thing happened. I had written a book published by Grant McIntyre called *The Knowledge Revolution; Making the Link Between Learning and Work* and another one called *Education Beyond School*. At lunch Brian Groombridge, Professor of Adult Education in the University of London asked if I had seen a review of 'The Knowledge Revolution' in *Education* written by Jack Mansell. I had not. He said I ought to look at it.

3 APEL in action begins

PREPARING FOR ACTION

Back at PSI I looked it out, read it and found 'If you have not read Norman Evans' *The Knowledge Revolution* then perhaps you should.' I noted that Jack Mansell was suggesting that further education was more inflexible than higher education if one thought of the possibilities of introducing the assessment of prior experiential learning. There and then I picked up the phone, found him at the other end and asked in as many words if that was what he was saying, what was he proposing to do about it. Come and talk, he suggested. So I walked across Westminster Bridge from Castle Lane to Elizabeth House, spent two hours with him explaining that I needed funding for some project to buy time until the Kellogg grant was forthcoming because I was reasonably confident that in due course that would happen. He explained that there was a desk job to be done urgently to examine all the entry regulations to award-bearing courses, particularly in further education but including higher education to see what they said about the use of the assessment of experiential learning. So within two hours I was walking back across Westminster Bridge knowing that I was more or less secure at PSI for a further seven months for the project the result of which was eventually published as *A Curriculum Opportunity: a Map of Experiential Learning*.[1] Time was bought for the Kellogg Foundation to make up its mind. And, far more significant than I realised at the time, the foundations were being laid for developments in APEL in Britain.

This was hardly the kind of developmental work I had anticipated undertaking but it served its purpose admirably in putting in the ground floor for much of the subsequent development. And it looked after funding until the end of July 1982.

The publication of *Curriculum Opportunity* in May 1983 brought unexpected, unintended dividends. The education correspondent of *The Times* misread or misunderstood the press release issued by the Further Education Unit and wrote a piece which included the implication that universities did little to admit older students without the customary education qualifications. Whether for this reason or not, some dozen provincial newspapers ran the story, which was of course quite inaccurate in that particular but it served as admirable publicity. Not surprisingly there were protesting letters from some universities, including the Vice-Chancellor of the Open University and indeed the Joint Metriculation Examinations Board for the North of England. All of which produced a flurry of activity and correspondence, but it indicated that we had touched a sensitive area.

The next move came from the Council for National Academic Awards (CNAA). Edwin Kerr had established within the Council a Development Services Unit to act as an R&D support force for the Council's activities. The Registrar was Dr Rita Austin. Very quickly she latched on to the potential significance of the assessment of experiential learning and showed a strong interest in wanting to promote developments down each of the two strands which flowed from it; that is the assessment of prior experiential learning for access to higher education and the assessment of sponsored experiential learning in relation to sandwich courses. For the first I was commissioned to undertake a piece of work on a part-time basis for twelve months which was published by CNAA as Development Service Publication Number 6: *Access to Higher Education: Non-Standard Entry to CNAA First Degree and DipHE Courses*, in August 1984.[2] This took the funding through until February 1983.

For the second we tried hard to interest some companies in tackling the assessment of learning from fieldwork experience, not only as a contribution to degree results but as a means of strengthening the curriculum as a practical exponent of the theory and practice rationale which underlay the provision of sandwich courses. It was too early to make headway with this second strand, fieldwork components of sandwich courses to produce assessable knowledge and skill which could become countable towards degree results. In 1981 employers were not yet generally attuned to the potential significance of on-the-job learning. Universities and polytechnics offering sandwich courses were in the throes of trying to win the argument with the DES that sandwich courses were worth funding.

Rita Austin had done a research project on the sandwich courses, the most significant issue of which was this. Asked the question 'Which in your view is the best timing for fieldwork experience, at the beginning, during or at the end of the academic course?', over half the tutors responding said in effect that it did not make any difference as far as they were concerned. At one stroke the theory and practice argument on which much of sandwich course education depended was demolished.

The long and short of the matter was that there was no reliable and attested educational justification for sandwich courses as a four-year degree programme compared with the standard provision of three years. What Rita Austin and I were after was a project which would demonstrate that the acquisition of assessable knowledge and skill from fieldwork experience was significant academically and to use that as an educational rationale for sandwich course provision. At the back of our minds too there was the strong possibility that if we could demonstrate that this was indeed the case, then it could be used as a curriculum development tool for looking again at the way theory and practice were combined in sandwich courses – in other words what was contributed from the academic provision within a university or polytechnic and what was contributed from the fieldwork experience – then it was not inconceivable that a four-year sandwich course might without detriment become a three or three-and-a-half-year sandwich course. Implicit in that thinking was the second possibility, that of improving the course. A more satisfactory combination of theory and practice and perhaps within that a strengthening of the contribution from the employer side of the sandwich course partnership, could mean that the argument with DES over funding would be stronger, and that in the employers' eyes the courses themselves would produce graduates who were more employable. But in 1981 all the actors in the sandwich course arena had their eyes on other things and so that one had to wait. Indeed it had to wait until 1986 when I managed to broker a project in Sheffield City Polytechnic funded by the then Manpower Services Commission (now TEED).

But the work for CNAA on non-standard entry to degrees and diplomas bought more time for negotiations with the W.K.Kellogg Foundation to continue. At that point however it became obvious that to combine the study tour facilities being sought from the Kellogg Foundation for British academics, institutional leaders and policy makers with some pilot projects on the assessment of prior learning in polytechnics could be a powerful instrument for development. Accordingly the Development Services Unit of CNAA and the Kellogg Foundation were both approached along those lines and in due course both funding agencies responded, after protracted negotiations. Internal reorganisations of CNAA slowed things up. Internal reorganisation in the W.K.Kellogg Foundation slowed things up even further.

In the background there was another factor at work. Peter Toyne, when Senior Lecturer at the University of Exeter, had undertaken the feasibility study for what eventually emerged as the Educational Counselling and Credit Transfer Information Service (ECCTIS). At Richard Hoggart's suggestion (while I was still at the Cambridge Institute of Education) he came and had a long session on the possible connections between the assessment of prior experiential learning and a computerised system of educational counselling and credit transfer. What neither he nor I knew or could know at that point, was the number of occasions on which our paths would intersect over the years in advancing our respective interests as they then were. But at different points of this story, Peter Toyne appears as a key actor.

ACTION BEGINS – FIRST STEPS

Meantime two other pieces of development work were funded. In 1982 the Wates Foundation awarded a small grant to run for two years to enable the first formally provided courses in the assessment of prior experiential learning to be launched, under the title of 'Making Experience Count' (MEC). And the Commission for Racial Equality agreed a two-year project under the title of 'Transitions: a study of possible access to further study' to run for two years from April 1983.

If Jack Mansell got the cement mixer to work on the foundations through curriculum opportunity, the Wates Foundation supplied materials for the first above-ground construction. Norbert Singer, Director of Thames Polytechnic and Richard Hoggart, Warden of Goldsmiths' College were enthusiastic about launching an experimental course. Through Colin Titmus, Dean of Community and Adult Education at Goldsmiths' college and Pamela Linn and Tony Hendry, Joint Heads of Continuing Education at Thames Polytechnic, we set about designing 'Making Experience Count'. It began as a combined exercise and from 1983 onwards it became two separate projects in the two institutions.

The Wates Foundation thus enabled us to take the first steps in Britain to do something with real live people about the assessment of prior experiential learning. There was a modest amount of money made available to each of the two institutions to help cover additional advertising costs and some additional staffing. The two institutions were keen, but what were we actually going to do? Who would the course be for? And how would we recruit it? This immediately posed the double problem of the content and conduct of the course itself and its underlying rationale. It was clear that the 'curriculum' for the course was going to be the accumulated knowledge and skill which the students brought with them. All that we had learned about the portfolio-assisted assessment of experiential learning from the Americans suggested that systematic reflection on that experience was the predominant methodology. It emerged quickly that there would need to be a set of triggers to get the course participants beginning to reflect on their experience. So themes such as childhood, organising family photographs, which were then complemented by suggested reading, were the initial list of starting points.

But however enthusiastic we might become about starting points for intended students or thinking about the assessment of their prior experiential learning in relation to access to higher education courses, the second and probably larger question remained. How were we going to persuade interested applicants that the course itself was worth undertaking? Faced with something new and experimental how were participants going to be made to feel that they were not mere guinea pigs going through certain motions, perhaps even tricks for other people's entertainment? In other words what were the possible benefits in prospect for any men and women who enrolled on the course?

We decided that there were six possible exit routes for those who completed MEC. To begin with we reckoned that it would be perfectly acceptable for people to complete the course, or indeed withdraw during the course in the quite clear conviction that they had had enough of formal education and there was nothing further for them in the notion of further study. Next it seemed possible that MEC might help people to get jobs. So employment was a second exit route. Then it seemed reasonable to suppose that some course participants might well conclude that further study was indeed appropriate for them but they simply were not ready to engage in preparatory courses for higher education. Something like a pre-preparatory course might make sense for any in this category. Next we saw that the courses offered under the general provision of access or preparatory courses at polytechnics might be appropriate for some. We thought it highly likely that some would be able to demonstrate through their prior experiential learning that they were quite capable of coping with degree courses and so for any in this category it was access to higher education which could be on offer. There were two other possibilities.

One was that the experience of MEC could lead to people wishing to undertake courses of further education and training offered by the Business and Technician Education Council or such as the National Nursery Examination Board. And we thought that there was a remote possibility that some might demonstrate that the knowledge and skills they had acquired without any formal certification could merit admission with advanced standing to degree courses.

It is difficult to overestimate the significance of MEC, because it worked. Apart from the last possibility of gaining academic credit towards a degree, MEC students have used all the other exit routes. And at that time it was particularly important to be demonstrating that people who thought they never had a chance of a degree in one September were actually on a degree course the next September.3 Beginning in 1982 it became part of the standard provision for adult learners in both institutions. As such it has provided a reference point for many other tutors in higher and further education who were interested in the portfolio assisted approach to the assessment of prior experiential learning, so that in some ways MEC became a working laboratory.

It had enormous significance for the Inner London Education Authority (ILEA). Early on in my time at PSI I had had long conversations with Alun R. Davies, Chief Inspector for Higher and Further Education in the Authority. Like me he had been principal of a college of education, in his case Bretton Hall and when I met him at County Hall and I talked generally about what I was trying to do with the assessment of experiential learning, he very quickly spotted the possible connection with further education. In 1982 he was seeing the large-scale changes on the horizon for further education and reckoned that introducing the assessment of prior experiential learning as mainstream provision could be an important influence for curriculum change, institutional change and indeed the professional attitude of staff. So when I told him about MEC he was more than interested.

Round about the time when I was negotiating with the Wates Foundation for the funding of MEC I found myself at a small meeting concerned with accreditation organised under the aegis of the Open College of the South Bank. This was in the very earliest stages of that attempted Open College, so just as I was new to the assessment of experiential learning, that small group was new to the implications of accreditation. Richard Gorringe happened to be at that meeting. And as I tried to give my account of where APEL could fit into accreditation he began as a persistent questioner and ended up as an enthusiast wanting to know more. The significance of this was that during the years 1982–4 Richard Gorringe was seconded from his senior lectureship at Brixton College to the Higher and Further Curriculum Development Unit of ILEA. So when he heard about MEC he saw it as an opportunity to learn about the business at first hand. I agreed that he could join the joint team with Alun Davies' approval. What I did not know until later was that an important part of Davies' remit to Richard Gorringe was to do whatever he could to develop APEL in ILEA further education colleges.

Something else that neither Richard Gorringe nor I could know, was that in January 1985 he was to be appointed as Staff Development Officer for Further Education in the Avon Education Authority. In true style there he set about propounding the virtues and value of APEL for further education, drummed up sources of funding for some special projects, found willing allies and got to work. This produced a series of initiatives within the Avon Authority. Most important perhaps was a Further Education Unit project 'Skills Assessment and Vocational Guidance for Unemployed People'. Working with Jenny Cronin and Anne Woodrow as Project Development Officer, this enabled Richard Gorringe to produce a series of working documents, the most important of which was a guideline document for use in the assessment of prior learning with unemployed people.[4] In effect at remote control the work begun as MEC, through the sponsorship of the Wates Foundation, got carried through ILEA down the M4 to Bristol and the Avon Authority.

So what the Wates Foundation was funding was a small-scale project which produced a steady ripple effect in both higher and further education. The one regret I have about it is that MEC was founded solely on the notion of portfolio-assisted assessment. I regret it because it was responsible for spreading the notion that necessarily the assessment of prior experiential learning was going to be a long-winded and expensive business. It was the point of departure for developments in Britain because at that time it was the strongest message coming from the United States, and until we got to work with real live students and staff here, there was no possibility of working out approaches which were more appropriate to students and institutions in Britain. But with that caveat *Making Experience Count* and *Curriculum Opportunity* were two important markers in this story. Each was more effective than I had even dared to hope.

I had the same high hopes for the Commission for Racial Equality (CRE) Project. They were not met. Reorganisation difficulties in further education colleges meant that of the five participants arranged with Alun R. Davies, the Central London Adult Education Institute (City Lit), Hammersmith College, Morley College, Hackney College and Vauxhall College, only Hackney and Vauxhall delivered. The second difficulty was a continual change of staff in the CRE of those officers who were connected with the project. This led to an unfortunate attempt to move the goal posts. Whilst it was entirely understandable, and indeed desirable that some CRE staff wanted to move from the terms of the project contract itself as reflected in the title 'Transitions: a study of possible access to further study for ethnic minorities', to wanting to collect evidence of discriminatory attitudes on the part of staff and institutions, there was a certain frustration for me as project director in insisting on sticking to the terms of the project and resisting attempts to add components to it which had not been negotiated either with ILEA or with institutions in the first place. This was more than unfortunate. The double problem meant that the total amount of evidence was nowhere near as substantial as I had hoped for and that it turned out to be not exactly what the CRE was wanting. Nevertheless this was a valuable piece of work for the institutions and, I trust, the CRE. It did deliver significant evidence of the way in which APEL can be of considerable service to members of the ethnic minorities.

On the way the FEU commissioned another piece of work. This was to produce a pamphlet for employers. It was to suggest how APEL related to retraining and updating. This was done between March and September 1983 and was published under the title of *Exploiting Experience*. Jack Mansell I learned was a hard financial task master but along with

Curriculum Opportunity even as two relatively short changed financially funded projects they proved of considerable significance. Altogether 20,000 copies of *Curriculum Opportunity* have been printed and 10,000 of *Exploiting Experience.*[5]

Meantime, Peter Toyne made his first appearance. Before he became Deputy Rector of the North East London Polytechnic (NELP), his Rector Gerry Fowler had involved me in the planning of a conference to be held in West Point, New York State on community colleges and community education. He had assembled a team of his own governors, some LEA staff, the Principals of both East Ham and West Ham Further Education Colleges with a view to showing them what a Community College could do as a means of stimulating action in his own area of East London. As a result of that conference he asked me to chair a series of meetings sponsored by NELP, to see how something along the lines of the assessment of prior experiential learning could be mounted as a way of enhancing the collaboration between the further education colleges and the polytechnic.

It was from these meetings that, under the leadership of Eric Williams, Principal of West Ham College of Further Education, a course was set up run by Paul Edwards[6], to help people joining the further education college with little or no formal educational qualifications to enrol in NELP's School for Independent Studies leading to a diploma of higher education or a degree. Two-thirds of the way through these consultative meetings, Peter Toyne appeared. Here was his first first-hand experience of the possibilities of APEL at work.

It so happened that by this time he was serving on the Steering Committee of the Development Services Unit in CNAA and was a determined supporter of the idea of carrying forward the work from the Non-Standard Entry Project into a scheme of pilot projects in polytechnics, doing it for real with real live men and women. In other words, he was both supportive and enthusiastically encouraging of what emerged as the CNAA pilot project programme. It is also worth noting that with Norbert Singer, Director of Thames Polytechnic he was in the first study tour under the aegis of the W.K.Kellogg Foundation.

That may be his first appearance on the cast of actors, but not of the thinkers. As mentioned already between 1978 and 1980 Peter Toyne did the feasibility study on what emerged finally as the Education Counselling and Credit Transfer Information Service (ECCTIS). When we met in the Cambridge Institute of Education, we dreamed dreams of ECCTIS, somehow managing to incorporate interactive computer programs to help people identify their experiential learning, something which is yet to happen. But it was from that meeting that a close working collaboration began.

ACTION – THE NEXT STEPS

Jack Mansell featured again and substantially. The number of initiatives in the assessment of experiential learning increased steadily but slowly. So he agreed to fund a further project to run from May 1984 until October 1985 to prepare a guideline document of the assessment of prior learning for lecturers in higher and further education based on reports by tutors of their own work with students from Goldsmiths' College, Hackney College, Heriot-Watt University, Hillcroft College, Middlesex Polytechnic, Sheffield City Polytechnic, Thames Polytechnic and Vauxhall College. This project produced the two publications *Assessing Experiential Learning* and *Case Studies*, both published by the Further Education Unit in 1987.[7] The idea here was to put together a set of working documents each describing what tutors had actually done with students in their attempts to develop schemes of prior learning assessment. As such it represented the first composite account of what was happening at that stage in higher education and further education. It landed me with a teasing task of extracting these pieces from those who had agreed to contribute them and then a delicate editorial task in shaping them for general release.

In the event Heriot-Watt's contribution was published separately by the Further Education Unit under the title of *Continuing Professional Development: A Learner-Centred Strategy*.[8]

The origin of that piece of work is in itself significant in this general story of a series of incidents which could on the one hand be seen as accidental and chancy, yet on another give evidence of how the assessment of experiential learning was an idea whose time was coming. Through Richard Bourne, who was then Deputy Editor of *New Society* and had written an encouraging review of *The Knowledge Revolution*, I was put in contact with Vernon Smith who was then Director of the Scottish Institute of Adult Education. In the spring of 1983 I was invited to lead a seminar sponsored by that Institute and the Scottish Vocational Educational Council on the assessment of prior experiential learning. Professor John Cowan of Heriot-Watt University attended, and asked a sharp question or two. He was at the point of worrying how to improve his post-experience course for qualified civil engineers and the assessment of prior experiential learning caught him where it mattered. The account he gives in *Continuing Professional Development: A Learner-Centred Strategy*, shows clearly how at Heriot-Watt he installed the assessment of experiential learning as the fulcrum for his post-experience course.

So it was that MEC featured in its two versions from Goldsmiths' College and Thames Polytechnic. So did the courses which Richard Gorringe had been influential in encouraging at Hackney and Vauxhall Colleges. Hillcroft featured for reasons already given. But the two highly significant additions were the accounts from Middlesex and Sheffield City Polytechnics.

Middlesex Polytechnic had for some time been offering credit in respect of previous experience and learning to older students who enrolled on their Diploma of Higher Education and Combined Studies degree. I had lighted on this during the work for *Curriculum Opportunity* and the CNAA study of the provision for unqualified entrants to CNAA first degree and Dip.H.E. courses. Anthony Turner, the Admissions Tutor, was an enthusiastic supporter of the general thrust of the assessment of prior experiential learning and so his account gave details of the first instance of academic credit towards an award being granted in this country on the explicit basis of the assessment of prior experiential learning.

Sheffield City Polytechnic was entirely different. It was the first attempt to work with an employer. Early on when casting around for support and possible openings I had discussed possibilities with Sir Peter Parker, then Chairman of British Rail. He asked for a one-page statement which he then circulated to all his fellow chairmen of nationalised boards as they then were. Derek Ezra (now Lord Ezra), Chairman of the National Coal Board (NCB), responded. Through him I found myself talking to Edgar Willie, NCB's Head of Management Development and Roy Harrison, Director of Education and Training. I was more than surprised and not a little gratified to notice when I went for my appointment at Hobart House, NCB's headquarters that *The Knowledge Revolution* and *Education Beyond School* were on Edgar Willie's desk. What is more he had read them. More important he approved of them. Indeed subsequently he chided me for being too diffident in the *Knowledge Revolution*. But this meant that there was an affinity of interests. The problem was how to mount a piece of work which did not cost anybody anything. This was in 1982. It was all a long time gestating, but eventually Edgar Willie and I conceived the idea of conducting a prior learning assessment project based on systematic reflection on experience for two groups of NCB middle managers. One group was to be based at Hobart House and the other in Doncaster. The London group foundered but the Doncaster group flourished, nurtured by John Buckle, Principal Lecturer in Law and Public Sector Administration. And it is an account of this work which is given in the Sheffield contribution to *Assessing Experiential Learning*. Again as with Middlesex I had lighted on Sheffield as a possible participant as a result of the work for *Curriculum Opportunity* and the CNAA project on non-standard entry. Just as Middlesex demonstrated that academic credit could be awarded towards a degree on the basis of the assessment of experiential learning, so the Sheffield City Polytechnic work with the

NCB in Doncaster demonstrated that APEL for employees held great possibilities. That Sheffield/NCB project ran over 1984 and 1985. And it was all done for love. Certainly the NCB contributed in kind through making company time available for some of the working sessions. Sheffield City Polytechnic contributed its tutors' time which was considerable but again no money changed hands.

ENGAGING HIGHER EDUCATION

By this time both the Kellogg Foundation and CNAA had delivered. Under the general title of Scholar Exchange Program, Kellogg provided funding for ten academic staff from Britain on study tours to see at first hand how some American institutions dealt with prior learning assessment. This was approved before CNAA had approved the project, the results of which were eventually published under the title *The Assessment of Prior Experiential Learning* in February 1988.[8] The CNAA project was 'to negotiate, establish, monitor and appraise not fewer than twelve schemes, in not fewer than six institutions for the assessment of prior experiential learning in polytechnics and colleges'. The courses selected were to cover as many main study areas as possible, including the Dip.H.E., and disposed so as to give a reasonable geographical sample within England. Each scheme was to develop procedures which would enable individual men and women who were technically unqualified to produce evidence of their uncertificated learning. The idea was that such evidence would enable admission tutors to decide whether or not to admit those individuals to the degree for which they had applied, and for both unqualified and qualified candidates, whether or not to grant admission with advanced standing. The aim throughout was to stimulate action, sustain it, describe it, try to identify what appeared to be the most effective approaches to the assessment of prior experiential learning, identify significant problems and produce a report to assist academic staff to develop schemes which fitted their own circumstances and their own institution.

The Kellogg funding was approved to begin in 1983. The CNAA project was for a two-thirds full-time working assignment to last two years, seven months, from April 1985 until November 1987. The problem was how to exploit the possibilities offered by the Scholar Exchange Program for the work envisaged in the CNAA project. I had a short list of possible participating institutions based on the work from *Curriculum Opportunity* and CNAA's non-standard entry project.

These were Newcastle upon Tyne Polytechnic where Gerald Dearden was then Assistant Director responsible for recurrent education, Bristol Polytechnic where I had found business studies an interesting possibility, the Polytechnic of North London, where Ray Hall, Co-ordinator for the Evening Degree had been an enthusiastic attender of meetings at PSI, Sheffield City Polytechnic, Middlesex Polytechnic, Thames Polytechnic and the North East London Polytechnic. In each of these institutions I had noted one or two individuals who seemed to me potentially interested in mounting a pilot project in the assessment of experiential learning in relation to their own discipline or department. Furthermore I knew the directors of these half-dozen polytechnics well enough to be sure that there was a steady backing in prospect for any project should we get as far as having it funded.

It was against this background that I gambled. Nearly a year before CNAA's Development Services Unit actually approved the pilot project I had begun to take people on study tours to American universities on the assumption that in time the project would indeed be funded. However, it is one thing to have a scheme in one's head. It is quite another to see how to put it into action. And it is another thing still to operate it successfully. On the whole this scheme worked pretty well. The gamble came off. I was able to demonstrate convincingly to the Kellogg Foundation that the money they had granted was put to excellent use in terms of institutional development. The CNAA project and the participating institutions correspondingly had the benefit of the opportunities offered by study tours to America. But there had to be a clear framework within which to use the study tour programme. There is something faintly glamorous about offering a short study tour to United States institutions. There needed to be crystal clear criteria. Participation would be by invitation only. No invitation was to be issued unless I was satisfied that the director or principal was fully supportive. And by that I meant having an understanding in general as to what the assessment of prior experiential learning was all about and then having some inkling of the longer-term implications for the institution should a pilot project prove successful. Wherever possible two study tour participants should go from any one institution, but on different study tours. This was on the standard grounds for any curriculum development that two people need to be able to support one another. Then there were three criteria against which individuals were matched. Study tour participants would be either those who were concerned with public policy or those who were institutional leaders, and clearly there was an almost inevitable over-lap between those two, or people who were actually working with real live students. In that way the invitations more or less sorted themselves out.

Once the study tour programme got going and I had the reactions of the first two or three groups of participants it dawned on me that one way of making the Kellogg money go further and increasing the number of study tour participants was to vary the amount used from the Kellogg money for any one individual according to an institution's capacity to pay. In other words, if I went to identify a member of staff who seemed well able to take a lead in the CNAA pilot project in a particular institution then the invitation was clear and if necessary the entire bill for the study tour would be met out of Kellogg funds. But if it was possible for an institution to make a contribution then I asked for it. To begin with the asking rate was £400, being about 50 per cent of the total, but that varied according to the exchange rate. When the Kellogg funding was originally negotiated the exchange rate was US $2.2 to the pound. Since then the variations in the exchange rate have meant on the one hand the value of the Kellogg funding has gone up but then the value of the British contributions has gone down – swings and roundabouts. It is an amusing thought that one unrecognised, unsolicited, gratuitous result of the 1980 years was to provide more money for the development of APEL in Britain than the dollar figures suggested.

The Scholar Exchange Program was not limited to higher education. Given the thrust Alun Davies had produced in ILEA there were a number of leading figures emerging in that authority. The first move was to include Richard Gorringe (through the support from the Sainsbury's Trusts) in an Institute of Adult Growth and Development organised by the Council for the Advancement of Experiential Learning (as it then was) in Washington DC, in the summer of 1983 amongst a group of five. Two, Pamela Linn and Tony Hendry went from Thames Polytechnic. And Ginnie Eley went from the North East London Polytechnic, so that was a fairly powerful quartet. Judith Hinman from Hackney College followed Richard Gorringe on secondment to the FHE Curriculum Development Unit, and she joined a study tour a little later.

Employers were a different matter. The sponsored learning idea was still alive in relation to sandwich courses. There were beginnings of significant developments of collaboration between employers and higher education in the USA under the general title of 'Joint Ventures'. CAEL had pioneered the Ford Motor Company/United Automobile Workers' College and University Options Program for blue-collar workers. It seemed possible that enlisting the support of employers might help stimulate comparable developments in Britain. One obvious approach was to include one or two employers in the study tour programme. Perhaps it was too early. Employers perhaps were not ready. Perhaps it was because of growing government interest in the private industrial councils and compacts which were developing in some urban areas and which have since become enshrined in White Papers and government policy. Perhaps more simply it was because I could not use Kellogg funds to subsidise employers. But the study tour idea for employers failed, save in one instance.

Martin Findlay, Vice-Chairman of Whitbread's, got interested. It was not quite what we expected. A Company Concorde flight one day for him, followed the next with feet in pools of water at the back of a battered Volkswagen Beetle, did not seem to worry him. He set aside two days of a US trip and we went to the Business and Training Development Center in Great Valley, the Scott Paper Company and Atlantic Richfield in Philadephia. In both the first two cases, CAEL was working with companies on a variation of human resource development. Atlantic Richfield was working in close collaboration with the Philadelphia Urban Center Program of the Great Lakes Colleges Association, offering internships to students on a four-day-a-week at work, one-days-a-week college seminars basis. What I wanted were answers from American employers to questions from a British employer around the general issue of why do you do it and what is in it for you? All the time I was listening for clues to approaches to British employers which might recommend APEL to them for their own employees and interest them in a different approach to sandwich courses. For companies, the difference quickly emerged in the needs of mature companies and young ones, and the effect of demography on each, lessons which are now being learned the hard way in Great Britain. Sure enough now, British employers are taking note of APEL as their American counterparts began to take serious note some five years ago. As for the internship/sandwich course and sponsored learning idea, that is the most recent initiative to have been followed up as a result of another study tour.

Later, Keith Davies, Youth Programmes Manager for IBM and Jeanette Anderson, Deputy Principal of Napier Polytechnic, were on the same study tour and listened to an explanation of the Philadelphia Center's Urban Center Program. Each was impressed from their differing perspectives. Both determined to undertake a small piece of development work. By bedtime that day, the three of us had worked out a draft proposal, as a result of which in January 1989 a Scottish Education Department funded project north of the border was being run cooperatively between Napier and IBM. This scheme formed a small part of a larger development funded by the TEED for developing work-based learning assessments within degree programmes. So all that took a long time to emerge.

However, no immediate action followed Martin Findlay's visit to advance APEL in employment. It prompted sharper thinking about what might be subsequent developments in APEL in relation to employment. One emerges in the later reference to learning contracts for employees. So, as with so many of the incidents in this story, the unanticipated is as important, if not more so, as the anticipated result of any effort.

THE RIPPLE EFFECT BEGINS

By the end of 1990 some hundred or so men and women from British institutions had been on these study tours.[10] The arrangement for each was more or less the same. During a seven-day period some seven or eight American community colleges, liberal arts colleges and universities were visited to talk about the various ways in which the assessment of prior experiential learning was being used. This first-hand information buttressed with sundry documents was part of the material in America for each study tour. To save time and money all of these institutions were strung out along the East coast between Boston and Washington, but between them they offered a rich variety of possibilities. But the raw material each study tour took with them was different. Take four or five people with a broad common interest in the assessment of prior experiential learning, each bringing with them different ranges of experience, of institutional setting and perceptions. Enable them all to have the same range of experiences together. Sit back and listen to the conversations which take place amongst the group over meals, or while travelling. Log the particular occasions when some American example seemed to turn on electric connections. Do a little gentle prodding about what might be done back home. And sure enough from each and every study tour some significant development takes place in terms of what an institution decides to do, and how it decides to do it for its own home constituency of students.

At the end of every study tour I asked the participants to send in a brief statement arranged in three sections: What did I learn; what might be relevant for short-term developments; and what might be relevant for long-term developments. Naturally some people did this rather better than others and some of course, not at all. Some got incorporated in large-scale official internal documents, others did what they were asked. A model answer was as follows:

I learned the following:

1 New insights into the way in which an open learning centre should be run including its incorporation into traditional courses.

2 That American institutions may not be any further forward that those in the UK concerning the use of management ratios to judge efficiency or effectiveness.

3 That there may be a number of opportunities for a college to develop outposts on trading estates or business parks providing the right contacts could be made with the developer.

4 That properly structured and incorporated work experience can have benefits well beyond those that I previously considered possible.

5 That a number of employers in the USA have been persuaded of the value of providing 'extra-mural' training opportunities for their employees both as a means of enhancing skills and as a means of raising their own esteem in the eyes of their workers. This may in turn favourably affect their staff turnover.

6 That despite the obvious progress made in the assessment of prior experience and learning, gatekeepers still exist and can have quite a debilitating effect on those trying to advance the course of APEL.

Proposed action in the short term:

1 Discuss with colleagues the very great impression that the Open Learning Centre at Bunker Hill made on me. I now have a clearer vision of what I expect for our own centre. At the time of writing these discussions have already taken place and I think we could have a centre operating in a very similar way to Bunker Hill by Christmas.

2 I shall organise a scrutiny of our trading estate developments with a view to floating some of the ideas we saw at Paoli.

Proposed action in the long term:

1 I hope to encourage more staff to develop open learning opportunities as part of their normal course structure.

2 I intend to open discussions, albeit tentatively, with some local employers to draw their attention to the experience of the Bell Telephone Company in developing education and training opportunities for its adult work force.

3 I propose to introduce a review of work experience procedures so that we can more clearly relate the experience to other parts of the curriculum and assess learning outcomes more objectively.

In effect each of these study tours was a staff development programme. As such it is highly suggestive of effective ways of spending money. Spending downwards of £1,000 to go for seven days to the United States seems a rather fancy way of spending money on professional development. The results demonstrate its effectiveness.

Here is a personal statement from one of the participants.

It must not go unstated that I have learnt, or more accurately, revisited through experience, the value of excellent organisation, appropriate briefing and careful selection of venues and purpose; at the same time it is important for me to say something about 'group learning' – four people from various backgrounds all sharing a common interest in

APEL, competency etc. do their own individual learning but also they can collectively learn so much as a result of being complementary to each other in function and able to discuss the visit during the period of being together.

THE RIPPLES EXTEND

Meantime there had been another interesting development. Something called the 'Experiential Learning Network' emerged. This arose because Rockland Community College from New York State had asked for help in promoting a service learning programme in Britain. The idea was to place American students through community service volunteers in what the Americans call human service agencies, but arrange their volunteer work on a learning contract which would earn the American students academic credit towards their degrees in their parent institutions in the United States. This meant recruiting a group of British tutors in the London area who would take on the supervision of these American students on their learning contracts. To set all this up Thomas Clark who was then Vice-President of Rockland Community College came across and ran a three-day training programme for about a dozen British lecturers I had invited as potential helpers on the programme and this proved one of the most effective in-service programmes I have ever had anything to do with. The result of this was that there was a group of a dozen or so people in the London area who were well and truly enthused not only with the assessment of experiential learning and the general curriculum idea underlying learning contracts, but were eager to go on meeting and talking about these things as a matter of their own professional interests and development. So it was that this nucleus began to organise meetings which I arranged in and through PSI. As the study tour activity began to bite, so other people began to join in. The news spread, and two or three times a year there would be meetings to consider various aspects of the assessment of experiential learning, attended by people mainly from London but also from many other parts of the country.

One of the most interesting things to emerge from these meetings were the different perceptions of APEL from staff in adult, further and higher education. Further education naturally tended to concentrate on access courses and part of their preoccupation was the difficulty as they saw it of getting higher education to accept the assessment of prior learning as an adequate alternative to formal educational qualifications. Higher education on the other hand saw no such difficulty, but was continually grappling with the question as to why older students should go through the whole portfolio preparation procedure when entry for mature students without formal educational qualifications was a standard practice in their institutions.

Adult education took a different line. And in part it stemmed from the affective strand to experiential learning which was part of my induction into the WEA. They tended to say that taking account of learning from experience was routine in their teaching, which of course it ought to be, and they were dubious if not downright suspicious of the idea of gaining formal recognition for learning from experience. The argument was that APEL means people laying their lives on the line, and that if they did not go on to get to the academic credit they sought, there could be an even greater sense of failure than failing in an examination. In effect failure at APEL would send the message, 'My life is a failure, I'm a failure'.

This was a serious objection but there was and is a solid answer. Seeking academic credit whether through formal examinations or through APEL always and necessarily poses the possibility of failure. So the fact that the learning to be assessed originated in somebody's life and working experience made no difference in principle to the question of failure. Much more important, what the question raised however, was the relationship between the reflection on life and work experience and statements of learning arising from it, together with evidence to support it.

These discussions were extremely important because they posed fair and square the issue of sustaining the integrity of the person whilst opening new opportunities to that person for the accreditation of the knowledge and skill acquired. But behind these discussions lay another factor. Traditionally adult education has not been concerned with academic credit. It has been much more concerned with study for study's sake, in the sense that it was all voluntary, that it covered a full range of studies, of attainments from basic literacy programmes through to higher education levels. That got mixed up with lecturers' and teachers' concerns in further and higher education about academic standard and credit producing all kinds of institutional questions, even fears. The funding arrangements for adult education were at risk. Adult educators feared that their cherished view of adult education might become submerged in further education, a prospect which many of them detested. So APEL became a cauldron of discussion for all sorts of anxieties and professional concerns of staff drawn from many institutions which had nothing to do with APEL for students.

Nevertheless the problem posed potentially by APEL for the integrity of individual students was shared by many in further and higher education as well as those in adult education. This was particularly true for lecturers working with classes for women returners such as Fresh Starts, Returning to Learning, New Opportunities for Women. Here the issues were posed in sharp and specific terms. Frequently it was the case that of the experiences from which women had learned most were intensely private, essentially personal. Experiences of being a single-parent household, of divorce, of abortion, were quite obviously occasions on which a great deal might have been learned. It would be outrageous, so went the argument, if those private experiences had to become public in order for learning to be recognised officially. Again this was a fundamental issue. There was a fundamental answer. The academic recognition of learning is concerned solely with the learning and the evidence to support a claim to have it. In those terms the experience is irrelevant. So the answer to a tutor worried about the risks of dragging personal experiences into a public arena was clear. There was no necessity or obligation for any student to reveal the experience from which any learning was derived. That is a personal decision for the student concerned. Assessment is solely concerned with learning and evidence of it. So if it turned out that in order to identify the learning which had come from an experience, there was a discussion between student and tutor, that was no different from the many conversations that go on between older students and tutors before, during and after classes up and down the country.

These discussions then all arose in the meetings of the Experiential Learning Network, and enormously valuable they were too. Given the expanding mailing list and the oscillating pattern of attendance from people in many parts of the country, they served as a useful dissemination forum.

There was no formal membership of the Experiential Learning Network. There was merely a mailing list which was compiled in PSI. That list contained, quite simply, everyone who expressed interest in the general ideas of the assessment of experiential learning and served as one small sort of dissemination system.

As the projects developed, so the numbers increased and so the mailing list lengthened. The Experiential Learning Network lapsed as local initiatives developed. By 1990 the Learning From Experience Trust's mailing list was some 450.

MOVING TOWARDS THE LEARNING FROM EXPERIENCE TRUST

The discussions in these Experiential Learning Network meetings turned regularly to the possibility of trying to create in Great Britain some organisation, broadly speaking analogous to the Council for the Advancement of Experiential Learning (CAEL) in the United States. CAEL was a development agency offering staff development training. It published the results of its own research and development work. It held national and regional meetings. Under a good deal of prompting from Richard Gorringe we arranged a first one-day workshop on the assessment of experiential learning for staff in higher and further education in July 1984. The expenses from this were borne by the Further Education Unit. Following the very successful training workshop given by Tom Clark (Vice-President of Rockland Community College), it was obvious that to include an experienced practitioner from the United States in workshops or seminars or conferences was not only valuable but a great attraction. So, as the study tour programme got going, and the number of senior figures in American institutions began to take notice of what was going on in Britain, the practice gently emerged of a number of senior figures from American institutions saying when they were going to be in London and offering to run seminars. This all served to fuel the interest of the growing band of British practitioners and incidentally fed the appetites of the Experiential Learning Network.

This one-day conference in July 1984 was followed by a four-day conference in July 1985. But by this time TEED was taking an interest and so developments were given an additional impetus. Here was another intriguing twist to the story.

It must have been through George Tolley that Derek Grover, a young assistant secretary in TEED came to one of the early meetings of the Experiential Learning Network. This put him on the mailing list. After the next mailing a different person turned up from TEED. He is now in charge of the Business Communications Branch. This put two TEED officers on the mailing list. In October or November 1984 a general information sheet sent out on the mailing list included a general question as to the amount of support that might be forthcoming for a more substantial summer conference in 1985. At about the same time I had written to Derek Grover suggesting that he might find it valuable to join in one of the study tours to the United States. Much to my surprise therefore I had a phone call sometime in that autumn from yet another TEED official called Jim Wiltshire. In quirky, unpredictable ways he had come across this circular letter sent out to the Experiential Learning Network and had picked up the reference to the possible summer conference. He declared an interest in it and asked if we could meet to discuss this mutual interest.

Late afternoon Jim Wiltshire and I had a cup of tea together in the Great Northern Hotel near Kings Cross when he not only declared an interest but offered sponsorship. That had never occurred to me. Provided we could work out a programme which was acceptable both to TEED and to the original idea behind the summer conference for the Experiential Learning Network, TEED would meet the bill. It subsequently turned out that the publication of TEED's *New Training Initiative* which Jim Wiltshire had had a hand in drafting meant he was looking at opportunities to convene groups who were prepared to think about the issues of progression and accumulation in further and higher education.

In July 1985 a four-day conference was held at PSI, which by that time had moved from Castle Lane to Park Village East behind Euston Station. It was divided so that the first two days were for practitioners and the second two days were for policy makers. Following the successful injection of American experience for the July 1984 conference part of the MSC sponsorship was to enable me to bring over four Americans as participants and contributors: Tom Clarke, Vice-President of Rockland Community College; William Craft, the Dean of Development, Bunker Hill Community College, Boston; John Strange, Founding Dean of the College of Public and Community Service, University of Massachusetts at Boston; Susan Simosko substituting for Pamela Tate, now President of CAEL. What was particularly interesting was that after the four-day conference, at TEED's request, we held a long seminar with the visiting Americans for what was the top team of six in TEED on the adult training side. The demand for a British CAEL became more insistent.

But this was only the beginning of TEED's involvement with the rising tide of development in the assessment of prior experiential learning. Jim Wiltshire also became involved. This meant that the net of knowledgeable, interested and committed people was widening, at policy level. Beginning with higher education, moving into further education, now TEED was the first government policy-making agency to be actively involved.

But Jim Wiltshire was more important than that. His interest led to the eventual funding of a manuals scheme which was to run from November 1985 to April 1987. This was an extension of the work developed by Sheffield with the National Coal Board and was piggy-backing on the CNAA project in both Sheffield City and Birmingham Polytechnics. The scheme was to prepare manuals for further assistance in the assessment of experiential learning in both business studies and mechanical engineering, as far as possible based on performance statements applying to both the workplace and academic courses and in the case of the business studies manual, to run a trial project for use in in-company staff appraisal procedures. In the event this meant Sheffield City Polytechnic working with the South Yorkshire Division of British Telecom.

While all this was going on, there were negotiations for two further projects with TEED, a second application had been submitted to the Wates Foundation and through CAEL and Morris Keeton an extension to the Scholar Exchange Program was requested. And those negotiations were conducted in the context of two sets of consultations. One in the Council for National Academic Awards (CNAA) led to the establishment of the Credit Accumulation and Transfer Scheme (CATS) and the other was the discussions which led to the establishment of the Learning From Experience Trust. But before giving an account of those matters there is a second strand of strategy to lay out for the development of the assessment of experiential learning in national terms.

It has already been made clear the way in which the CNAA project was stimulated and advanced by relating it deliberately to the Kellogg Foundation's Scholar Exchange Program. The only way of conducting that project itself was to rely heavily on the voluntary additional work undertaken by members of staff in the participating institutions. The Scholar Exchange Program enabled them to have some sort of thank you and reward for their initiatives, but behind that there was a broad strategic intention. It simply was that through putting so much work and responsibility on tutors in the institutions the first line of dissemination about the assessment of prior experiential learning in higher education was secured. In other words instead of having a central team that did all the work, the pattern was support, advice and encouragement from the centre but the work put out where it could best be done. The nature of PSI as a research institution made this imperative. The funding from CNAA at that time could not include any contribution towards staff time taken in institutions. So in a sense this pattern of working was imposed by circumstances, but it coincided with what seemed the best strategy for development available. And it is a pattern of working which has been adhered to, used consistently in all projects which have involved work with students. Once the desk studies, *Curriculum Opportunity* and *Non-Standard Entry* were completed, it was development work which was the central requirement. And development only makes sense if it is undertaken by people who are committed. They need to own it.

This lesson was drummed home from the American experience. There despite the very extensive practice of the assessment of prior experiential learning there is a standing risk that it remains peripheral to the work of an institution rather than central. This is because so often APEL work is undertaken by continuing education departments and therefore tends to be separated from the mainstream academic work of full-time faculty members. Since the mainstreaming of APEL was the target in Britain that lesson was well learned.

APEL AS A NATIONAL SERVICE

Credit accumulation and transfer was most certainly not a new idea in 1983 for those who had thought about continuing education in relation to higher education. Anyone with experience of higher education in the United States knew it as a working system. Ray Ricketts, Director of Middlesex Polytechnic was one such. He is an important figure in these developments which in some ways were a culmination of his efforts in the various institutions he served from the mid-60s onwards to promote the CATS idea. Richard Hoggart's final report for the Advisory Council for Adult and Continuing Education in 1982 had urged its case. But nothing had been done to translate an idea into day-to-day practice. So the moves towards establishing a Credit Accumulation Scheme are worth recording and it is impossible to overestimate the national significance of its press launch in March 1986. Edwin Kerr the Chief Officer of CNAA is its unsung hero. Sometime in 1983 he convened a residential seminar to consider the future of CNAA awards. There was much discussion about credit accumulation but largely in terms of credit accumulation within individual institutions. Cross-institution credit accumulation featured, but not prominently. Sometime after that Norbert Singer addressed a meeting in the Polytechnic of North London convened to consider the proliferation of part-time degree schemes in the London area. The discussion at that meeting concentrated largely on the need for an additional information service for the benefit of the London population. Probably it was from that meeting that the South East England Association of Colleges eventually emerged. Talking to Norbert Singer at the end of that meeting I urged on him the case for a cross-institutional credit accumulation arrangement. We agreed that CNAA was the only body which could take the initiative in such a matter. At that time we both were sitting on the Academic Policy Committee of CNAA and Norbert was on the Council. So we agreed that I would draft a letter to the Chief Officer setting out a proposal and asking him to take the initiative. I took the draft letter to Edwin Kerr to check whether it was the kind of proposal that he would be able to accept. It was more or less in line with his vision of the future, and no doubt others were putting similar ideas to him. We cleared the draft. It then went under the signatures of Ray Ricketts, also a member of CNAA's Academic Policy Committee and Council, and Norbert Singer from Thames Polytechnic and myself. From that point onwards Edwin took on the task of getting the proposal approved in principle by CNAA, and setting up a consultative group to work out a scheme in detail. Those consultations went on for eighteen months and included the Master of Birkbeck College, University of London, the London Regional Director of the Open University and a representative group from polytechnics.

They were not easy consultations. With every good reason polytechnics were anxious about the establishment of any scheme which looked as if it would in effect rob them of potential students. At length the case was argued that this was not so and along the following lines: that the scheme would be a service to individuals not institutions; that the information guidance and counselling facilities in the institutions would be fully used; and that in any case the proposal would be for a pilot scheme for the

London area only to test the underlying assumption which was threefold: that there were a number of potential adult students who would best be served by being able to take their courses from more than one institution in composing an academic programme; that there was a considerable number of potential academic students who for one reason or another were either not able or not interested in the institutions' existing academic programmes, and that with an increasingly mobile population there could well be increasing numbers of students, part-time and full-time, who needed to take their credit with them. At the CNAA Council meeting in July 1984 the scheme was approved together with a budget to develop what would be an additional registry in the Council itself.

The assessment of experiential learning featured prominently in the scheme. Academic credit based on APEL was to be available at both bachelor's and master's degree levels. In a few sentences therefore a national seal of approval had been given to APEL. Incidentally also at one leap we jumped right over the Americans in including APEL at master's level. This was and is a facility available nationally, which is only rarely available to Americans through their own institutions. There are two other national documents which lay in the background; other influences were at work. In the summer of 1984 both the University Grants Committee and the National Advisory Board for Local Government Higher Education published papers approved by working parties on continuing education. Each referred to the need for institutions to develop procedures for dealing with the assessment of experiential learning and urged that this was a vital component in improving the services for adult learners. So APEL in the Credit Accumulation and Transfer Scheme was a natural development, but there was then a pause in opening the CAT Scheme. CNAA offices were chronically overcrowded and there was literally nowhere to put the CATS Registry. So it was not until November 1985 that a Registrar for CATS was appointed. Edwin Kerr had chaired the National Advisory Board Working Party and had sat on the UGC Working Party. That early experience in American University, Washington DC was working its way through into the main stream of British higher education.

Throughout the discussions leading to the establishment of CATS Edwin Kerr assumed personal responsibility for steering things to a satisfactory conclusion. And at a very difficult time in the development of CNAA itself this was a visionary at work in his own quiet perceptive way. The establishment of CATS means no more and no less than a powerful instrument for changing the face of higher education in Britain. Its significance goes beyond that. For it opens the way to forms of collaboration between the world of work and the world of formal learning which are not only new but potent. The assessment of prior learning at both bachelor's and master's level implied that the in-house provision of companies became eligible for academic credit. So did the on-the-job learning of employees. During the first four years of CATS activities, both these facilities have come into full operation and both have been helped through development projects negotiated at first under the aegis of PSI and then from The Learning From Experience Trust.

THE LEARNING FROM EXPERIENCE TRUST

The establishment of the Trust was the realisation of a long-standing idea. As has already been mentioned, early on in the discussions of the Experiential Learning Network the demand had been made consistently for the establishment of some body in Britain broadly speaking analogous to CAEL. The case was urged most powerfully during the two-day summer conference in July 1985, spurred no doubt by the presence of American contributors. And negotiations for further projects made the idea seem feasible.

Very early on at PSI I raised the question with John Pinder the Director, directly. What would be his reaction I asked, to the establishment of some small public body under the wing of PSI. He welcomed the possibility. Changes in PSI and the slow pace of early developments meant that the idea was not pursued. But in the autumn of 1985 Sir Charles Carter reckoned the time had come to do something. Frequently we had talked about these possibilities but somehow the time and opportunity had not seemed right. Now it was.

There was the question of preparing all the papers for submission to the Charity Commission for the establishment of a new educational charity. Then there was the matter of financial backing and last there was the question of premises. On the first Patrick Coldstream, now Director for the Council for Industry and Higher Education, and Stephen O'Brien the Chief Executive of Business in the Community were able to help. Trying to draft a paper which gave an accurate and convincing account as to the reasons for establishing a new educational charity with a clear statement of its purposes was a piece of experiential learning for me. Edwin Kerr again featured as a principal actor. There was a consultative meeting or two with Sir Charles Carter, Edwin Kerr, Stephen O'Brien, Patrick Coldstream and myself. And eventually we got things to the point where it was possible to ask David Bosanquet, a long-standing solicitor friend from Kent well experienced in these matters, to undertake to steer the matter through at the Charity Commission. Sir Richard O'Brien, then chairman of PSI; Shirley Williams; Stephen O'Brien, Chief Executive of Business in the Community; Frank Whiteley, Deputy Chairman of ICI; Edwin Kerr and Andrew Rutherford the Warden for Goldsmiths' College agreed to become Trustees and so the paper side of the work was completed. At the first meeting of the prospective trustees for the new body we settled on the title of The Learning From Experience Trust. Interestingly enough at that point in 1985/6 to use the phrase experiential learning was risky. Now it is in common use but early on there was something rather alarmingly offputting about the word 'experiential'. For many people and particularly for employers it indicated a rather groupy, touchy, feely notion and as such was disconcerting. However, now it is all different; experiential learning has come into the language.

As for money there were three ways of looking at it. First, PSI saw no objection for those funded projects which were incomplete being transferred to a new body. Second, those projects which were currently under negotiation could easily be switched to the new body as the financially responsible agent. Third, there was the problem of finding a start-up of the funding since to pay for premises and some full-time administrative/secretarial help would obviously incur greater expenditure than paying for the same range of facilities through PSI itself. Here the Joseph Rowntree Memorial Trust was encouraging and supportive. An application for £180,000 over two years was rejected but in its place an initial offer of £70,000 for the first year with possibility of returning for a further £70,000 in the second year proved our salvation. As for premises, through the good offices of Shirley Williams, who at that point was a governor of Regent's College, an American-initiated replacement for what had been Bedford College of the University of London in Regent's Park, we secured some half-basement rooms as the working premises for the Learning From Experience Trust.

In the summer of 1986 I moved out of PSI and into The Learning From Experience Trust as its director. It was a somewhat ominous move. After we had loaded all the files into the lift on the top floor of PSI in Park Village East the lift broke down midway between floors 3 and 2. The only way then of transferring the files was to hand them up from midway between floor 2 to floor 3 and carry them down. A somewhat exhausting business but at least it braced us for opening a shop in different premises, which we did on 1 September 1986.

We needed an Administrator. Michèle Bailleux's arrival at the Trust has been one more chapter in the story of happy coincidences. I first met Michèle in 1980 at PSI. She was there as Personal Assistant to Shirley Williams, having moved with her from the House of Commons in 1979. At that time I was looking for possible APEL customers and by chance learned that Michèle might well become one. She moved on from PSI in 1981 and I heard nothing about her until in the spring of 1986 I gathered from Shirley Williams that she was looking for another job. A phone call, a quick quiz about salary, a pub lunch when I endeavoured to explain what the Learning From Experience Trust was intending to do, and that was that. No letter went in either direction. No formal arrangement was made. But it was all settled and on 1 September we both began.

The basic premise for the Trust which must inform all its activities was and is:

'Most people know more than they think they know if only they knew that they know it.'

That phrase appeared in the Trust's first brochure which set out its overall position as follows:

The Learning From Experience Trust (LET) is an education charity established to develop ways in which people can make maximum use of their knowledge and skills, however they acquired them. It seeks to develop procedures for identifying and evaluating learning which has not been formally examined and to encourage their use in higher and further education, training, industry, commerce and the public service.

Learning can be privately planned, sometimes incidental, even accidental. It does not all have to come through schools and colleges.

Learning can come from employment, leisure, private reading, television and radio, DIY, friends and other experiences in life.

Learning can take place in formal education settings or in employers' education and training schemes but this intentional learning may not be certificated or result in formal qualifications.

All this is **Prior Learning**, describing the accumulated knowledge and skills a person carries with them.

The Assessment of Prior Learning (APL) can be as reliable as the assessment of formal certificated learning acquired through classrooms and lectures.

The Trust's business is to enable individuals, companies and educational institutions to make best use of learning from experience to become better learners, better employees, better employers.

Most people know more than they think they know if only they knew that they know it.

LET seeks to encourage the development of learning programmes which combine theory and practice.

Learning is most effective when the learner is in direct contact with what is being learned.

LET seeks to encourage the development of reliable procedures for assessing learning derived from practical experience as part of a course.

Recognition of Learning Achievement is the purpose of the identification and assessment of prior learning.

Systematic Reflection on experience is the basis for identifying prior learning and can lead to:
A general learning autobiography through portfolio-assisted assessment
Sharply focused accounts of learning in a specific field
Self-assessment and education, career and life planning
Greater employability
Career development

Progression in further study and occupational development can be assisted by the assessment of learning acquired from experience.

A Portfolio is a folder of evidence of a student's learning that has taken place either inside or outside of educational institutions designed to show the skills, qualities and knowledge that students have acquired appropriate to study or work.

There were two beliefs behind the idea of establishing the Learning From Experience Trust. The first was that its justification would lie in undertaking development work in the borders between the world of employment, life and leisure and formal education. Schools did not come into the thinking nor at the outset did youth training. Essentially at the beginning the focus was on older learners and ways of improving services available to them beginning in that border zone. So through being concerned by definition primarily with older learners, the assessment of prior experiential learning led inevitably to related issues critical for older learners, concerning the curriculum, pedagogy, methodology, means of delivery, and ultimately institutional change and by extension improvement of the systems of further and higher education.

The second belief was that the Trust might be a useful catalyst for those developments, always seeking ways of getting them incorporated in mainstream work and activity. APEL could be an influence for organisational and institutional change. Concentration on individuals might result in affecting systems. Promoting interesting, even exciting developments at the margin was of no interest. And a clear implication of that position was that the success of the Trust might lead to its own redundancy. At the point where sources of funding for development projects dried up, it could well be that the job was done. As time has gone by the possible areas for application of APEL have expanded year by year. So how far that view of the Trust's life will prove realistic is yet to be determined.

Alongside the Trust, Capability Assessment was registered as a limited company. The idea was that as development projects led to proven and usable techniques they could be offered through Capability Assessment on a fee-for-service basis, the income of which would be covenanted to LET to support further developmental work. So far CA has remained dormant. Again time will tell whether its activation is desirable let alone possible.

The Learning From Experience Trust began its work as an independent body. The Credit Accumulation and Transfer Scheme was operational. A combination of these two developments meant that the general promotion of the assessment of prior experiential learning in Great Britain got an additional impetus.

In the meantime negotiations on the next wave of projects continued. The Kellogg Foundation extended the Scholar Exchange Program for a further three years taking it up to 1988. The Wates Foundation had agreed to fund the development work with employers over three years which in the event took up 1986, 1987, 1988. And the Manpower Services Commission approved two further projects. One was a small three-month scheme in relation to the Youth Training Scheme (YTS) which ran between February and April in 1987. This project used tape recorders in portfolio preparation as a record of achievement to enhance basic skills in under-privileged trainees. It is written up in a separate publication of the Trust.[11]

The other was a more substantial exercise which was only possible because of the establishment of CATS. This was 'Learning Contracts for Employees'.[12] It was to run from November 1986 until October 1988. This idea was to use a period of full-time paid employment as the basis for negotiating a learning contract to be assessed at first-degree level and registered with the Credit Accumulation and Transfer Registry at CNAA. Along with the CNAA project, Learning Contracts for Employees has proved an equally sharp development. Just as the former produced solid evidence not only of the credit worthiness of the assessment of prior experiential learning both for admission to first degree courses and for credit towards them, so Learning Contracts for Employees has demonstrated that men and women in full-time employment have earned academic credit towards both bachelor's and master's degrees without realising it, and can capitalise on that learning for formal qualification purposes. This means that there is a body of evidence which can be referred to both for higher education and for employers as to the validity and reliability of the assessment of prior experiential learning for academic purposes.

Another MSC-funded project then emerged suddenly. One of the interesting consequences of the establishment of CATS was a degree of interest declared by employers. Quickly many saw the possibilities offered in terms of establishing an academic credit rating for some of their in-house courses. CATS simply did not have the staff to cope with these enquiries, let alone do any development work based on them. So it was that The Learning From Experience Trust was funded by the MSC for a relatively quick-fire operation for a project on the *validation of companies' in-house courses* to run from December 1986 until March 1987.

Following the strategy outlined already this work could only be done by putting it out. A call to Norbert Singer revealed that Professor Brian Currell at Thames Polytechnic had just been appointed as Head of Continuing Education. He was a scientist, was able to pull together a team of colleagues to undertake this work and became the Trust's agent for completing this project. This resulted in recommendations for academic credit being made at bachelor's or master's level for:

- Brewers Society
- British Telecom International
- Glaxo
- IBM
- Independent Broadcasting Authority
- International Computers Ltd
- Jaguar Cars Ltd
- Training Agency (Manpower Services Commission)
- J. Sainsbury plc
- Woolwich Equitable Building Society

By this time the volume of work was more than a one-man job even with the support of staff from many institutions of higher education. Gerald Dearden, who by that time had retired from Newcastle Polytechnic, joined as Deputy Director and undertook to manage the Learning Contracts for Employees project. That was in January 1987. By agreement with the Warden of Goldsmiths' College, John Storan, who had been a staff member there throughout Making Experience Count became a Professional Associate of the Trust on a shared appointment with the College. He undertook the small YTS project and was at hand to undertake a further MSC project with YTS supervisors. This project was approved to run from January 1988 until March 1989. Jeffrey Braham joined the Trust in May 1988 to manage a Joseph Rowntree Memorial Trust project: 'YTS Into Higher Education'. Then Linda Butler joined the Trust in September 1988 with the task of developing programmes for women and employment and exploring the possible harnessing of information technology to APEL. She also worked her way in on the first stage of the FEU project 'APEL in the Context of Student Services'.

The first initiative concerned specifically with opportunities for women was funded by the National Council for Vocational Qualifications (NCVQ) as a small exploratory project into the possibilities of appraising for National Vocational Qualifications (NVQ) competences acquired in the domestic workplace[13]. This opened up a whole range of issues connected with opportunities for education and occupations for women which are being explored in further projects elsewhere. Later Michèle Bailleux became a Deputy Director to run a project on 'Senior Secretaries into Management' and to look after publications and dissemination. Meantime, the *Validation of Companies', In-house Provision stage 2* began with Gerald Dearden as manager. John Buckle began to manage a CNAA-funded extension to the APEL project to explore possibilities for mathematics and science in higher education. Stage 2 of the FEU project began in November 1989 managed by Corinne Henebery who had been associated with the work from PSI times in Castle Lane. And four other TEED projects of considerable significance began as well. At last Universities enter the APEL arena with a two-year project broadly analogous to the CNAA one, working to the title 'To explore the potential of APEL in Universities'. A British version of the American Joint Ventures Program appeared as the Employee Development and Assistance Programme (Ford UK) and the Trust was commissioned by TEED to do some work under the title 'Opportunities for Further Education and Higher Education arising from the EDAP (Ford UK) Programme'. The third was based learning for Academic Credit in non-sandwich course degrees. And perhaps of greatest importance of all, because of its implications for employment attempts to produce support materials for the Staff Development Line Managers and supervisors.

So after twelve years of various stalkings, cornerings and trying to net experiential learning, this is where the personal story has got to. Three years at the Cambridge Institute of Education, incubating. Six years at the Policy Studies Institute hatching and watching to see if there was sufficient food for survival. Five years at the Learning From Experience Trust trying to promote the full cycle of incubating, hatching and nurturing. Some sort of stocktaking seems appropriate before moving into Part 2 which is more of a factual account of the various stages of action referred to already, and which also can serve as a trailer for some of the issues which are explored speculatively in Part 3.

4 Reflections

All the time that personal story was being lived there were developments of national significance. It was as if script and stage set kept changing while the play was acted. Those national developments provide the context for the next section, but before turning to that there are a series of reflections on some of the issues which have arisen as APEL practice has expanded, which can form a bridge between a personal story and what follows. It is an attempt to stand back and draw out some of the lessons which have been learned.

The first group of reflections begins with convergence. Considering the relatively sharp difference of interest shown by higher education, further education and adult education in 1981, there is a sense in which by 1989/90 their interests in APEL are converging. To begin with, higher education saw APEL in terms of access, only of marginal interest because entry regulations meant, in effect, that higher education could admit who it wanted. Interest quickened at the prospect of APEL facilitating admission with advanced standing. And the introduction of Credit Accumulation and Transfer Schemes has increased the impact. Further education's initial interest was in access, first to higher education then to its own courses, and then in relation to work with the unemployed. Later The National Council for Vocational Qualifications transformed everything for further education. Adult education's interest, to begin with, was somewhat disdainful, distant, sceptical and sometimes hostile. But now, through links with open college federations, it is becoming a significant factor. Each of these three shifts in different sectors of education has been stimulated in part by those two watchwords: progression and accumulation.

The shift in the thinking and understanding of employers is sharper. Instead of the standard line in 1981 'I am not interested in qualifications; I just want to know if they can do the job', now it is more like 'Yes, interesting. I can see that says something about recruitment and retention.' The connection with youth training is obvious. The 16+ young men and women who do not go on to higher or further education will only stay in the learning business and resist the blandishments of employers offering good wages simply to get good workers for what may turn out to be dead-end jobs, if their further learning looks and feels nothing like the formal education system they have rejected. And that means focusing their minds on learning from experience as the core of any learning programme.

So the first reflection is that it has turned out that APEL has an almost limitless range of applications. The second reflection is about balance. To some academic staff APEL offers a strong intellectual appeal as a way of thinking about adult learners and their potential. Most staff who have worked with older students, know the emotional satisfaction, the sheer joy of it, at helping men or women who thought nothing of themselves as learners, grow in confidence, flourish and produce high quality work. For them, APEL speaks to the heart and mind. And of course this is where the portfolio approach can be so valuable. But all the reflection on experience, the conceptualisation of what has been learned, the collecting of supporting evidence which amounts to a documented learning autobiography takes a great deal of student time, staff time and there is no certain result in formal assessment terms. So whilst this portfolio-assisted approach may be excellent seen as a formal class or at an organised drop-in centre, it clearly is not appropriate for large numbers of people.

Many potential APEL-style students want the quickest, cheapest fix. If someone wants an engineering degree, outstanding ability to cope with geriatric grandma may be interesting but it is strictly irrelevant unless it happens to be engineering applied to some new-fangled Zimmer frame or a self-help bath lift. For people who have that clear view of the qualification they want, a direct instrumental approach without frills is what they want of APEL. And that is where a sense of balance becomes so important, because it is not a question of either or. The question is the best mix for an individual. Ideally, there needs to be a range of approaches for individuals to choose from, with help where necessary, offered moreover by an institution organised so that each approach is handled with the same professionalism. It is a tricky balancing act. It has all kinds of academic, as well as administrative and financial implications. And this is where the sense of balance is so vital. For further education the arrival of the National Council for Vocational Qualifications both makes it more important to achieve that balance and possibly makes it more difficult to achieve.

This leads directly to the third reflection: guidance. It is there in the middle of the question of balance. It is proven beyond all reasonable doubt that through following the APEL sequence, many men and women come to know themselves better, are better equipped to make decisions about their future. Frequently they discover, somewhat to their surprise, that as a result of APEL they have changed their minds; what they thought they were sure about as being right for them, has turned out to be inappropriate and sometimes actually wrong. All of this is unpredictable, but it is very important. It gives added significance to the question of balance. Guidance both as purpose and as a possible outcome of APEL is central to any accurate understanding of what APEL is all about.

Staff development comes next. And the points about balance and guidance back it up. There may be an intellectual appeal about APEL for many staff. But this does not necessarily mean that they are competent, or even could become competent at doing it. This is not a matter of judgement, or detecting faults and deficiencies. It is a matter of observation. Just as the brilliant lecturer at whose feet students know they are privileged to sit – they do not need telling – can be a hopeless tutor – and the students do not need telling either – so the first-rate formal teacher can flounder in the uncertainties of APEL. And it is easy to understand. For APEL the curriculum is what is in the body and mind of the student, the learner. Teacher, the staff member had nothing whatsoever to do with its content or acquisition. So it can appear that the teacher is more of an accessory to the learner rather than a principal provider. Understanding that this is not necessarily the case, that APEL requires an explicitly collaborative style of learning and helping, encouraging, supporting, facilitating are the ways of describing the staff role in APEL up to the point of assessment; this is the core of any professional development programme to help staff prepare themselves for working in this rather different mode. But there is no doubt about it, some form of deliberate preparation is a necessary prerequisite for launching any APEL scheme.

One of the topics which crops up in any professional development programme for APEL is assessment. And this is another reflection in this attempt at some mental stocktaking of APEL matters. It is clear that, as with so many other aspects of education, assessment in APEL raises questions which go way beyond frontiers of APEL. Before expanding a little on that as one of the checklists of reflections, there is one generalisation about academic assessment with APEL which is different from academic assessment in general. It is: there needs to be a clear separation of function and person between staff who help in the preparation of prior experiential learning for assessment and staff who do the assessment, make judgements about the quality of the work and evidence being offered. In shorthand terms, this is simply to avoid confusion in the minds of staff and students alike between advocate and judge. It is an important principle to bear in mind for APEL.

Beyond that, assessment in prior experiential learning moves into interesting areas. There is the question of evidence – what counts? Then there is the question of the quality and quantity – what level of academic credit and how much? There is the more contentious question of grading – can two equal APEL claims be separated into some priority? All these issues have to be faced in any modular, unit, or credit accumulation scheme. In any of those schemes the problem is to avoid getting locked into a highly sophisticated computerised system which records faithfully all marks and at the flick of a switch produces what appears to be a professional result, which in the view of some academics can turn out to be unprofessional rubbish. Trying to fit APEL mechanically into some such system can produce equally silly results.

The fundamental point which APEL raises about assessment is the central fact about professional academic judgement. Whatever the system, its checks and balances, in the last resort everything rests on the judgement of an academic. After all, that is one of the things an academic is paid to do, make academic decisions. But it is too easy to jump from that to assuming that it is necessary for every assessment to be fine-grained, distinguishing say between 57 and 58 per cent in figures. That is not a strict necessity. It is a practice which has adhered to assessment like some external accretion. APEL's assessment stands as a reminder that learning is not confined to precise terms which can facilitate judgements differing by 1 per cent – there is a place for those fine-grained assessments of course, but for most purposes a five point scale will suffice admirably.

This is particularly important for APEL, because for perfectly understandable reasons, indeed entirely proper reasons, academic judgements about uncertificated learning must stand scrutiny in exactly the same way as any other judgement. In order to achieve this there is a tendency for some academics making assessments of experiential learning to compare the evidence in front of them with some of the best work which they mark in the formal system rather than considering it against the entire distribution range which they customarily employ. To put it at its baldest, the basic consideration needs to be: does this work in front of me merit a bare scrape-through pass in the same way as some of my other students are going to get bare scrape-through passes.

Trying to refine all this is another way of saying that one reflection prompted by these years with APEL as a quarry, is that there is a great danger at present of there being far too much emphasis placed on assessment procedures. Too much money, too much time, resources in general perhaps being wasted. Do the users of assessments gain so much that it justifies the huge amount of investment devoted to producing these assessments? Could the resources to this part of education be put to better use?

The last of this group of reflections is more to do with the general problem of getting anything done with complicated institutions and human beings working in them. In a way, it is near throughout to questions about institutional change. In the many different ways there are of thinking about institutional change one thing seems absolutely clear: detailed plans to effect change in institutions rarely, if ever, work in practice as intended. Some of the important factors taken into consideration when developing the detailed plan will have changed by the time the plan goes into operation, changing the entire dynamics of the effort. Outline plans which leave plenty of room for changes of direction or emphasis are much more helpful. But that presupposes that outline plans are based on some principle of organisational structure which is strong enough to tolerate such changes. It is a different kind of strength. Much of that is pragmatism.

Pragmatism is usually thought of as reaction to circumstances. However it can also be spotting the possibility of creating the circumstances likely to make some desired action possible. Pragmatism can get a bad name as the venal interpretations often put on the word manipulate, unless it is based on some clear-sighted sense of direction. But at its best it seems as good a way of thinking about change as any other. It also is a means of getting things done. Of course it is risky. There is no guarantee that things will work out beneficially. Its great advantage is that it is active. It means searching continually for openings, registering abilities and working out how to make the best use of learning.

It really goes back to the beginning. With the help of PSI, and then through The Learning From Experience Trust, with great encouragement and support from so many different people and bodies, it seems exactly what has happened. Throughout, the style of working has been to attempt to identify an area where the application of APEL is untried. Then somehow find funds to run a pilot project with the twin purpose of starting some development in its own right and of producing evidence which other people can consider and make their judgements about, but all as the first line of dissemination. And it has been a bit like steadily trying to work around the circumference from the centre of a circle. First, polytechnics and colleges with support of CNAA; then further education in alliance with various bodies; then YTS, both trainees and supervisors; then employers; most recently NCVQ and universities. Others have tackled the unemployed. And of course NCVQ, on a larger scale, has put into an APEL project almost as much as the entire resources used in the work of this ten-year period. Open college federations are doing marvellous work with adult education especially with much neglected groups: women and volunteer work in voluntary bodies. Nothing would have happened unless the timing was right. And the 1980s were a time which was right for the development of various applications of APEL.

All this can be very frustrating. Nowhere has it emerged more clearly than in years of effort to engage employers in some pilot projects. At the beginning it was rather like trying to enlist the support of academics. A small group of senior executives from Legal and General the insurance company, the Wellcome Foundation, Whitbread's, the National Coal Board and Business in the Community met fairly regularly over a couple of years but found it impossible to move from general discussion about ways APEL related to the problems of redundancy, early retirement and career changes which were beginning to face employers, to specific projects for working with their own employees which could attract funding from community affairs budgets in companies. This was the case for women office staff particularly. All agreed that many staff were working way below their potential – ability being under-used – and that personnel policies would be improved if some acceptable route for career advancement could be mapped. But apart from the NCB initiative which was more or less in this area, nothing happened.

There seemed to be two reasons for this. The first was timing. For employers, the early 1980s were too soon for the obvious implications of APEL for recruitment, retention and career development within personnel policies to move up the list of priorities of short-term issues. And as has been mentioned already, that is no different from APEL generally. Now its time has come; then it had not come. The second is institutional. It is the difficulty of knowing how to deal with a set of institutional practices and procedures which are not only different, but are of a different order. This is the reverse side of employers complaining that they can easily find it difficult to deal with academic institutions. Is it the training manager, the personnel manager or the group community affairs manager who is able to take action or promote action? Or is it an educational advisor, an educational affairs liaison officer or who? And having completed that mapping exercise for a particular company, what are the committee procedures? What is the brief given by the board to the relevant committee which might even suggest that some APEL projects might be entertained? Only when all these various items are clarified and plotted is it possible to introduce APEL through the central approach route – what is in it for the employer? What tangible benefits are there which in the longer term affect the company's balance sheets? Without a clear answer to that question there is nothing to talk about. It is all pie in the sky.

So a second group of reflections follows. Searching does not lead inevitably to finding, even when the openings look promising. Pragmatism is bound to produce some failures. There are four initiatives which in different ways did not produce the results which were hoped for; the Commission for Racial Equality project, the manuals project, the YTS projects, and a maths and sciences project. For reasons already given the Commission for Racial Equality project was not very successful. It was particularly disappointing because in the mid-1980s it would have been valuable to have collected a solid mass of evidence about ways in which APEL could help ethnic minorities and especially blacks, make better use of their abilities and of the educational opportunities which are there for them to use. To have been able to write a major report, as in the case of the FEU and CNAA projects, with wide dissemination, could conceivably have been helpful in the early stages for the various open college federations and consortia which have emerged in the past five years. More specifically, as with higher education and some polytechnics, it could have spurred on the thinking about access, before all the rhetoric began to pour forth from education ministers. The need is so urgent for engaging blacks more fully as learners in any form of post-secondary education. A strong confident report on APEL backed by the CRE may just possibly have helped.

The second relatively disappointing project was the one on manuals. Retrospectively, there was one serious mistake in the original idea and one hazard which could have been anticipated in working with an employer. The design fault was to assume that it was possible to write a how-to-do-it manual for business studies and engineering at first degree level which intending students could use on a distance learning basis. That was half wrong. It turned out that while it was (and is) possible to produce a guide which takes students by the hand and gently inducts them into systematic reflection on experience and gets them going down the APEL path, it is not possible to produce a guide suitable for general use for the second stage in the APEL sequence, when specific statements of learning must be framed in direct relation to the content of a particular degree course. The reason is simple; it ought to have been foreseen. It is just that despite broad similarities in the content of mechanical engineering and business studies degrees there are considerable differences in the syllabuses as written, so that a handbook intending to help intending students sort out their prior learning claims for academic credit towards a degree in one higher education institution may not be of much help in another. So while the manuals project produced a handbook/student guide[1] at a general level, it could not in the event produce anything of general use at a specific level.

The hazard encountered was inherent, as is now clear, from working with a major employer. The idea was to use the general handbook as part of a staff appraisal procedure of the company. The idea worked. Where supervisors got the hang of APEL and encouraged their juniors, supervisors and juniors alike benefited. Strengths and weaknesses were identified. Career development possibilities were plotted. Ways of gaining further qualifications were scouted. Where supervisors were not supportive, even resistant to their juniors working through the handbook, it exposed starkly to the executive responsible for developing staff appraisal procedures for the company, just what problems had to be solved before the appraisal system could fulfil its job, benefiting both individual and company through improving information about performances and potential.

All of that worked. What did not, was producing a definitive report. There was no difficulty with the academic side of the work. It proved well nigh impossible to get an evaluation from the company. It is one of the hazards of working with employers. It is no-one's fault. Promotions, company reorganisation producing a different chain of command, different geographical boundaries for regional responsibilities and so on, meant that undertakings to send in reports at particular times simply could not be met. As a result, as with the CRE project, no well-founded account could be written and published on APEL as an element in staff appraisal for companies. And the pity of that is that just at the very time when reskilling, updating and retraining were becoming ever more important, one contribution has been missing from the search for the most effective ways of achieving those ends.

The work with the Youth Training Scheme illustrates another problem of working with employers. Work with YTS supervisors and largely with trainees, is only possible by agreement with the employers. That is not only as it should be, but must be. Any satisfactory work depends on the employer, the supervisor or trainee as well as the project worker recognising that there is something in it for them. It follows that where there is a strong company commitment to training, any project will get a relatively smooth run, especially where it is a large company. Smaller companies are obviously more affected by short-term staffing problems so that the most carefully planned assignments for work with employees' projects can get aborted. Those are all of a piece with a smaller company having less fully embedded provision for training. The complications this can produce when working with YTS supervisors are obvious. A line manager who is also a YTS supervisor can easily find that the circumstances of the day mean that the mainstream company requirements override YTS supervisory duties. Whatever may be the personal inclination, company business must come first.

These kinds of issues affected projects with YTS trainees far more seriously. Here a combination of the beginnings of a smaller number of 16+ men and women as fully waged employees (demography at work) and government encouragement to move trainees to employed status, meant an increasing tendency for employers to treat YTS trainees more as employees and less as young people in training. The effect of this on the YTS into Higher Education project was very serious. It meant that time and again a project worker turned up for an appointment, a trainee was going to move into another stage thinking through, planning and then moving on from being a YTS trainee into further or higher education, only to find that the trainee was working and not available. Some illness or staff absence required the trainee to work rather than keep up training. Once again this was no-one's fault. But we learned the lesson as is set out in Part II.

All this illustrates, not the difficulties to be overcome in applying APEL with employment, but far more serious, some of the problems endemic in trying to establish employee training and development as a serious national undertaking. What emerges is that there is just as serious a question about staff development in employment as there is in further and higher education. Every time work experience, or preferably, work-based learning is explored as a means among others of attempting to improve the general level of skill and performance throughout the work force, there are serious implications for line managers and supervisors. It is rather like the employer side of YTS writ large. This issue gets explored further in Part III.

Mathematics and science is another relatively disappointing story: disappointing that is as a failed attempt to produce successful examples of relating APEL to both admission and admission with advanced standing to degrees with components of mathematics in their requirements (not specialist mathematics degrees) or in combined science degrees. This project was an extension of the CNAA effort resulting in the assessment of prior experiential learning which did not include any APEL work done with mathematics or science. In some ways it was an attempt to take further the initiatives with mathematics taken within engineering projects, and move beyond information technology which had featured in that project. The idea was to test the APEL possibilities in those disciplines on the assumption that there were non-graduates working in technical roles in laboratories, engineering design offices and people considering career changes who might become candidates, given the prominence accorded to the need for larger numbers of scientists and technologists. Out of four participating institutions only one managed to find science candidates for APEL (a second discovered through surveying those already enrolled on a course that some might have claimed credit successfully had the facility existed) and only one found any mathematics candidates, and those were people who had already enrolled on an applied science programme. A different Science programme proved the validity of interviewing as an effective way of making APEL judgements as is described in the next section. Both of the two institutions which failed to produce any candidates at all went through fundamental institutional reorganisation during the period of the project, so that despite good intentions, it proved literally impossible for them to put them into practice. The staff concerned who were eager to develop APEL schemes, simply did not have the time to do so. Both of those institutions will develop those schemes in time so the project contributed in a small way to their institutional development. And in one case those developments should include a very important element; seeking to give academic credit for qualified Registered General Nurses enrolling on a combined science degree.

In the other two institutions great efforts were made with mathematics, but they ran into the sand largely because of curricular matters. It seems that there are two questions which can be asked about those wishing to study courses which require a significant level of mathematical knowledge and skill. The first is: is there evidence that the candidate possesses the requisite knowledge and skill to cope with this course? The second is: is there sufficient evidence that this candidate can acquire the knowledge and skill requirement to follow this course? It is the first question which is usually posed. Were the second question to be posed, the APEL results might be forthcoming in mathematics. Unfortunately it proved impossible to devise APEL schemes based on that second question.

As a lesson learned however, all was not lost. As with any developmental project the evidence of what does not work can be as important as that of what can work. And for mathematics what did not work seems to point to the much larger questions of mathematics curricula generally at any and every level. The second lesson was that it is more difficult to convey the APEL message of opportunity to men and women who might become candidates in mathematics and science than most other disciplines. General advertising did not produce the response looked for. It could well be that recruiting through employers would be more successful. After all employers have their own reasons for wanting employees qualified in mathematics and the sciences. And that perhaps is a fitting point on which to end this second group of mistakes made, and lessons learned.

The last reflection at this stage is this: the mystery of time and place. This is an account of how things happened as accurately as can be managed. Easily it could have been told by another, if time and place were different. Suppose that tutor due to go to America with students in 1977 had not gone sick. I would never have been connected with CAEL's early efforts at APEL. Someone else would have done, sometime. Suppose George Tolley had found himself chairing an inquiry into vocational qualifications before chairing the FEU group which led to the Open Tech, instead of the other way round, as it happened. NCVQ or something like it would have been spawned years earlier. APEL would have been propelled into further education generally earlier.

The story would be different. The story would have been different again had the economy been stronger with companies spending more on training, if there had been a change of government and so on. The point is that fortuitous combination of time, circumstance and an idea which happened to fit in with the needs of the day has resulted in this story being told: sometime it would have been told by another in any case and told differently. And in the 1990s there are many stories to be told by many people.

What always would be the case, is that the context for developing approaches to the assessment of experiential learning would be the long tradition of adult education and progressive education stemming from earlier writers such as Rousseau, Dewey, onwards. There is nothing new about the benefits of learning by doing. Throughout, that tradition has placed great value on the affective aspects of experiential learning alongside the cognitive. Paying due attention to that aspect of experiential learning within schemes for the assessment of experiential learning is something yet to be achieved.

Part II
A decade of APEL

5 Introduction

It is not easy to think of another decade in the twentieth century which has been so crammed with initiatives about education and training. Not even in the nineteenth century when education reform ran through the progressive establishment of a national education system to revisions and reform at university level with all the accompanying tensions between religious and secular provision, has there been such frantic activity. Most of it has been promoted, even forced by a government which has been in power for all of the 1980s, beset by anxieties about the economy and increasing worldwide competition, together with its determination to reduce wherever possible the overall size of the tax-funded public expenditure. Beneath that there lie demographic trends and governments so far in Britain do not control demography. Other bodies have played their part such as the National Advisory Body for Local Authority Higher Education as it used to be called, and the University Grants Committee before it was reconstituted, the Council for National Academic Awards and the Further Education Unit, the Royal Society of Arts, and most recently the employer-funded Council for Industry and Higher Education and the Confederation of British Industry's seminal work on 'Towards a Skills Revolution'.

For higher education the 1980s began with the creation of the National Advisory Board when the then Secretary of State for Education and Science dodged holding the nettle of funding arrangements for poly-technics through their local education authorities, whilst for universities there were the first of draconian reductions of funding. The Lindop Inquiry followed to review the workings of the Council for National Academic Awards. Years of continual sniping went on until the 1988 Education Reform Act established both the Universities Funding Council and the Polytechnics and Colleges Funding Council (PCFC) to work either side of the continuing so-called binary line with the abolition of tenure in its customary role and newly-established governing bodies for PCFC institutions which were removed from local authority control and given independent corporate status, in parallel with powers devolved to them by CNAA to conduct their own academic affairs with hands-off remote supervision. Meanwhile the TEED introduced its 'Enterprise in Higher Education' programme as financial bait to persuade higher education institutions to develop programmes designed to help students become more employable and effective as graduates.

For further education there was the removal from local government control of a large slice of funding which was transferred to TEED and used on a contract basis to try and force the speed of change in further education to meet the increasingly felt needs for sharply focused ways of improving the skills of the workforce. During the decade as the Manpower Services Commission became first the Training Commission, then the Training Agency and then the Training Enterprise and Education Directorate of the Department of Employment. There was first the Open Tech to develop distance learning materials for skill updating and enhancement, then the Open College as a national vehicle for distance learning and vocational subjects at further education level, and the National Council for Vocational Qualifications with its brief to establish national standards in occupational competence in all areas of employment. Then, too, further education was affected by the Education Reform Act. College governing bodies were reconstituted to ensure a majority of business people, whilst simultaneously they were to take charge of their own budgets under arrangements for local financial management. All this time further education was heavily involved in the succession of Youth Training Programmes from Youth Opportunities Programmes to one-year and two-year Youth Training Schemes and for adults the Job Training Schemes and their successor Employment Training.

Meantime the Department of Education and Science established its Professional Industrial and Commercial Updating Programme (PICKUP) programme applying to higher and further education alike. There was the Unit for the Development of Adult and Continuing Education as a ginger group with the National Institute of Adult Continuing Education and REPLAN as an initiative for the unemployed.

The Management Charter Initiative, which emerged from the inadequacies of British management as identified by research groups funded by government, produced a flurry of activity affecting both further and higher education. And most recently the establishment of the Training Enterprise Councils, and there are supposed to be eighty-two of them by the end of 1992, as a means of government trying to manoeuvre industry and commerce into a position of discharging local responsibility for the training needs of their own area and paying for much of it themselves, something which government proved incapable of doing at national level, has introduced a joker into the pack of cards, shuffled to ensure that tax money is spent on national needs.

And if all that was not enough, Richard Bird, Deputy Permanent Secretary at the DES wrote another report of the workings and future of the Council for National Academic Awards, top-up loans so-called were introduced in higher education to compensate for the freezing of student maintenance grants, training credits were introduced on a pilot basis as a means of funding training for younger people through the Training Enterprise Councils.

It is this decade that saw the assessment of experiential learning become part of many people's vocabularies. Higher education, further education, adult education, trainers and employers, people from all these spheres now commonly talk about experiential learning. So do government departments. The Department of Trade and Industry uses the phrase when talking about the problems of getting more engineers. The Department of Education and Science sees that experiential learning is important when it talks about increasing access to higher and further education. The Further Education Unit energetically supports developments in different applications of experiential learning. TEED has come to realise that experiential learning is a factor to be taken into account across the broad range of its programmes from the Youth Training Scheme, New Adult Training Scheme, its Further and Higher Education initiatives and on into Employee Training Schemes, Management Development and services for the unemployed. The University Grants Committee and the National Advisory Body report in 1984 on continuing education urged universities, colleges and polytechnics to busy themselves with experiential learning. The Council for National Academic Awards has been a steady proponent of experiential learning. It has sponsored research and development work, disseminating the results and offered guidance to its associated institutions. And employers: the Brewers' Society, Jaguar Cars, JBS Computers, Wimpy International Foods Division of United Biscuits, the Woolwich Building Society, Sainsbury's, the Hotel Services Training Unit of the National Health Service, the Training Agency itself as an employer, among others have all begun to incorporate the assessment of experiential learning in their own staff development and training initiatives.

It was not always so. Only a few years ago the eyes of the Permanent Secretary to the DES glazed over after three or four minutes on the subject. Higher education institutions generally were sceptical. Further education saw the point but did not know what to do about it. Employers tended to think that experiential learning was an interesting topic but had no particular relevance to their own affairs with an eye on red and black figures on the balance sheet. That was in 1981. In 1990/91, ten years on it is all very different. There are activities based on experiential learning in each and every sphere.

One of the reasons for this is that through APEL academic credit towards formal qualifications can be gained without formal study in a recognised educational institution. In other words APEL is a route towards the accreditation of uncredited knowledge. Accreditation here means recognising formally that a given body of knowledge and skill counts towards a particular qualification, is credited towards it. Accreditation is first cousin to accumulation. Taken together they mean arrangements whereby formally recognised knowledge and skill, accredited, can be banked as and when the accreditation occurs, accumulating until there is sufficient credit to meet the requirements for the award. Accreditation applies principally to formally provided courses. Applied to prior experiential learning it brings uncertificated knowledge and skill into the certificated category. It facilitates credit accumulation.

APEL also facilitates progression. And this is another reason for the attention currently being paid to it. Until fairly recently, academic progress along any formal qualification route has been more a game of snakes and ladders with the dice loaded against the player, than an articulated scheme designed to produce onward movement. Children understand the point immediately. At degree level it was only the most persistent full-time student that could move from one polytechnic, college or university to another without serious loss. That loss was usually expressed as a loss of time, but in reality it was a waste of academic achievement. To transfer from the end of a first-year course in one higher education institution straight into the beginning of a second year of a similar course in another institution was extraordinarily difficult to manage. There were perfectly understandable institutional reasons for this, but nevertheless it was an inhibition against orderly progression. For part-time degree students usually the position was even worse. To be locked into a part-time course lasting four or five years in one institution and find it almost impossible to transfer that amount of first-degree learning to another part-time course in an institution in a different part of the country just seemed obscure if not bizarre, given the changing circumstances of individuals in their domestic and employment positions. At sub-degree level there was no ready way of transferring the results of either a City and Guilds' Certificate or a Business and Technician Education Council Award or an award of the Royal Society of Arts to a different one of those three bodies with full credit recognition as the starting point for undertaking a higher level course of study. At bachelor's and master's degree levels this is now possible through Credit Accumulation and Transfer Schemes, either in the CATS Registry at CNAA or in individual institutions. And at sub-degree level, so far, the National Council for Vocational Qualifications has the brief of facilitating that kind of progress. In the case of CATS, APEL is a facilitating agency for progression. The same is true for NCVQ. Unless it devises ways of using APEL procedures for the award of its National Vocational Qualifications it cannot possibly fulfil its statutory brief. And it knows it. So for progression to mean much throughout, APEL is essential.

Yet another reason for the steady acceptance of APEL is its role in educational guidance for adults. One of the prime benefits of giving adults the opportunity to reflect systematically on their experience is that they come to have a better understanding of their own capabilities, their strengths, their weaknesses, and indeed what they want to do in the future. Over and over again this has been proven. Indeed, frequently older men and women will say that it is the self-assessment strand to the APEL exercise which is more valuable to them than any question of formal academic credit. Increasingly the need for adequate education guidance for adults is accepted as a vital part of any programme of retraining, updating and skill development. And since the need is ever more pressing for more and more adults to become more effective in their occupations and work, the extension to APEL is receiving increasing attention.

The background to this rising interest is of course demography. On present estimations, by the year 1994 there will 1.1 million fewer than at present in the 16 to 24-year-old age group. That debit will be balanced by two credits. By the same year, there will be 600,000 more than at present in the 24 to 48 age group. And in the 48 to 58 age group there will be 1.6 million more. Within those figures lie all sorts of conundrums, but two things are reasonably certain. The first is that there will be an increasing number of women in full-time and part-time work. And second, the health of the economy depends heavily on more and more older people learning more and more so they can contribute more, whether in production or service industries, the professions, administration, local and central, all because numbers of younger recruits are not going to be there. This is the price demography will exact if the country is to remain relatively prosperous in a governable society. It points to the need for human resource development to become a central preoccupation for management and correspondingly for higher and further education.

It took higher education a long time to get there. The diminishing number of 18-year-olds means quite simply that the buoyant level of applicants to some universities, polytechnics and colleges is likely to dip. This is not to say that all of these institutions are going to experience that equally. But quite clearly some are bound to, even if many do not. The evidence has been there for a long time. Various predictions from the DES about numbers in higher education have contained higher and lower expectations both based on demography. The problems coming round the corner have been preached high and low, but it is only recently that institutions have begun to reformulate their admission arrangements to taken full account of these facts.

This averting of the eyes from evidence is both unsurprising and surprising. It is only rarely that people positively welcome launching into the unknown. Most people prefer to ignore the uncomfortable uncertainties the unknown suggests until it stares them in the face. The fact that it is academics who have practised this aversion from the evidence, for so many years, is no more surprising than it is for car workers caught up in the complexities of multinational competition. What is surprising however is that it has taken so long for the institutional leaders of higher education to force attention on the evidence. Now the attention of many is focused sharply on that evidence. There is an active search for new potential groups of students which necessarily means turning to the men and women age 25 and upwards and rewriting pamphlets to try to attract them. Steadily the point is being taken that APEL has a lot to say to institutions and their potential older students in these circumstances.

Further education has come to demography later still. During most of the 1980s they have drawn significant numbers of young people to their GCE courses at 'O' and 'A' level (GCSE is too new as yet to assess its impact on further education) from the schools where many of these young people could have continued had they wished to. From the mid-1980s onwards, further education colleges had to cope with the consequences of a quarter of their funding being switched from the DES to TEED and tender for funds on a contract basis. In its heyday the Youth Training Scheme provided a significant amount of funding, but for all the obvious reasons that is now a declining asset. Various forms of community programmes, first alongside the Job Training Scheme for Unemployed Adults and more recently that which got incorporated in employment training for adults was a potential source of steady funding. Since all TEED funding is on a short-term basis this meant increasingly that further education colleges were engaged in an almost perpetual juggling game of resources, staff and students. However, local financial management as provided in the Education Reform Act of 1988, has given a new twist to all these problems. So just like higher education, further education is now having to be much more energetic in positive recruitment efforts to attract older learners.

It may well be thought that employers are a different matter. It turns out they are not. The same demographic evidence has been there, but they do not appear to have taken it much into account. Again this is both unsurprising and surprising. In addition to the unsurprising factors mentioned during the 1980s, employers have been understandably preoccupied with the intense commercial and financial pressures bearing on them in the search for greater efficiency, cost effectiveness, with all that means for reducing the number on their payrolls, regrouping in more efficient premises and all the rest of it. But it is surprising that the training arm of the Confederation of British Industry confessed to the same problems in getting employers to face demography as has been the case in education. Now they have to take account of the declining numbers of young people who are going to be available for employment. This poses the twin problems of recruitment and retention. Securing an adequate number of recruits at all levels of employment is one thing. Holding on to them is something else. Shortages are bound to produce poachers. And here again employers are turning increasingly to the opportunities they are able to offer their employees through various applications of the assessment of prior experiential learning as one way of trying to cope with these difficulties.

It is no surprise then, that the assessment of prior experiential learning is an idea whose time has come. Concern for the learning attainments of people however they have acquired them makes more and more sense in a fast developing technological world. Overall it is reminding formal educational institutions that there are more ways of learning than walking through their front doors and being formally taught. It is also reminding employers that, whether they recognise it or not, they too are in the learning business every time they find a need for some of their employees to master new skills, adopt new attitudes, come to terms with new processes.

6 The assessment and accreditation of experiental learning

Experiential learning is learning derived from experience. That is the fact of it, but of itself it is not very helpful. All learning comes from experience; being in the classroom, being instructed directly is an experience. So the focus needs narrowing, sharpening. The experiences from which experiential learning is derived are for the most part experiences which lie outside those provided by formal education institutions. In those terms, experiential learning is informally acquired learning. It may have come through employment, on-the-job learning, through domestic responsibilities – running a home, through hobbies and so-called leisure which can range from do-it-yourself, building your own garage, installing your own double glazing, to taking Caribbean holidays or getting fascinated with Mayan archaeology in the Yucatan of Mexico. This extends the range of experience which may lead to learning. And all of it is learning which has been acquired by individuals, without any reference to formal learning arrangements.

However the focus needs changing again, to have an inclusive view of what experiential learning refers to in the present context. Currently in Great Britain it also refers to learning which may have been gained through formal teaching in formal educational institutions which has not been certificated by any established validating or examining body. In other words uncertificated learning whatever its source can come under the label of experiential. That is if it is prior experiential learning. The point of that label 'prior' is that it refers to all the accumulated knowledge and skill which is uncertificated and which a person has acquired before joining a formal learning programme which involves certification. And it is this prior experiential learning which is attracting so much attention.

There is another category of experiential learning which is attracting increasing attention, and that is the learning derived from any form of practical experience which is part of a course or formally arranged learning programme. We can refer to this as 'the assessment of on-course experiential learning'. Sandwich courses leading to a degree or Higher National Diploma are an example of this part-of-course or current experiential learning. It is a requirement of sandwich courses that students spend periods of work experience in a place of work such as an office, in an engineering plant, or on a social work placement, interspaced with periods of formal academic study in a university, polytechnic or college. Many other courses include this type of experiential learning. Access courses for example; often course tutors ask their students to undertake different kinds of practical work which can produce experiential learning. But little if any of this on-course experiential learning is formally certificated and accredited towards qualification results. And this is the essential difference between prior experiential learning and on-course experiential learning. The difference becomes self-evident when there is any question of accreditation.

Prior experiential learning can stand instead of or be a complement to, formal academic qualifications and serve to support applications for admission to formal courses. It can also be used to produce academic credit towards the completion of a course. Naturally in each case the experiential learning has to be assessed academically before it can be taken into formal consideration. That will be discussed fully later. It only counts where a suitably qualified member of academic staff says it counts. At that point prior experiential learning can be accredited.

Generally on-course experiential learning does not become countable in that way. It may be a requirement of the course; students cannot receive the qualification they seek at the end of a course without undertaking periods of practical experience. Only rarely does the learning that may come from that experience count towards the qualification itself. It is not assessed academically, so it does not normally contribute towards an academic qualification – not yet. It may in the future.

However, there is more to APEL than accreditation. Experiential learning cannot be accredited without being assessed. It cannot be assessed unless it is identified. It can only be identified by extracting it from experience. It can only be extracted through systematic reflection. And it is this systematic reflection which can become sufficient unto itself, or be the first stage towards accreditation via formal assessment. These are not strict alternatives. They are essentially complementary but they do point to two different ways of thinking about experiential learning and its assessment.

APEL can be seen in terms of curriculum and/or in terms of assessment. These twin understandings of APEL, implicitly or explicitly run through every scheme which has been developed. And to a substantial extent the curriculum implications are indicated by the emphasis made on 'portfolio' as an approach. A portfolio concerned with experiential learning is an individualised approach through which an individual records the results of systematic reflection on experience, expressed as what has been learned from it. As such, it is frequently used in community groups or Fresh Starts or Return to Learning style courses where the rebuilding of self-confidence is the pre-eminent need as encouragement and motivation to learn more. This is a pedagogical matter, a method of teaching to stimulate people to learn for themselves. The content of this curriculum is what men and women bring with them. The teaching is concerned with helping them to learn what they already know. And as a teaching method it can be notably effective. In the process of discovering what they already know, men and women learn not only about how to learn, but they learn a lot more as they do it. They begin to make connections between what they already know and the additional knowledge and skill which may be related to it. For example, the mother of a disabled child can begin to articulate what she has learned from day-to-day experience with, for example, items of public policy concerned with building regulations in public places or the design of public transport. She can develop the vague understandings she has anyway into some coherent understanding. She can become better able to use more effectively what she has learned from her day-to-day experience.

In many ways, this curriculum mode of looking at APEL is very similar to what good primary school teachers do. Quite simply, they try to begin with what children know and understand, make connections with what is to be learned next and go on building additional learning in that way. Applying that principle of teaching and learning to adults is what APEL is about in curriculum terms. It is a process of learning.

Assessment is different. It is a matter of making independent judgements about the level and quality of learning which has been reached by an individual at a particular time. As such, APEL is no different from assessing a student's performance on the basis of formal taught courses or distance learning programmes or an Open University course.

What these twin understandings of APEL mean in practice is explored in a variety of contexts in the remainder of this part of the book.

PRIOR EXPERIENTIAL LEARNING

So prior experiential learning is countable academically and this is why it is attracting so much interest. If it is to be countable, however, clearly there are several earlier stages. It is one thing to say that someone has learned through the experience of putting up a garage or installing double glazing, or visiting the Yucatan or the Vatican. It is quite another to talk of someone without the normal formal entry requirements being admitted to a building management or archaeology or history degree course, let alone being awarded academic credit towards those qualifications.

The way prior experiential learning is brought to the point where it can be considered for formal assessment and so to accreditation is easy to describe. It is more difficult to accomplish. And it is the individual who has to accomplish it. All kinds of help, support and encouragement can be given. But the responsibility rests squarely on the man or woman for converting the experiential learning which is locked up within them into an external account of what it is.

There is a sequence of tasks which have to be completed. The first is psychological. Most people without formal education qualifications do not believe that they are much good as learners. This is true at most levels. They may be confidence itself in dealing with their work, their domestic and personal lives. Indeed many without formal qualifications are more successful in most respects than those with qualifications. But all that confidence can evaporate if they get anywhere near a college or meet any circumstances where they have to learn formally. This is one of the great problems about further training and updating in employment. There may be a variety of reasons why people have not reached the formal quali-fications level; many of them are not necessarily to do with the person's capacity to learn. And this first task, psychologically, is to believe there is a possibility that people can know more and do more than they or anyone else gives them credit for.

No-one can accomplish this task for anyone else. Everyone has to be helped to do it for himself or herself. Some need more help than others. There are different ways of helping. It all depends on what an individual wants to do. Of course it can work the other way. Some people are so confident they know a great deal it is very hard to convince them that they are relatively ignorant. That is a different issue.

Take the do-it-yourself and archaeological examples; anyone wanting to undertake a building management or archaeological degree will have to satisfy admission tutors that as well as being interested and knowing something about the subject, they can actually cope with the course once they have begun it. There is little point encouraging people to study or even allowing them to think that they can study at a particular level if the evidence is that they cannot.

Take the people who are least confident. By selecting some topic that interests them, and everyone has an interest of some kind, it is usually possible to enable people to prove for themselves and to themselves that they know far more about it than they realised. Everyone went to school. Most people have families. Many people read books. A proportion of people are unemployed, go on holiday, see films, watch television, listen to music. Many interests can serve as a trigger or starter for beginning to move through the psychological barrier and believing in oneself as a learner. Others who are confident that they have learned from their experience have a jumpstart. They just need helping to articulate what it is they have learned. All this can be done in individual conversations, through completing simple questionnaires, through working through checklists of knowledge and skills. It is a highly individual business. It can be done. Once that psychological stage is over the real work can begin. The real work is to reveal the prior experiential learning which is concealed.

There are three subsequent stages for an individual wanting to identify prior learning with a view to accreditation. The first is to review the past experience and attempt to isolate those incidents when it seemed that an experience resulted in something being learned. This can only be done through reflection. So systematic reflection on experience is the first stage of the work.This can begin once an individual has grasped the possibility of being more knowledgeable and more competent than had been thought.

At this stage no experience need be excluded; the only restrictions on the nature of experience to be used are those which individuals may wish to impose on themselves. Anything can be included if it has led to some learning. This stance is necessary to avoid the danger of blocking off at the outset access to some potentially significant experiential learning. In the event some of the learning identified is likely to be more obviously relevant than other, so some fairly stringent selection needs to follow systematic reflection. This attempt to extract significant learning experiences from the overall life and work experience of an adult is an essential preparation for the tough intellectual task which follows.

The second of the three steps, then, is to begin to lay the basis for making a claim to possession of certain knowledge and skills through isolating significant learning drawn from the experiences which have been isolated previously. The transition from describing experience to formulating statements of learning is again a tough intellectual task, but it is essential if the claim being made is going to be formally assessed. Once the claim has been made in clear unambiguous statements we leave the second stage.

Then comes the next stage – prove it! This third stage is the collection and documenting of evidence. Obviously whatever evidence is offered must seek to substantiate the claims being made. There needs to be a direct connection between claim and supportive evidence. The form of evidence and indeed its content are likely to be influenced heavily by the purpose of assessment, whether or not it is for guidance in relation to academic study of some kind. Sometimes it is helpful to produce a portfolio of learning in the form of a learning autobiography, something which is often referred to as portfolio preparation leading to portfolio-assisted assessment. For others, it can be more helpful to list competences and count off what has been learned.

Once the evidence has been collated with the claims being made then things move into the role of assessment. It can be at this time that self-assessment is sufficient. This is because systematic reflection on experience is liable to lead to a greater understanding of self, therefore can easily influence decisions about what to do next, and for some that is the end of the matter. The job is done. Further study, they conclude, is not necessary or appropriate.

But for others, formal assessment is the target. How the evidence is handled then becomes the responsibility of the assessor, with two important questions about the nature of evidence. Documented previous work, references, artefacts, all may be submitted. But the vital point is that it must be open to the assessor to call for whatever additional evidence is necessary. So tests, essays, and comprehension exercises may be imposed by an assessor who judges that he needs supplementary evidence before making a judgement.

At this point, prior experiential learning is assessed and ready for accreditation.

At the beginning, each of these steps and the compiling of evidence was seen as portfolio-assisted assessment. Later other approaches were adopted, but that is where the first attempts began in Britain to practise the assessment of prior experiential learning. All approaches conform to the four-stage sequence:

1 Systematic reflection on experience for significant learning;

2 Identification of significant learning, expressed in precise statements, constituting claims to the possession of knowledge and skills;

3 Synthesis of evidence to support the claims made to knowledge and skills;

4 Assessment for accreditation.[1]

Those first efforts were made in relation to higher education. The idea was to conduct pilot projects, collect evidence, argue the case on the basis of that evidence and hope that APEL as a day-to-day experience would begin to enter the bloodstream of higher education.

7   APEL and higher education

Maybe there was a car accident involving the owner of a car, who was driving, and two friends who were passengers. The driver, unfortunate soul, found himself involved in a dispute with his insurance company afterwards because it turned out that the other vehicle involved was an uninsured car whose driver simply disappeared. Reflecting on that protracted experience the driver realised that he had learned a good deal about the law as it affected his position and entitlements with the insurance company. He had begun to read carefully relevant sections of the newspapers and magazines he bought. That prompted him to go to the local library and browse through some books. He even got into conversation with a solicitor in a pub one day and picked up a few leads to follow.

One of his passengers landed up in a casualty ward of a hospital. It so happened that she was thinking about reading for a degree in social sciences, because her children had flown the nest, she had decided that she would like to work somewhere in the social and care services. She had not been seriously injured; however, while waiting what seemed an interminable time to be seen by a doctor, she began to notice, unconsciously at first, and then with deliberation, the different ways the receptionist reacted to a succession of patients who arrived after her. She began to make mental notes of the demeanour of the people waiting; men and women, young and old, couples trying to comfort one another and so on.

The other passenger, an older man was sitting in the back of the car. He thought of himself as an armchair psychologist. Once he had got over the shock of being thoroughly shaken up from the collision – he'd been daydreaming peacefully, enjoying the country lanes and fields he had been driven through – he found himself a victim of his own reactions. Here was he, he thought, recently made redundant and wondering whether to seek another job or just move into retirement gracefully, savouring the balm of the countryside, feeling his anger for his former employer draining away, and then he was suddenly jerked into bewilderment by the car halting in the ditch. What's more, having to restrain himself from joining in a furious exchange between the driver and the front seat passenger about whose fault the accident was. The phrase 'stress management' kept running through his thoughts. He had read about it. Here was how to do it.

Now suppose each of these three imaginary figures was interested in the possibilities offered by higher education. Having reviewed their lifetime experience, they might have singled out this car incident as an occasion when they had learned something.

If they were engaged in APEL they would then move towards the next stage of work. They would need to shift from thinking about the experience and describing it to giving an account of what they had actually learned. The driver was quite clear that he had learned a good deal about insurance and law. He had also become quite skilled in ferreting out the information that he needed from books and cross-checking it so that he could not be caught out if it came to an argument with the insurance company. It so happened that the lady who entered the casualty ward had been so intrigued with watching the receptionist and the reactions of the patients generally that she wondered what sort of a training if any the receptionist had been given to help her do her job properly. She worked backwards through the patients waiting with her and thought what would be helpful to them, so that when she tried to work out what she had actually learned from her casualty ward experience it began to seem like an embryonic proposal for a receptionist's training course. The armchair psychologist had no trouble in setting out what he had learned from the car accident which had broken his reverie. He had acquired first-hand knowledge and could express the effects on different people. He could still visualise it all very clearly.

The final stage for these three people involved in the car accident, if they were able to use prior experiential learning in relation to formal study, would be to produce evidence of what they claimed to have learned. If certain experiences lead to acquiring certain knowledge and skill then it is the individual's responsibility to prove it. Claims to learning have to be substantiated.

Now in the case of the driver, the evidence was easy. He had all the documents that he had collected and all the correspondence between himself and the insurance company relating to his dispute, the steps that had led him to threaten to go to the Small Claims Court and the terms of the eventual settlement. The insurance company paid up in full. The lady in the casualty ward had remembered in surprising detail most of the people who had been waiting with her, and she listed what she took to be their characteristics and then drafted a training programme. The armchair psychologist could offer no tangible evidence, but he produced a booklist of publications dealing with stress management saying that he had read them all.

At this point several different things could happen to our three imaginary people. The sorting out of significant learning experiences has led to a set of statements about what was learned and those claims have been supported by evidence relating directly to the claims being made. What happens next is something for the individual to decide.

Following the story of our imaginary trio we could easily find that the older man was so pleased to have it confirmed that he was a good learner that he returned to his reading as all he required. However, being redundant he might decide that further study had a great appeal and so he was advised that he could apply to read a degree in psychology with a good chance of getting a place using his prior experiential learning to support his application. He had no 'O' level passes to his name, let alone 'A' levels.

The lady interested in the social services and finding her appetite whetted, felt she was not ready to begin studying as an undergraduate; she thought she needed evidence of prior learning for gaining entry to an access course. Her idea was that if she was successful on that then she would know for herself that she was ready to become an undergraduate.

The driver of the car was a middle manager for a mail order firm. He was restive. He had worked out that promotions seemed to come to graduates and he was not one of them. He had made enquiries about business studies degrees but had been discouraged to find that he would have to spend two nights a week for four or five years attending classes. Then he heard of the Credit Accumulation and Transfer Scheme at the Council for National Academic Awards. Having read its regulations he realised that here was an opportunity of gaining credit for the year he had spent at the University of Newcastle upon Tyne before family circumstances had overwhelmed him and he had moved to the south for employment. He also realised he might be able to get additional credit for his prior experiential learning. What was more he understood that he could take the courses he was required to study at times convenient to him and in different institutions including the Open University. So he decided that he wanted to submit his prior experiential learning and have it assessed, not merely citing his insurance knowledge but the knowledge of cost accounting, marketing and business management he had learned at his work.

So what an individual chooses to do with the evidence of prior experiential learning depends to a large extent on why they are engaged in the business in the first place. The case of the car driver is clear; an express route to a degree. The lady knew she wanted to follow a social science course but needed to prove herself to herself and to gain confidence for the attempt. The armchair psychologist was generally interested in the APEL idea, and then was content to wait and see what it all suggested to him. So much for our three imaginary individuals.

If all that work is the responsibility of individuals, to produce not only the claims for prior experiential learning but the evidence to support it, assessment is the responsibility of academic staff. In considering evidence purporting to support claims to prior experiential learning, academic assessors must be free to use any means they consider most appropriate. For example, the assessor of the business studies candidate who applied through the CATS Registry noticed first of all that a course in the first-year programme at the University of Newcastle upon Tyne, covered more or less the same ground as the material submitted about insurance and the law. So that was ruled out. Double counting is banned, obviously. The material about cost accounting, marketing and business management was convincing, but there was not much evidence of understanding of the underlying principles. So he set the car driver a couple of essays to write, with a short-list of recommended reading. The essays were good; academic credit was awarded.

The admission tutor of the access course was intrigued by the scheme for a training course for hospital receptionists that the social science applicant had submitted and the interview was taken up with discussing how she had come to formulate it. She produced the notes that she had made afterwards. They impressed the tutor so much that he suggested that she could apply for a degree place straight away. She demurred, wanting to take her own time to be sure of her ground as she went along.

The psychology tutor had read the material in front of him, looked at the booklist attached and pondered. Many of the books on the list were required reading for his first-year students, with some for the second and third-year students. If the man really knew what those books were about he would be a valuable student to have in the classes. He telephoned the older man applicant, he formed a good impression and invited him for interview. It turned into an interesting discussion about psychology, but the tutor noticed that the interviewee shied off anything statistical. So he offered the man a place on the full-time course, explained the student grant arrangements that could apply to him as someone having been made redundant, and gave the older man three books on elementary statistics and told him to study them.

Those vignettes are obviously related to the general theme of access to higher education. The sequence of tasks undertaken by individuals, and the response of academic staff on behalf of academic institutions remains more or less constant whatever the level of knowledge and skill in question and the kind of work an institution is responsible for. So these are the respective responsibilities. Individual students or prospective students as learners have the sole responsibility to make claims about the learning they have acquired and produce evidence to substantiate those claims. They may be helped, but the responsibility is theirs alone. Staff have the sole responsibility for assessing the claims and evidence submitted to them. However, just as learners need help, so do staff. More of that later. But the helpful rule to observe generally for staff engaged in these procedures is this: those who help students prepare their claims and evidence generally speaking should not be involved in making assessments of the students they have helped.

APEL AND ACADEMIC CREDIT TOWARDS A DEGREE

This is particularly important for accreditation in higher education. Regulations for all degrees, diplomas and certificates in higher education specify procedures whereby courses are approved by academic committees before they are offered, for: content, structure, methodology, resources and methods of examining. The sections dealing with examining will indicate the composition of the board of examiners and include a requirement that an external examiner is appointed. Unless and until the external examiner signs the schedule of final results, no awards can be made. Since the external examiner has the authority to scrutinise draft examination papers, call for samples of course work and completed examination scripts, interview students and moderate mark sheets, increasing or decreasing the marks awarded by internal examiners if necessary, this is no idle matter; or should not be. In the final meeting of the board of the examiners to determine results, discussions about students' performance are concerned essentially with academic performance. Advocacy, or special pleading for a student by a member of staff who has taught that student is a delicate business. APEL results are handled throughout in the same way as results of any formal study. Given the nature of APEL and the involvement of staff with the preparation stages it is vital to ensure that its assessment is by an independent third party. The integrity of academic standards is at stake. The accreditation of APEL for higher education awards can have integrity only if it is subject to the same scrutiny as all other modes of learning.

This separation of role and function between staff who help students prepare their prior experiential learning for assessment, whether directly or not, and those staff who make the assessments is less important, indeed even inappropriate at other levels and categories of education and training particularly in vocational courses. These issues are explored later.

Looking backward for accreditation at APEL raises a different range of questions. They all flow from the requirements made upon institutions for validation. Validation bodies have rules. Those rules guide institutions in designing their courses. One of the critical sections of the rules concerns the admission of students to study courses. Now admission can either be at the beginning of a course, leading to a qualification, or to a later stage of the course, the student in effect being credited with part of the programme which they have learned before joining it. Technically this is admission with advanced standing.

APEL poses no difficulty for straightforward admission. All degree regulations whether for universities, polytechnics or colleges include clauses which are intended to enable applicants without whatever may be the formal education requirements cited to be admitted. So APEL is catered for. The same is true broadly speaking for Business and Technician Education Council (BTEC) courses. It is more or less the case that institutions have the responsibility for admitting whichever students they deem suitable.

Admission with advanced standing is a different matter. The general regulations to a degree lay down the conditions for admission with advanced standing. Usually they specify that candidates may be admitted direct to the second year of a study programme and exceptionally to the third year of a study programme, but rarely if ever to half way through the third or final year of a course. In other words whatever accreditation a candidate may bring to admission, at least one third of the programme must be completed through formal study at the institution. However, regulations for particular degrees may have a narrower interpretation. For example in engineering degrees usually, there is a sequence of courses to be followed with prerequisites. A course in the second year can only be followed if the specified course in the first year has been completed satisfactorily. Other degrees such as some in business studies have a part 1 which ends at the end of the first year, all of which must be completed before proceeding to part 2. All of this gets more complicated where programmes of degree studies are organised in modules or relatively short courses, three or four of which are studied simultaneously. Frequently modular programmes allow students in both years 1 and 2, or years 2 and 3 to take the same course simultaneously. In other words students in years 1 and 2, or years 2 and 3 are sitting side by side in the same lecture, listening to the same tutor, being examined in the same way. It is more complicated still when different combinations of studies are possible, say some business studies and some French or Spanish studies, or some information technology with some management courses.

Dealing with all this for regular full-time or part-time registered students going through the conventional admission procedures, can be complicated for staff and students alike. It is obvious that a good deal of information has to be mastered to pick an appropriate path to the various opportunities and choices presented. So when it is a question of APEL being considered for accreditation and admission with advanced standing to degree courses, things can be very complicated indeed. This is not to say that it cannot be handled satisfactorily. But it is quite obvious that the educational advice, information and support services an institution provides for its students become increasingly important when the academic organisation of an institution is modular. It becomes more important again when APEL comes into the reckoning.

Some Variables[1]

During the last ten years of steady developmental work, it has become evident that there is a series of variables which largely determine the characteristic features of any APEL scheme. Retrospectively, it is obvious that this must be so. To begin with, this tended to be obscured because of the initial concentration on portfolio-assisted preparation. As tutors in polytechnics and colleges of higher education have tried to come to terms with the potential students who wish to study degree programmes covering most of the disciplines on offer within the curriculum, so understanding of the tasks involved has sharpened. And the bald realities of resources, staff–student ratios, unit costs, devolved financial responsibilities and cost centres have forced on to centre stage this essential question – how best to conduct APEL effectively, efficiently and economically? Within a tutorial system there is no special problem posed by APEL. But since that one-to-one tutorial provision is not affordable for all, what then?

It all depends on the particular way the variables combine. There is the initial intention of the student. There is the evolving and settled intention of the student. There are the characteristics of the discipline or area of study in question. There is the way an institution does its business: structure, academic organisation, modes of learning on offer, and so on. And the best buy for any discipline for any institution depends on how all of those factors come together.

Variable 1 – initial intentions of individuals

So summoning up the imaginary trio who were in the car incident, whilst the sequence being worked out can make the assessment of prior experiential learning seem long-winded, complicated and requiring a great deal of staff time to be given to each individual seeking assessment, that is not necessarily so. Earlier, considering the imaginary trio, it became obvious that everything stems from the intentions of the individual concerned. Where someone has a clear eye on a future target, say an engineering qualification, clearly the only prior experiential learning which is worth documenting for assessment is that which has been learned previously and relates specifically either to the entry requirements for the engineering qualification or to parts of the engineering course if there is to be any question of going for academic credit towards the qualification itself. In that case systematic reflection on experience can be stimulated, supported and progressed by the use of handbooks, manuals, checklists and examples designed for the job in such a way that with minimal staff involvement the tasks can be completed at home. This saves the student time and effort. It concentrates the mind wonderfully. In other words, portfolio-assisted assessment is only one approach among many.

Conversely, where someone has a sense that further study makes sense but doesn't have a settled view on what for, then APEL's direction-finding self-assessment strand is the central issue. In which case while manuals, checklists, interactive computer programs (if we have them) can be a great help, there is no doubt at all that the group support possible through regular class meetings with a staff member as facilitator is the best way of tackling the tasks. The dividends in terms of student learning are rich. Being taken through some systematic reflection on experience by the tutor, picking up clues from other students, gaining confidence in self as learner, partly through listening to the accounts of learning from experience given by other students, and partly through recognising the extent of the learning already acquired is a marvellously motivating experience. And it all becomes essentially self-assessment. Understanding and recognition of self, that comes first. For people engaged in that task the complicated, lengthy procedure is indeed 'necessarily so'.

This shows the first of the variables which is likely to influence the nature of any APEL scheme: the initial interests and purposes of an individual man or woman.

Variable 2 – Settled Intentions of Individuals

The second variable is the evolving purpose of that individual. In between stands systematic reflection on experience and its potential importance as an arena for self-assessment.

It is important to say that formal assessment is by no means the be-all and end-all of taking APEL seriously. Long before there is any question of formal assessment, something of greater significance has been going on: self-assessment. The mental activity of reflecting systematically on experience is a means of a person finding ways of expressing a whole mass of knowledge and skills which previously was taken for granted, or at best was vaguely sensed. So attempting to articulate clearly what a person knows and can do becomes a means of a person revealing to her or himself in rather different terms than previously, who they are. Frequently we are not aware of the import of things we have learned informally, incidentally, accidentally until reflection reveals it. The vignettes earlier in this chapter show this at work. For example, although it is becoming a commonplace observation it is worth repeating, that many women do not make the connection between what they do day-by-day domestically – looking after children, catering and cooking, maintenance of house and equipment, entertaining and so on, whether they work for wages or not – and paid employment such as the managing of a shop, office, agency in day-to-day activities. They are not all that dissimilar. Once a woman has made that connection then it is likely to change the way she thinks and looks at herself and the way she views possible developments in her future. Self-perception sharpens from systematic reflection on experience. Self-assessment can provide map and compass bearings for future activities. So what an individual decides to do and how he or she sets about it, is the second variable.

Some Guiding Principles

Before commenting on some other variables it may be useful to set out a second set of guiding principles.

1. The student makes the claim

For APEL the most important guiding principle throughout is that it is the student or applicant who is making claims to have acquired knowledge and skills. It follows that the responsibility rests with the student for making a claim and supporting the claim with appropriate evidence. That is not to say that many applicants or students do not need considerable help in preparing those things and in understanding what might be sensible claims to make, but it is vital to recognise where the prime responsibility lies.

2. Learning not experience

The insistence throughout must be that the experience of a student is significant only as a source of learning. The intellectual task of moving from a description of experience to an identification of the learning derived from that experience is demanding. But if it cannot be accomplished there is no learning to assess, however important to the individual that experience may have been.

3. Identification comes before assessment

A third guiding principle is that there is a clear separation between the identification of prior learning and organising it into forms fit for presenting for assessment, and the assessment itself. The identification of prior learning comes through systematic reflection on experience. And there are three stages within that.

- First: The scrutiny of experiences to select those where something was learned.
- Second: The writing of clear statements about what was actually learned.
- Third: The collection and collation of evidence to support the statements of what was learned.

4. Assessment and academic responsibility

Academic assessment is the responsibility solely of academic staff. This is the fourth guiding principle. It is open to staff to employ any procedure they think most appropriate to arrive at an academic judgement about the evidence of prior learning submitted, and to ensure the maintenance of academic standards.

5. The nature of evidence

The fifth guiding principle concerns the nature of evidence submitted for assessment. As with all academic assessments the method of assessment needs to be appropriate for what is being assessed. Hence academic staff may choose to rely on the written evidence submitted. They may decide to probe through an interview either in person or on the phone. They may require additional work assignments to be completed, sometimes related to specified readings.

They may examine artefacts. They may observe performance. Whatever manner of assessment is used, it must be such that the judgement made can be considered by external examiners and boards of examiners alongside and with the same degree of confidence as other more traditionally assessed performances such as formal examination results.

6. Two academic functions

As a general rule and as a sixth guiding principle, it is wise to separate the two academic functions; helping students prepare evidence of learning and assessing that learning. In other words staff who help students prepare evidence should not normally have any part in making academic judgements about that evidence. The simple point here is to avoid confusion between advocate and judge.

Those guiding principles provide a framework for thinking about the different approaches which may be taken to the identification of prior learning and after that the different approaches to its assessment.

Variable 3 – Differences Between Disciplines

The next variable is the nature of the academic discipline, or the area of study concerned in its institutional context. The identification of prior experiential learning can be approached in several ways. Students can work together in a group or in a formally organised class. Work can be done through tutorials. It can be done using instruments and manuals devised for the purpose. Or prior learning can be identified through interviews.

Quite obviously, if it is possible to refine interviewing techniques so that tutors are able to identify significant prior learning, this is a cheaper, quicker and more simple approach. It is worth quoting therefore two concrete examples of assessment occurring simultaneously with identification on the basis of an interview.

In the first case, a member of staff for production engineering found that through careful and systematic interviewing for admission it was possible to identify likely areas of prior learning which might be creditable. Applicants on the part-time course tended to be recommended by their employers and have extensive work experience in some of the topic areas covered by the course. All 'non-standard entry' applicants were interviewed at the workplace by college staff.

Close collaboration between college and employer frequently meant that the college could deduce from the work experience of applicants what they were likely to have accomplished as learning on the job. A phone call or two between college and supervisors in companies could supplement the interviews and provide sufficient reliable evidence for admission. In some cases that approach has proved strong prima facie evidence for admission with advanced standing.

In the second case, the context for using interviews for approaching the prior experiential learning of applicants to the computing and information technology degree is different. Staff of the faculty held a series of 'open house' evenings during the year which were arranged specifically for people to explore what opportunities courses offered in computing and related study areas. This often meant that, when applicants were considered formally for admission, they might have already known a good deal about the content and structure of the course, and in turn they might well have been known to the interviewing tutors, having met them at an 'open house' meeting.

Four other factors underlay the use of interviews for identifying and assessing prior experiential learning. The modular structure of the course, in relatively small units, meant that investigations of prior learning could be sharply focused. The content of each section enabled tutors to form reliable judgements of an applicant's expertise in any of the study areas covered by the course. The interviewing tutors had always had experience of teaching a wide range of the units in the course. And interviews were conducted by pairs of tutors. In these ways reliable and valid academic judgements could be made about the creditworthiness of applicants' prior learning.

But there were risks. The first was the combination of facilitator and examiner. Interviewing in pairs may have been reliable and valid for the assessors. Not all students saw it as such. The confusion of roles mentioned earlier caused some problems. So that was the first refinement. The separation between preparation and assessment had to be self-evident to students. Then to clarify things as completely as possible, the tutors worked out a strict routine for preparing the students, and for the students to prepare themselves, for documenting what went on, so ensuring that the tutors fulfilled the role assigned to them.

All this was set out on a part-time student's admission records sheet. There was a section for initial counselling. There was a section for the admission interview. There was a section detailing the checklists which were to be given to applicants after counselling, and that came in two parts. The first was for candidates who were advised to proceed direct to interview and had listed all the documentary evidence that they were required to take with them. The second was for 'candidates advised to prepare a portfolio in lieu of formal qualifications'. This section had a simple set of instructions on how to use the guidelines for preparing a portfolio which they had already received, right through to the stage of making a formal submission. All this was supported with a series of explanatory notes giving the background as to why portfolio preparation was being offered for the assessment of experiential learning, giving examples of the kind of evidence of learning the admission tutors would be looking for, prompters to help people reflect on their work, and life experience which was not necessarily associated with information technology, but which might be of some good to them. And all that was put together with a description of the degree course, its components and the modes of study and so on.

Now the important thing about those refinements to the original approach to simply using an interview for the assessment of prior experiential learning, is that they show an institution evolving its procedures to take full account of the circumstances it finds itself in. It represents a deliberate attempt to establish a set of procedures which gave the maximum sense of security, not only to students, but to academic staff, whilst seeking to exploit the possibilities of recruiting older learners through offering differing possibilities in the pattern of study – self-paced learning was combined with a student-centred organisation of the academic course. And APEL is a catalyst for all these developments.

Nevertheless the question arises as to how far this approach to the identification of prior experiential learning can be developed for use in other disciplines to produce results which are equally valid, or reliable, or how far interviews can be used when combined with other approaches. For example work is beginning on the assessment of prior experiential learning for mathematics and science. It seems that the central issue is how far mathematicians should be assessing mathematical capabilities which have already been acquired and can be demonstrated, or how far it is a question of trying to assess individuals' propensity and capability for learning mathematics even if they have not grasped the mathematical concepts which are judged as being a prerequisite for beginning a course. This becomes an increasingly important issue given the number of courses in higher education which contain mathematical components. Successful study of the mathematics required for a life sciences degree is likely to be of a different order from studying a pure and applied maths degree. Can interviews do the job here? How large a contribution can interviews make in doing the job? That question has to be answered for all disciplines.

A Science Tutor working on the maths and science project answered this convincingly. Direct interviewing did not work very well. So she had an idea of walking applicants round laboratories, pointing out various items of equipment, commenting on their use, all the time watching, listening, waiting for the candidate to make connections between what was in the laboratory and what went on in day-to-day employment. Once the ice was broken, conversation flowed. A visit to a lecture in progress took the process further. As a result candidates revealed information on which decisions were made about admission and admission with advanced standing. This approach to enabling candidates to begin to identify their knowledge and skill in relation to what was involved in studying science formally gave time and space for candidates to relax, grow in confidence so as to do themselves justice. Apart from anything else it is first rate teaching. Skilfully APEL was put to work.

So the nature of the discipline heavily influences the most appropriate approach to the identification of prior learning. These variations between the disciplines also can produce different approaches to assessment. When it comes to assessment just as there can be a wide variety of approaches to the identification of prior experiential learning, so there are different approaches to formal assessment.

It has been emphasised already that systematic reflection on experience lies at the heart of any APEL scheme. Frequently this means that students undertaking APEL develop a fuller understanding of themselves, their capacities, their strengths and weaknesses, and often they change their minds about what they want to do in the future and so about the area of study they may wish to undertake. Tacitly there is a self-assessment being conducted by individuals whatever approach to APEL is followed. This means that self-assessment by students is likely to be the forerunner of any formal assessment. Indeed part of that self-assessment is often the decision as to whether or not to go for formal assessment at all.

Broadly speaking there are three approaches to formal assessment. There are variations on conventional procedures. There is interview and performance observation; and interviewing alone.

Many institutions have used all their customary approaches with individual variations. And these were based on the clear separation of the two academic roles, facilitator and assessor. One way is to use performance observation as a complement to interview. Another is to use interview alone. In these last two cases there was no such division between facilitator and assessor.

Another alternative is to submit a completed portfolio of learning to admission tutors who are asked to take it as evidence to support an application for admission. The applicant is then interviewed. In most cases the admission tutor would consult the course tutor, but the admission tutor's decision is final.

It is important to note, however, that for this to work effectively arrangements need to be made in advance through extensive briefing and discussion to ensure that admission tutors are willing and able to receive portfolios and deal with them in this fashion.

But whatever approach to assessment is used there is one essential difference to note between the assessment for admission and the assessment for admission with advanced standing. For admission all that is happening in simple terms is that admission tutors are being provided with an additional range of information about candidates' attainments as learners to that which they would be considering anyway. Some of that additional information is in a different category from the usual kinds of evidence offered by applicants in that it is unlikely to fit neatly into the syllabus content on which examination results are based. Hence the need to ensure that admission tutors are given proper preparatory briefings in what is involved in the assessment of prior experiential learning. But since the admission tutors' decisions are fully provided for in the entry regulation of the institution, this is a relatively straightforward business.

Admission with advanced standing, though, is a different matter. The principles for assessing experiential learning are the same as for admission. Self-evidently the stakes are higher all round. The argument that the assessment of experiential learning endangers academic standards can only be answered convincingly by insisting that those assessments are subject to the same academic scrutiny by examining boards and external examiners as any other results. This means that any academic staff member who judges that assessed experiential learning has demonstrated a candidate merits the award of academic credit towards the degree itself, must feel absolutely confident that the judgement can be fully justified. The same applies when degree regulations enable students who are already enrolled on the course to seek academic credit for their experiential learning and so reduce the number of formal course requirements they need to complete. And in each of these cases the separation of the two academic functions (see Guiding Principle 6) becomes of paramount importance.

For all these cases academic credit can be awarded either on the basis of equivalence to the content of components of the course itself, or where regulations permit, as credit under the rubric of optional studies or project work.

Some examples show all this in operation.

In one institution the evidence presented in a portfolio is considered for the award of academic credit towards the completion of the degree. The portfolio is presented at a panel interview for evaluation. The panel is composed of the subject tutor, an independent assessor and the course director or a representative. Decisions about academic credit made by that panel are then taken as recommendations to the examining board.

Alternatively, the evidence to be used for the assessment of prior learning can be drawn from the critical incident interviews, complemented where necessary with literacy and numeracy tests. Assessments are made separately by the course tutor and the appropriate subject tutor who conducts his own interviews with students seeking academic credit. This is assessment for academic credit and/or exemption.

The validity of the decisions on admission with exemption or credit is ensured first through using two academic assessors and second through assimilating assessments of prior learning to the normal internal academic procedures for examining laid out as requirements for conduct of the degree course.

In another institution a different assessment procedure was established. The appropriate board of studies adopted a formal paper: *Assessment of Prior Learning for Accreditation,* which established a set of criteria devised to guide assessors:

- Authenticity: that the student really did what is claimed in the proposal;
- Directness: that the focus of learning was sharp rather than diffused;
- Breadth: that the learning was not isolated from wider consideration;
- Quality: that the learning had reached an acceptable academic level; and
- Currency: that the student had kept up to date with recent developments.

The first step towards final assessment was for all the assessors to meet with the co-ordinating tutor to discuss the criteria. Although at that time assessors would have received proposals, the essential purpose of the first meeting would be to clarify the criteria.

This was an essential point about this assessment procedure because of the range of proposals which could be considered at any one time. A random selection of proposal titles made this clear:

- Manager of estate agent's office for four years; knowledge of housing law, marketing, office management;
- Israeli dance, extensive teaching and choreography;
- Extensive experience in the (then) Department of Health and Social Security, plus counselling for a voluntary agency;
- Fundraiser and project organiser for major conservation agency, 10 years' involvement;
- Edwardian society, and access project.

There were two assessors for each proposal. Assessors read the proposals and conducted a joint half hour viva voce with each student. They were free to set questions requiring written answers or to test the acquisition of skills. This was rarely necessary, though it is worth noting that for dance proposals a wide range of evidence was accepted including both live and videotaped performance. The assessors then made a short written report on each proposal and in all cases finished with a recommendation for the amount of credit to be awarded.

An alternative example was concerned essentially with evidence of previous learning which might have commanded academic credit. The framing of the entry regulations meant that the assessment procedure began with the application forms themselves. Forms were considered in two phases. First those that passed a screening by the degree scheme office were sent directly to subject tutors who interviewed the students and made a decision on admission and programmes to be followed and made recommendations for credit. Then recommendations from tutors were assembled in the co-ordinator's office and submitted for formal approval to the scheme's student programme committee. This provided the opportunity for awarding credit for optional units in addition to those necessarily tied to subject requirements.

Students who wished to claim additional credit sought an appointment with the co-ordinator to establish the feasibility and subject areas. Further tutorials could then follow to consider a draft of the claim to be made. The completed portfolio was then sent to a subject tutor for assessment. Recommendations to the student programme committee then followed, in the normal way.

These differences between the disciplines as a variable, crop up even within the same discipline. It is instructive to consider the three different schemes in business studies. In the first, formal assessment of APEL occurred only for those who were already enrolled on the course and were seeking academic credit so that they could complete the course more quickly. Formal assessment was not part of the admission procedure despite the fact that considerable weight was put on prior experiential learning as revealed during the admission interviews. The second showed a different emphasis. For new applicants formal assessment of prior experiential learning preceded admission to the course and was either for admission or admission with advanced standing. Formal assessment was also offered to enrolled students as a means of getting exemptions. In the third, the accent was on admission with advanced standing.

Correspondingly, the approach to the identification of prior experiential learning varied between the three. The early stages of the first two schemes are diagnostic: goodness of fit between applicant and course, as much for the benefit of the individual applicant as for admission tutors. Only subsequently is the focus sharpened on prior learning for potential credit, if an individual seeks it. The third poses the question, 'Does this applicant meet the requirements of this particular unit of study and so merit academic credit?' These variations reflect different views about the purpose of helping individuals identify their prior learning. All are valid. But they all indicate how the context of degree course and institution dictate different approaches and, most important, different clientele in their respective areas.

Something similar can be seen in considering two mechanical engineering cases. The first example has a steady number of applicants who are sent by their employers to join the degree course, so recruitment via APEL is not a prime interest. In the second example it is. The first relied on interview supported by close contacts with candidates' employers. Furthermore it appears that regulations facilitate admission with advanced standing, whereas in the second example they inhibit this.

Assessment can take a different turn in some disciplines such as social studies. There the content of courses may be general, say on social policy, rather than neatly specific as in engineering. Academics making decisions on the assessments of experiential learning for admission or for credit – admission with advanced standing – can find themselves considering evidence of knowledge which is clearly at an acceptable level but which does not equate exactly with the various sections of courses taught for the degree. Obviously sometimes the evidence they consider is course-related. But in other cases what they are doing is making judgements about conceptual grasp and understanding rather than in relation to content coverage. And that then is the basis of their assessment.

So the characteristics of a particular discipline can be the most powerful determinant for devising any scheme of APEL.

Variable 4 – institutions

The next variable is the institutional structure and the organisation of courses and the curriculum. Credit accumulation schemes are the key factor.

The central concerns for institutions are the resource implications which have to be balanced against educational benefits. From the institutional point of view again there are two ways of looking at APEL. It means either the use of interviews, manuals, guidance handbooks, checklists and the like, or an organised class or seminar. It is possible to use a mixture of these different approaches in which case the seminar is a relatively small demand on tutorial time. Ideally all should be on offer. But what an institution is concerned about primarily is cost and use of resources. Now it is obvious that providing a class or seminar incurs the usual costs of formal class: tutorial time, use of space, overheads and all the rest. But manuals are not free. Either they have to be prepared by an institution's own staff so that there are development costs to be met one or way or another or they must be bought. There are now a few manuals and handbooks available. But there is a snag. Some handbooks can cope with the general approach to APEL and the specific requirements in relation to a particular course. Others are only good for the general approach. Anyone who is new to the general idea of reflecting on experience to produce clear statements of what is being learned, organised systematically, needs help in getting into the mental stance of being able to do it. A handbook can do that job admirably. But depending on the type of course and the level of learning involved, there are particular ways of relating that learning to particular competences, capabilities, knowledge and skill. Here there are several factors to deal with. Say the course being considered is in catering or office skills. Most courses on offer, in different institutions will have broadly similar content. So a published handbook or set of checklists may well cover the ground of the specific requirements. But when for example it might be a degree in say hotel management or business studies, the content of one course may be significantly different from another offered in a different institution. Then it is by no means clear that published checklists could apply generally to all courses. In those cases it often means an institution developing its own set of checklists or learning requirements for its own purposes. Straight away that raises the question of start-up funds. The preparation of checklists takes considerable time. That staff time has to be funded somehow. True enough once the checklists are prepared they can stay in use for as long as the course exists unchanged. The money may be well spent. But it has to be found from somewhere in the first place.

This is where the organisation of courses and their administration becomes so important. It is quite obvious that accrediting the assessments of prior experiential learning is much more manageable in relation to shorter programmes of study rather than longer programmes of study.

Where an institution's academic provision is based on a unit or modular organisation, the assessment of prior learning is easier to handle than where courses are organised in large sections. This is obvious. And it is particularly important where the assessment of prior learning is conducted by comparing it with the content of formally taught courses. So in some ways modularisation or a unit structure is a facilitator for the assessment of prior learning.

The accreditation of prior experiential learning is further facilitated where programmes of academic study can be followed on a part-time or occasional basis. Mixed modes of learning are in vogue and for good reason. The demographic factors lying behind the expectation of increasing numbers of older learners lead to the need for institutions to enable older men and women to match their rhythms of academic study to the changing rhythms (sometimes unpredictable) in their employment and domestic lives. So an ability to move from full-time to part-time study and vice versa, take time out and pause before returning, in other words, all forms of student-paced learning become a necessary part of an institution's repertoire. And again this obviously can facilitate the accreditation of prior experiential learning.

There is an aspect of modes of study provided by an institution which has a direct connection with facilitating the assessment of prior experiential learning. This is essentially a curricular matter. When courses are written in terms of learning outcomes such statements can serve as the basic instrument for assessment. That instrument of assessment can be used by students and academic staff alike. The self-assessment sketched as one of the possible benefits of systematic reflection on experience can be put to firm academic purpose by the student concerned, thus saving the time of the academic assessor. Suppose a student, say in social science, has significant experience as a social worker and is seeking qualified status. If the various components of the qualifying course are expressed in terms of learning outcomes in addition to syllabus descriptions then it is quite possible for this unqualified social worker to go and check for him or herself how far what has been learned from experience equates with the requirements of a particular course component. Here again, the evidence is clear. Where institutions are adopting this style of course description, the assessment of prior experiential learning is more readily manageable.

While there is no way of conducting APEL without arranging for individuals to work through the three stages there are ways of simplifying procedures for all concerned. It is not necessarily the case that long and apparently complicated procedures with lots of tutorial time have to be devoted to each student undertaking APEL. It is necessarily the case that simplified procedures require staff time and therefore take resources to begin with.

Running through all these applications of APEL there is the same sequence of mental tasks for individuals: getting psychologically tuned to the APEL business; systematic reflection on experience to identify significant learning; the expression of significant learning in concise statements as formal claims to certain knowledge and skill; and the collation and organisation of evidence to support those claims in forms which can facilitate assessment. For each individual the process and the product can become either a component of educational guidance and counselling, and orientation and access to further study, or a route towards admission or admission with advanced academic and professional standing, or academic credit towards a final qualification.

This is the case whether the 'student' is a bookmaker who is seeking to have the financial skills of his trade converted into credit towards a business studies degree or an experienced manager, who got his first appointment on the strength of a degree in classics and who now feels the need to equip himself with a formal education in management, and wishes his knowledge of management gleaned the hard way through trial and error in his job to give him a flying start.

So the evidence is clear. The approach adopted is governed by a combination of the interests of individual participants, the characteristics of a discipline, the way the course is organised and the perception tutors have of it within their particular institutional context.

APEL IN SANDWICH COURSES

This is talking about what the Americans call sponsored experiential learning. Right at the beginning of efforts to insert the assessment of experiential learning into higher education practice, this seemed a sensible thing to tackle – sandwich courses. In Great Britain there are hundreds of sandwich courses with thousands of students taking them in a wide range of disciplines and occupational areas: engineering of all kinds, business studies, construction, surveying, hotel management, catering and so on.

Every student on these courses is required to spend what amounts to a year, in a work-placement. Some do a continuous year, some do a couple of six-month periods. There are thin and thick sandwiches served up in a variety of patterns. But whatever the arrangement that work-placement and experience is under the direct control of an academic institution. It is a degree requirement. That is what sandwich courses mean. And yet in few cases[3] for any sandwich course student does formal assessment of what might have been learned from that year's worth of work experience count academically to the classified degree result. In other words, a quarter of the course of a four-year degree learning programme is excluded from academic assessment.

Now of course there are some assessments. The most prominent form is where a certificate of performance in the workplace is issued as a statement complementary to the classified degree result. Often work assignment projects on the tasks are set by tutors which are either work-based placement experience or related to it. And of course, efforts are always made to relate the theory taught in the classroom or lecture to the practical experience of the student. So it is not that the learning from work experience is ignored in relation to formal assessment of students on sandwich degree course programmes. But it is the case that to only a very limited extent is the work experience required to be undertaken by students laid out as a source of intentional learning which is susceptible to formal assessment. So it is that few of the assessments associated with the work experience component of sandwich courses can be described strictly as the assessment of experiential learning.

It took until 1986 before anything happened on this front. Then some liaison with the principal of Sheffield City Polytechnic and TEED led eventually to the funding of a three-year project under the title of 'Facilitating and assessing placement learning'. Sheffield was not an accidental choice. The principal, the head of what has become the Business School, the principal lecturer who had pioneered the work with the National Coal Board and worked with the Trust on learning agreements and validation of companies' in-house courses and the principal lecturer who was to undertake the project had all been on study tours. They had all seen at first hand some ways in which American institutions awarded academic credit for the work-experience period within co-operative education programmes, the equivalent to sandwich courses. In the event the project worker felt unable to demonstrate how for British degrees academic credit could be awarded for the experientially acquired knowledge and skill from work experience and that was a profoundly disappointing result. However, the thorough work that went into working out systematically how students, academic tutors and employers can best be prepared to get the most out of a period of work placement produced what may well turn out to be a definitive set of guideline documents. And although none addressed the award of academic credit directly, they provide an admirable basis for taking further the debate about academic credit. Moreover the discussions exposed a general range of issues about assessment for any academic credit, whatever the mode of learning, whether lecture room, mediated, distance or independent study.

That project finished in September 1989. A further project, funded again by TEED then began at Napier Polytechnic in Edinburgh. For this too the Trust played something of a facilitating role. The deputy principal of Napier Polytechnic and the manager of IBM Youth Programmes UK were on the same study tour. Like the Sheffield quartet, they had seen an American programme of sponsored learning and they were enthusiastic about trying to develop something comparable in Scotland. On the train between Philadelphia and Trenton, New Jersey we hatched a scheme for a new form of collaboration between IBM and the Polytechnic, the purpose of which was to work out ways of awarding academic credit for work-based learning during a sandwich course. In 1988 the Scottish Education Department funded a limited project. And this was followed by a full-scale development project to extend the principles evolved throughout the Polytechnic in many parts of its curriculum. The assessment of sponsored experiential learning was on its way.

APEL AND EMPLOYMENT

Any new idea, new way of working, new procedure to be followed, has a chance of being successful if there is something in it for everyone, some benefit perceived for all the people involved. Even a sceptic can deduce that applying that notion to higher and further education shows that everyone wins, no-one loses. Potential and actual students gain through having their self-confidence boosted, being enabled to make better choices, strengthening their case for admission and at best getting their course shortened in respect of what they had learned already. Individual members of staff benefit in several ways. Personally they can enjoy a sense of being more professional; getting a better fit between what their institution has to offer and the individuals who come to it. That better fit is likely to improve the retention figure in their classes; fewer students will leave because they are dissatisfied. They also gain from the benefits accruing to the institution. When demographic graphs throw doubt on recruitment levels, any means of attracting not only more applicants from the older age groups, but applicants from socio-economic groups which are currently relatively unrepresented, is a boon. Only then can staffing levels be sustained and with them all the resources which enable an institution to function professionally. At a policy level, wherever that is found, either in central or local government or in a governing body, it is ultimately recruitment figures which influence overriding funding policies. So everyone wins, where the assessment of experiential learning is conducted effectively in further and higher education. But it is not always seen as a financial issue.

In employment it is. It has to be. Then the 'everyone wins, so that no-one loses' argument is essential. At first sight that may seem improbable. The argument goes like this. And it begins with demography, just as for education. Employers now recognise that they need to make the best use of the adult employees that they employ for the simple reason that there will be fewer younger men and women available for employment as the next twenty years go by. This poses a set of conflicting pressures. On the one hand they have to be able to keep their workforce up to date with developing production techniques, organisation and administrative procedures and that means investing in updating and retraining programmes. On the other hand, they worry that the people they have retrained may use their improved skills to move to another employer for a better job. So rather like education establishments, employers face the dual problem of recruitment and retention.

The assessment of experiential learning fits into this picture. Remember that its central message is that an individual is likely to know more and be able to do more than there is any formal evidence to show. Remember too, the dual strands running through any assessment of experiential learning: self-assessment and formal assessment. In the context of employment this offers two strands of possibilities. Assessment without thought of accreditation is very close to staff appraisal. Systematic reflection on experience can reveal capabilities in an employee of which neither the employer nor employee was consciously aware. This can be valuable when an employer is facing staffing problems arising from making promotions, the needs for redeployment, or in anticipation of redundancies. That is obvious. What is not so obvious is that it can be a direct help to an employee. Employees who have compiled a portfolio of their attainments as learners, present themselves to their line managers with far greater confidence. Through their own self-assessment they have a better sense of their own worth. So this strand of possibilities arising from the assessment of experiential learning in the workplace can flow into the main stream of managerial responsibilities. The accreditation strand of possibilities fits into those responsibilities as well.

Learning contracts for employees shows this at work.[2] This scheme involved enlisting volunteers in full-time employment in Jaguar Cars Ltd, JBS Computers Ltd, the Manpower Services Commission as it then was, and Wimpy Foods International Ltd and negotiating with each one of them learning programmes which took them on from what they already knew at either the level of a bachelor's degree or a master's degree, but with a three-way reference.

The programme of learning had to be acceptable and of direct interest, not only to the employee but to the employer. In other words, there was something in it for everyone. These arrangements were possible because of the establishment of the Credit Accumulation and Transfer Registry at the Council for National Academic Awards. That Registry offers facilities to individual applicants to qualify for CNAA degrees by assembling programmes of study from a number of sources undertaken in a mixture of patterns. 'Credit may be given for previous formal courses of study or learning gained by experience' [CATS regulation, CNAA] (assessment of experiential learning). These facilities meant that credit acquired from the assessment of a completed learning contract could count towards either a bachelor's or a master's degree.

The CATS regulations also meant, however, that the volunteers could acquire additional credit for their experiential learning if they chose to do the work of preparing statements of that learning with supporting evidence for assessment. In this way they were undertaking the same preparatory work as they would have done had they been in formal attendance at an education institution. Once the volunteers got the hang of the Learning Contracts Scheme, realising that they were on an accelerating track towards the degree they were seeking, then about half of them asked that their prior experiential learning should be assessed. This amounted to saying no more and no less than that their on-the-job learning in their day-to-day work assignments, whether on the production and design side of engineering, software engineering, restaurant management or administration, should be assessed. It might well generate academic credit which was additional to whatever credit they might obtain from their negotiated programme of additional learning. Learning Contracts for Employees exposed two additional sources of potential academic credit for the volunteer employees. The first was that implied in the quotation from the CATS regulations. Anyone who had say, completed a Higher National Diploma, or one year of a higher education degree programme, or had completed some Open University courses, could apply to have credit assigned. And provided it did not amount to double counting, repeating evidence of learning which was being assessed for credit already, it would be counted.

Company in-house education and training was the other source of potential academic credit. And that includes any provision made by the employer whether literally in-house or brought in or provided externally on a commercial basis. And such courses which have been validated academically and given a credit rating by a team of academic assessors, and approved by CNAA through the CATS Registry, or by higher education institutions can feature in an individual applicant's papers as claims to credit towards the award being sought.

Learning contracts for employees therefore demonstrate that without leaving the employers' premises, employees who are prepared to do some work in their own time (in employer's time if it is granted) have three sources of potential academic credit in their hands; a negotiated learning programme, the assessment of experiential learning and in-house courses of education and training. It follows that the employers have these three sources of potential academic credit available to them for their staff development, updating and retraining purposes. With this essential difference: that without doing anything significantly additional to their normal activities they can offer their employees a route towards qualifications which exploits what has been learned already, whatever its source. It sets fair to save everyone time and money, and all within the general provisions for ensuring the academic standards commensurate with higher education at bachelor's and master's degree levels.

As with the self-assessment strand to the assessment of experiential learning, this version of assessment for accreditation fits into managers' concerns. Whether in the context of learning contracts or taken by itself, the proposition that on-the-job learning can become creditable in degree terms means that managers have another factor to consider in relation to their policies for recruitment and retention. Whether interpreted as inducement, benefits or opportunities for advancement is a matter of emphasis. What is absolutely clear is that this way of looking at the possibilities for making best use of the learning attainments of employees offers an employer a cost-effective way of looking at retraining and updating needs. For a start, it is far cheaper to pay for the academic consultancies involved in the three categories of potential academic credit cited, than pay the full cost of the fees for attendance at formal courses which can produce the same amount of academic credit. And then if attendance at those courses occurs in the employer's time, there is a considerable cost to be borne for the loss of employee time.

But there is another financial advantage. Many employers bear the full cost of enabling their employees to study for a formal qualification and whether that is full-time or part-time study the costs are high. At the end of a learning contract and taking into account the three sources of possible academic credit, it is unlikely that a candidate would have satisfied all the requirements for the award. Some additional study will be required almost certainly. There are many ways that additional study can be completed. It could be through attendance at formal courses in an institution. It could be through enrolling with the Open University. It could be through a further learning contract or a project, depending on the nature of the study involved and the level being attempted. The point is that whichever of these possibilities was chosen to complete studies for the award, it would involve less study time than would enrolling at the beginning of a course leading towards the same award. Less study time means less fees to pay. And where an employer either pays in full or contributes to those costs, that clearly means a smaller expenditure figure in the training budget.

Hence it seems reasonable to assert that the assessment of experiential learning for employees and employers is an advantageous financial proposition read against the employers' overriding responsibility for the annual income and expenditure accounts. It is cheap at the price.

The learning contract project was not simply a one-off. It was a deliberate attempt to pioneer an additional way of seeing collaboration between employer and higher education as a series of benefits for employee/employer and higher education alike. And so it has proved. Each of the four polytechnics began to seek other employer partners with whom to arrange learning contract schemes. TEED itself has fastened on to learning contracts as another way of approaching, updating, reskilling, staff development and training generally and is busy promoting additional projects.

Nor was the validation of companies' in-house provision a shot in the dark. Several of the companies involved have gone on to develop extensive collaborative programmes with their polytechnic partners. The Brewers' Society, the Woolwich Building Society and Sainsbury's to name but three have followed up the initial validation work undertaken for them with Thames Polytechnic to work out what are essentially degree completion programmes. Their in-house courses for their own employees have been combined with the assessment of on-the-job learning (APEL) and courses jointly planned with the Polytechnic as a route towards a bachelor's degree. And it is all arranged to be of the greatest convenience for employees and employers. Distance learning programmes, residential weekends and attendance patterns generally seek to minimise the interruption for the day-to-day work of the company. And has led to further collaboration between the Polytechnic and a range of older employees.

Similarly Sheffield City Polytechnic has used both learning contracts and validation of companies' in-house courses for further developments.

Both feature in subsequent collaboration with TEED, which sees the value of both sources of potential academic credit in relation to its own personal development programme for employees. And Burton's, the men's outfitters chain, has gone into partnership with the Polytechnic for the validation of in-house courses. Wolverhampton and Leeds Polytechnics are going along the same path energetically. Others are at earlier stages. It is fast becoming a major institutional undertaking.

APEL AND MANAGEMENT EDUCATION

All of these possibilities feature in the various attempts to improve management education which have followed the publication of *The Making of Managers*, which was the Handy Report, published by the National Economic Development Office in 1987, and funded jointly by TEED (the Manpower Services Commission as it then was), and its companion document, *The Making of British Managers* by John Constable and Roger McCormack. According to the reports the scale of the need for the development of managers is phenomenal. Some 90,000 people become managers each year, so we are told, and of them only some 12,000 have any sort of formal academic preparation for the role. If that calculation is extended across the total work of managers in Great Britain, then it is difficult to avoid being scared for our economic future, given the dramatically different proportions of trained managers in Japan, the USA, Germany and France, and increasingly in other South-East Asian countries. Unsurprisingly then, the initiatives taken by the Council for Management Education and Development (CMED) renamed National Forum (NAFMED) and the Chartered Management Initiative and the burgeoning number of business schools concern approaches which incorporate two imperatives: building on the knowledge and skill which have been acquired through experience of managing (APEL in one form or another) and minimum disturbance to the work and domestic lives of the managers who have to be persuaded of the need to become better at their jobs. So flexibility, open access, integration with work, employer involvement, appropriate assessment methods and appropriate learning methods are the watchwords for any schemes which anyone can think up. And since everything we know about the assessment of prior experiential learning speaks of its potential power as a motivator for additional learning and study, and as a confidence builder which encourages further study, then it is hardly surprising that APEL must be a central factor in attempts to foster the development of managers. Quite apart from anything else the scale of the operation means that both for logistical and financial reasons opportunities of the kind demonstrated by learning contracts have got to be exploited to the full.

In 1983, when the first piece of work with the assessment of prior experiential learning was launched with a group of middle managers in the National Coal Board, as it then was, at Doncaster, it was clear that APEL connected with a whole range of management development issues as well as staff appraisal. That small group of middle managers demonstrated that systematic reflection on their experience assisted their occupational development because it enabled them to reveal to themselves their strengths and weaknesses, and as a result to have a better understanding of what makes sense for them in the future. Whether their next decision was to undertake additional formal study or change career direction, or seek internal promotion with greater assurance, they all agreed that the APEL procedure was valuable for them in terms of their own personal and career development. Exactly the same is true of the middle managers from TEED itself, who were volunteer participants in the learning contracts for employees project. As has been mentioned earlier, the scale of the needs now being cited for management education is such that means have to be found of capitalising on on-the-job learning of the managers thought to need to acquire additional management skills so as to become better managers. Straight away this is talking about the assessment of their experiential learning. That was taken forward by another TEED-funded project, 'The Experienced Manager'. And as institutions up and down the country design their new certificates of management and lay plans for diplomas and MBAs almost automatically APEL features one way or another.

APEL AND CONTINUING PROFESSIONAL DEVELOPMENT

Management education is a component of something larger – continuing professional development (CPD). The need is obvious. Keeping up to date for doctors, engineers, lawyers and social workers is every bit as necessary as it is for British Telecom technicians, and production workers in an automated car manufacturing plant. Some companies are busy developing their own CPD programmes. Most universities, polytechnics and colleges provide CPD courses, often tailor-made for a particular sector or employer. And the pressure for CPD is increasing. The introduction of PICKUP in 1982 showed the government's concern for this level of retraining and updating and all the career changes that go with it, just as more recently, NCVQ indicates concern with the levels of skill in the workforce in general. Pressure comes not only from the need to keep up to date, but from a growing tendency to move towards mandatory CPD as a means of ensuring that the licence to practise of a professional remains a proper protection for the public and ensures appropriate professional standards. And all of that is underlined by 1992 and the arrival of increasing winds of competition from the other countries in the European Community.

So far there is little formal academic assessment within CPD of APEL. Non-graduate applicants for a master's degree in education can be admitted on the basis of their assessed experiential learning. The design of the CNAA master's degree for professions includes provision for credit based on APEL. If companies' in-house courses are validated and learning contracts/agreements for employees are included, then APEL relates to CPD and can come into the reckoning.

But the general impression is that it is the curricular strand to APEL rather than the formal assessment strand which is being developed in some CPD programmes. The Engineering Council, for example, used PICKUP funding to develop a small handbook called *The Career Manager*. The foreword includes the words

The Career Manager will help you in the following ways:
- To review systematically your present development needs
- To provide preparation for discussion with your employer/careers adviser
- To devise a realistic career action plan
- To record your actual progress against that plan.

I believe that you will find this approach both stimulating and effective.

The handbook which is rather like a largish diary takes an individual through all that in twenty-two pages, most of which are blank spaces with headings. It is self-assessment with a vengeance. And it is certainly CPD.

Doctors and architects are edging their way to some form of APEL in their respective schemes for professional development. Provision for general practice doctors sometimes concentrates on simulations and role play. Pretending to be a patient, trying to feel the anxiety, insecurity, perhaps panic, the need for reassurance which is what so many people experience in the doctor's surgery, all this is quite different from reading about it or coping with it in real life. The intention of the CPD is to encourage self-assessment. Like the engineers, it is all based on experience. Formal assessment of what has been learned from those experiences, however, becomes a teasing issue for the examiners for membership of the Royal College of General Practice (MRCGP). The examination has four components. There is a multiple-choice question paper, an essay examination paper based on case study examples, a critical reading question paper requiring comment on a provided text, and an oral examination. As in many other academic contexts where theory, and practice are the twin strands of study, assessments tend to be weighted heavily on the formal examination of knowledge of theory, producing results which sometimes seem less than satisfactory as a report on a person's fitness for licence to practise. Excellent results in formal examinations and mediocre practice standards in the consulting room clearly are unsatisfactory. Yet because formal examinations are so much easier to handle this kind of imbalance produces a continual tension. It is not unlike the discussion of sandwich courses. For the MRCGP examination, however, the compulsory oral examination is increasingly seen as a way of attempting to correct the balance. Investigating what someone has to say about their day-to-day practice could produce a set of results which would complement those derived from formal examinations and add up to a comprehensive account of an applicant's professional competence. It would be APEL by another name. And because there is discussion about the possible formal accreditation of the MRCGP so it might become a requirement for professional practice instead of its voluntary state at present, APEL could become a central feature on medical education and training.

Similarly the Royal Institute of British Architects (RIBA) is concerned to incorporate APEL in the provision of its newly designed master's course in association with Thames Polytechnic. This is designed explicitly to take account of the practice as well as theory, shifting the focus away from the purely academic. To this end APEL is being introduced as a means of acquiring academic credit, and so are negotiated learning agreements and credit based on the validation of RIBA's in-house courses. Again APEL is becoming part of the provision of continuing professional development for architects. The Central Council for Education and Training in Social Work (CCETSW) has taken similar decisions. It has approved regulations for its credit accumulation provision for post-qualifying awards which include provision for granting credit on the basis of APEL. The chartered accountants have become interested in APEL following the Hotel Catering and Institutional Management Association. The City and Guilds of London Institute is incorporating credit for assessed experiential learning in new awards at first degree and master's degree levels partly as a spur to the development of the professionals working in the wide range of occupations it exists to serve.

This does not imply that all CPD is related to APEL. It is absolutely clear for, say, solicitors, that there is a straightforward information service required about recent statutory provision with some sharp-minded academic commentary on it. And the same is true for many other professions. It is saying that since CPD concerns the improvement of day-to-day practice, careful identification of what has been learned already from professional work is a secure base from which to strive for that improvement.

The context for all these developments in higher education relating to

APEL is the rigorous application of quality assurance procedures designed to ensure the preservation of academic standards. Every scheme, whether for individuals as students, or for employees or for companies, is subject to the searching validation procedures pioneered by CNAA twenty and more years ago, and now either used directly via the Council or deployed through accredited institutions, responsible for their own academic affairs. So it can be said that APEL has become mainstream activity in many higher education institutions, and is becoming so in many more. A CNAA CAT Newsletter (Number 1) showed how fast these developments are. It told that sixteen polytechnics had CAT schemes already in place, with eleven more schemes operational by September 1990, four following by September 1991 and far more later on, and that agreements had been negotiated with ten universities.

8 APEL and further education

Primarily all that concerns higher education. Further education is different. It has to be, given the huge range of services it offers to such varied groups of potential learners. But the principles remain the same. To a larger extent than is sometimes recognised, so too are the applicants and potential students coming from the same categories of people. But because further education colleges are concerned primarily with sub-degree work, accepting the amount of BTEC higher national diploma work undertaken is significant, it works from within a different tradition, substantially vocational. It has different institutional structures and procedures, and generally considers itself to have less direct responsibility for the design, content and examination of the courses it teaches. That is how things were until the establishment of the National Council for Vocational Qualifications. Of which more later.

The case for the assessment of prior experiential learning in further education was and is the same as elsewhere; that many men and women who appear as older applicants may well bring with them accumulated knowledge and skill for which there is no formal evidence but which may well be academically significant. The case is most obvious in relation to access courses which offer routes towards higher education. And as with higher education itself the purpose of identifying the prior experiential learning people bring with them is to strengthen the applicants' case for admission to an admission tutor. But within each scheme it is important to remember that the twin strands run: that leading to self-assessment and that running towards formal assessment.

There are a variety of ways that this is being done. One approach is to provide a timetabled course for a class meeting, say thirty-three weeks for three hours a week. The course takes as its content the life and work experience of its students, themes such as childhood, schooling and organising can be used to stimulate reflection on experience. Considerable written work is likely to be required as take-home assignments. Students can be encouraged to compile a portfolio of learning as they go along.

General discussions are supplemented by individual tutorials. The general thrust of a course can be towards enabling students to make informed choices about their futures which for some includes applying for higher education.

Quite a different approach was adopted for a specialist entry course to an access course for the B.Ed. degree. Students were required to compile a portfolio of their experiential learning drawn from their experience of short placements in schools and community settings, any related work they might undertake while on the course itself, such as part-time youth work or voluntary work, and from any reflections they might care to make about their childhood, adolescence and post-school years. There was a threefold purpose behind this injection of the assessment of experiential learning into this particular course. It was to provide a focus for integration and assimilation of the many aspects of the course that are about theories of child development and education. It was an attempt to help students to deepen their understanding of their personal reasons for wanting to teach or do youth work, and to work out how much and in what way they wanted to share their own experiences with others, for example youth club members. But also and perhaps most important of all it was to help build confidence in the value of their own experience of class, sexual and racial identity, in order to help them survive in the very different social and institutional climate of a higher education institution.

To help students prepare their portfolios the college drew up a list of qualities and competences, with corresponding examples, which an applicant could be expected to have before being admitted to the access course itself. The first quality listed was 'appreciation of some of the personal and academic implications of undertaking an Access course leading to a B.Ed. Honours degree'. The example given as to how evidence might be covered in a portfolio read 'indication of efforts made to gain information about the course from the reading of literature; talking to students; autobiographical account of reasons for seeking course; awareness of implications of five years of study.' Another required competence or quality was 'the ability to write at an appropriate level of accuracy and complexity'. And the example given was 'range of writing in portfolios; samples of writing from work, letters, courses'. And then 'the ability to display flexibility of interpretation and tolerance in the face of others' arguments and cultures' was listed as a competence. And the example given of evidence which could be used to support a claim to having acquired that flexibility was 'testimonials; tape of live discussion; evidence of interest in own and/or others, ethnic backgrounds.' The same institution organised what it called a Portfolio Preparation Workshop. This was a drop-in workshop for adults offering two two-hour sessions a week during the whole academic year. The idea here was to provide a workshop setting where adults who were thinking of returning to education could produce a portfolio of their learning achievements. This would contain evidence of what they had learned from experience other than or in addition to what had taken place in formal educational institutions. The assumption was that this would serve two useful purposes for students. As a process it could provide a framework for self-assessment for confidence building and extended careers guidance and planning. As a product the portfolio could assist where possible entry to a chosen course by offering selectors a substantial record of the student's knowledge and skills.

Behind both of these developments in providing opportunities for students to assess their prior experiential learning lay some institutional concerns. Tutors were aware that sometimes the courses students chose to attend and indeed the courses they were accepted on, were on a rather random, haphazard basis. So they were concerned to give adults the widest possible information, choice and support in planning their futures. Tutors were also aware that although due lip service was paid to the value of students' experiences, frequently little use was made of those experiences as the starting pad for launching into new areas of knowledge. Nor did the tutors think they did enough to help students make connections between the experiential learning which they had already acquired and the more formal study material of the courses.

The tutors recognised that their own entry requirements, like many others, asked adult students to offer some indication of 'relevant experience'. However, other than by subjective impressions at interview there was no way of evaluating the learning that had taken place as a result of the experience, whatever it was. Also at interview applicants are sometimes judged on unstated criteria, like perseverance or open-mindedness, about which they could offer evidence for experiential learning if they were given the opportunity to do so. So it was these five concerns which prompted the development of these two approaches to the assessment of prior experiential learning.

A variation on this theme of incorporating the assessment of experiential learning within access courses comes from a course for adults seeking professional training in social science or youth and community work. In this case the portfolio was used as an integrating tool for the entire course. And the variation is this. The portfolio was to provide a record, not only of prior experiential learning, but current experiential learning based on placements offered as part of the course. Indeed portfolio preparation became the unifying theme for the course as a whole. At first it was chiefly a device for documenting previous learning experiences and recording the results of assessments carried out. Later in the course it broadened to become a means of structuring and unifying otherwise disparate although not unconnected learning experiences. As such it had a major role in achieving curriculum integration. Structuring the portfolio as a record of competences achieved is itself a discipline and useful intellectual skill. So as well as providing a framework for this purpose the portfolio itself became evidence of the depth a student had achieved in analysing and recording learning. The portfolio itself therefore became not simply a record of competences, stated in an assessable form, but a record of an unfolding learning process.

REPLAN was another government initiative, introduced this time to help with unemployment. Based in the National Institute of Adult and Continuing Education, REPLAN works closely with the Further Education Unit and a whole series of development projects have been launched in colleges of further education. One such was 'Skills assessment and vocational guidance for unemployed people' in the County of Avon. The brief for the project was to work out ways in which prior experiential learning could be put to the best use for helping unemployed people find their way back to employment. One of the most important results of that project was the development of a handbook which the Further Education Unit published in 1987 as *Building Your Own Portfolio*?. This was a simple straightforward set of questions, examples and exercises designed to help unemployed people deal with the things they find most difficult: to think purposefully and positively about the possibilities offered in jobs which were quite unfamiliar to them. So often the shock, confusion, numbness and blow to self-confidence brought on by being unemployed means that people find it almost impossible to picture themselves in a job which is not like the one they had previously. The very fact that this slim publication has proved such a popular FEU issue shows how APEL for unemployed people spoke to the preoccupations of so many further education staff.

The abortive Job Training Scheme and the equally dubious successor Employment Training (ET) have also involved many further education colleges. The somewhat unsatisfactory division between training manager and training provider has only underlined the significance of reflection on experience. The entire planning period for ET is supposed to produce a training programme on an individual basis. An individual training programme can only be produced on the basis of a review of the past, attempts to sort out strengths and weaknesses, further attempts to work out what might be the most appropriate type of employment to try to go for, and then the evolving of a programme of training to get from here to there. And if that does not look like APEL it is hard to know what it is all about.

One of the most telling developments in non-advanced further education has been the emergence of open college federations. They have been powerful advocates of APEL. In their different ways the Manchester Open College Federation (MOCF) and the Sheffield Open College led the field in these initiatives. MOCF undertook a project funded by the DES through the Unit for the Development of Adult and Continuing Education to spread the news and stimulate similar developments throughout the country. Sheffield's efforts have been more localised, but are equally influential in spreading the open college federation idea; wherever there are any open learning systems designed essentially to open opportunities for adults, they see APEL as one of their vital ingredients. As they set out to try to encourage those who do not automatically turn to further or higher education, alongside flexible learning approaches, credit accumulation and progression they send the message to all who will hear that they value what men and women can bring with them. And that is precisely what APEL is about. When NCVQ appeared on the scene it presented open federations with an additional range of issues as it has done for further education as a whole.

The National Council for Vocational Qualifications has given another twist to the assessment of prior experiential learning in further education. Broadly stated, NCVQ was established in 1986 by government with a brief to try to produce usable pathways through the jungle of vocational qualifications. This meant thinking up ways of producing a coherent structure which would accommodate not only the generally-known examining and validating bodies like the Business and Technician Education Council, the City and Guilds of London Institute, the Royal Society of Arts and the Pitmans Institute, but also the scores of bodies such as the Chemical Industries Association, the Construction Industry Training Board, the Engineering Industry Training Board, the Hotel and Catering Training Board, the National Examinations Board for Agriculture, Horticulture and Allied Industries, and so on.

It was and is a tall order. The brief given to the National Council for Vocational Qualifications by government is to:

- Improve the value of vocational qualifications to employers and individuals alike;
- Encourage individuals to develop their vocational competence by improving access to vocational qualifications and clearly defining progressional routes;
- Encourage the provision of more and better vocational training through vocational qualifications which meet the real needs of employment and prepare individuals for changes in technology, markets and employment patterns, thus contributing towards improved national economic performance.

And that of course is the whole point of NCVQ: to improve national economic performance.

NCVQ's chosen method of tackling its tasks was to settle on the notion of competence as the integrating tool to facilitate the hallmarking of National Vocational Qualifications. For NCVQ the fundamental requirements of a competence are:

- The area of competence to be covered must have meaning and relevance in the context of the occupational structure in the sector of employment concerned.
- The statement of competence must be based on an analysis of occupational roles within the area of competence to which it relates.
- The statement of competence must encompass the underpinning knowledge and understanding required for effective performance in employment.

For NCVQ, a competence thus is:

A statement of competence clearly relevant to work and intended to facilitate entry into, or progression in, employment and further learning issued to an individual by a recognised awarding body. Each statement of competence for a national vocational qualification should be determined and/or endorsed by an acceptable group with responsibility for maintaining and improving national standards of performance in the sector(s) of employment where the competence is practised.

What this means in practice is that employers in designated industry lead bodies are being required to set out statements of competence with standards attached in their particular occupational area. Everything will be set out in a hierarchy of competence going through Levels 1, 2, 3 and 4 and may be higher for the professions. Quite clearly this is involving these industry lead bodies in a great deal of work. And it is only after their work is completed that competences can be publicised nationally so that the system is fully operational.

For further education colleges, all this means a demanding set of new requirements. The same is true for the examining and validating bodies that colleges have worked with over the years: BTEC, City and Guilds, RSA, Pitmans and so on. What this means in practice for the examining and validating bodies is that their qualifications need to be submitted to the NCVQ so that they can be hallmarked for particular competences. Since not all courses leading to qualifications have been constructed on the basis of demonstration of competences, this too is requiring considerable additional work. But it all faces those colleges and examining and validating bodies with broadly speaking a similar range of problems to solve.

Accumulation and progression are the watchwords of the NCVQ enterprise. This becomes of fundamental significance since NCVQ is only interested in evidence of competence, it is not concerned with how those competences have been acquired. In other words, for the colleges there is a disaggregation between any courses leading to recognised qualifications and the demonstration of competences which alone will merit a National Vocational Qualification award. Inevitably and inexorably this introduces the assessment of prior experiential learning. Since it is only the demonstration of a competence at a particular level which can enable an individual to get a National Vocational Qualification, it matters not in the slightest that somebody seeking recognition for a competence at Level 3 has done nothing whatsoever to gain formal recognition for any competence at Level 1 or 2. In other words, it now becomes an individual's right to seek recognition of competence at an appropriate level more or less on demand.

For colleges of further education this poses a set of tricky and indeed sensitive issues. Instead of teaching courses which begin at the beginning of an academic year leading to a formal qualification and working according to neatly organised timetables, institutions and their academic staff will now have to recognise a competence when they see one. Or rather, because it is more complicated than that, they will have to be able to recognise a unit of a competence, a subset of a competence, assess it and then determine what additional acquisition of knowledge and skill is necessary as 'top-up' study, to enable that individual to reach the full competence in question. So at one bound to come to terms with NCVQ and all its works, institutions will need to reorganise the way their learning programmes are put on offer to potential students, rethink the content of those learning programmes so as to comply with the NCVQ requirements of competences, usually in collaboration with BTEC, City and Guilds, RSA or the Pitmans Institute, and moreover be able to cope with all that is implied by accumulation and progression. And this of course is where it connects directly with the assessment of prior experiential learning. Since there is no obligation on an individual to have completed competences in Levels 1 and 2 in order to undertake assessment in competences at Level 3, then straight off this involves the certification of uncertificated learning. APEL has come full circle.

Clearly this is a massive undertaking in terms of a national system capable of delivering NVQs. It requires significant changes in the ways in which all the various bodies concerned do their day-to-day work. To this end the TEED and NCVQ launched a two-year project in October 1987 working with five further education colleges and one skill centre 'To explore the accreditation of Prior Learning (APEL)' in relation to vocational qualifications. The project had five primary objectives. First of all it was to determine the feasibility of using evidence of achievement from previous experience to recognise current competence. That meant working with participating awarding bodies to develop guidelines, procedures and support for assessment and for the assessment and accreditation of prior learning. Staff development was a prerequisite for any of these developments; the project was also to devise briefing and training workshops. It was also concerned to make observations and comment about the monitoring of progress during the project by the awarding bodies, the potential demand amongst different client groups and the costs of implementation. Last and perhaps most significant of all the project was designed to attempt to determine the impact of APEL on organisational change within the participating colleges. As with some of the other projects mentioned this set up a ripple effect both within the colleges and outward from them to others. Colleagues in colleges got interested and began to develop their own approaches to APEL. Various conferences served as a general dissemination exercise. So via NCVQ interest in APEL in further education has both quickened and widened. Some £300,000 was invested in this project and that alone gives some indication of both the importance attached by the government to all these developments on the one hand, and on the other the large range of issues it all raises for the colleges, the examining and awarding bodies and indeed for NCVQ itself.

It also raises fundamental questions for employers. Since the central purpose of NCVQ is to strengthen the workforce, and this is to be achieved by institutions helping people to reach competence levels which are themselves decided by employers, then quite obviously this is talking about a new form of collaboration between employers and further education colleges. Demography comes in here. So does local financial management, as specified according to the Education Reform Act of 1988. Briefly it means that colleges will have to work hard at recruiting older men and women as students. Local financial management means that they are going to look increasingly to employers for as many students as they can manage to get. And that will not be easy. It is one thing for industry-led bodies of employers to determine standards criteria and formulate statements of competence. It is quite another thing for employers in the immediate area of a college to understand what NCVQ is all about, let alone be willing to pay tuition or assessment fees involved, if their employees are to attend that college.

Indeed the position is more complicated than that. The establishment of Training Enterprise Councils with the responsibility for organising the training in their own area, will drive colleges into competitive contractual arrangements in order to sell their wares. No-one knows yet how all of this will work out. But it is quite clear that the simultaneous arrival on the scene of national vocational qualifications as organised by the NCVQ and Training Enterprise Councils as established by parliamentary statute, is going to change the world in which further education colleges live.

One of the difficulties all these colleges have is to keep a sense of balance between vocational and non-vocational provision. On average, colleges have about 60 per cent of their work which is vocational and about 40 per cent which is non-vocational. Regional and institutional differences mean that some colleges have far more courses such as 'New Opportunities For Women', 'Return to Learning', 'Access to Higher Education' than others. And of course, the amount of GCSE and 'A' Level work varies considerably according to the way in which 'A' Level work is being organised either through a tertiary college, a sixth-form college, a community college or through colleges of further education. Furthermore, in some areas adult education has been assimilated to further education colleges and in others, community provision may be operated as a separate service. Newly established institutions such as the Manchester Open College Federation and the South Yorkshire Open College exist specifically to create pathways towards further study, sometimes on to higher and further education only some of which begins as vocational work, whatever direction an individual may choose to take further along the learning road.

NCVQ emphasises the point quite correctly: despite the significance of its National Vocational Competences, underlining the urgency of colleges equipping themselves to make full provision for NVQ assessments, and with the enterprise being fuelled by extensive funding by the NCVQ itself and the TEED for developmental projects in colleges, it is important for further education as a whole to continue to see the world as it did before the arrival of NCVQ. That world was and continues to be a world where the vocational lives alongside the non-vocational. In other words, NCVQ is posing the problem for colleges of continuing their provision of both liberal and vocational education whilst assimilating the vocational training assessments which are the essential foundation for NCVQ.

For APEL this is a fundamental matter. The disassociation of learning from assessment which is the principle on which NCVQ is founded is totally inappropriate for many students in further education who find APEL a rewarding and empowering way of learning. And there is a danger that undue emphasis on NCVQ can distort APEL and risk diminishing the contribution it can make to the education and training of adults.

Increasingly the combination of these various pressures is prompting colleges to revise their registration and admissions procedures, to investigate the implications of college admissions rather than registration on courses. As with higher education APEL is one bit of yeast, leavening further education provision. Asking the question in contemporary circumstances, how best to improve the services for the various demands made by differing groups of potential students can produce answers in further education which show APEL helping to change the system.

APEL AND YOUTH EDUCATION AND TRAINING

The assessment of experiential learning features in another department of employment: the Youth Training Scheme (YTS). The linchpin of the YTS scheme is the on-site supervisor. Not all of them are enthusiastic about it, understandably. Employed as supervisors of mainline activity within the organisation, frequently these supervisors find themselves lumbered with the additional task of supervising YTS trainees. Having that responsibility with the accompanying tasks of completing record sheets and making assessments of their task performance is a very different thing from supervising full-time employees who work within conditions negotiated between management and union. Nevertheless, it is the on-site supervisor of a YTS trainee who is likely to make the most effective contribution to the overall quality of the training offered to YTS trainees. So anything which could boost the morale and enthusiasm of YTS supervisors would be helpful. The assessment of experiential learning came into play again. There was a twofold intention in introducing it. First it went on other evidence of the benefits arising from people being able to demonstrate to and for themselves through systematic reflection on their experience, that they knew more than they thought they knew. It therefore seemed likely that enabling YTS supervisors to articulate what skills and knowledge they used supervising their trainees and to identify where and how they acquired that knowledge and skill would be a useful experience, and also potentially valuable in encouraging them to improve their performance as YTS supervisors. As an extension of that, it seemed possible that in the process some might be so pleased to discover that they were rather better at learning, and more successful learners that they had assumed previously, that they might be stimulated to undertake some form of further study and training for the sake of their own occupational development and their personal growth.

And so it proved. There is nothing surprising about that taken in the light of the accounts of where and how the assessment of experiential learning is being conducted in a range of other arenas. It is, however, an important indication of the way assessment of experiential learning can work to the benefit of so many different categories of people both in formal learning in institutions and in the day-to-day world of life and work.

There was a bonus to conducting assessments of experiential learning with YTS supervisors. Some claimed that as a result of their efforts to sort out for themselves what they were doing as supervisors of YTS trainees they found that they thought they became better at their mainline supervisory duties. In other words there was some transfer occurring between what they thought about in one context and what they actually did as wage earners in another where they were responsible for other wage earners' performance. That was new. It was important. It has profound implications for the way training programmes are arranged. And even more important it has great bearing on the way employers view the demands being made on them to shoulder more of the national responsibility for training the next generation of employed people.

The YTS into Higher Education project, funded by the Joseph Rowntree Memorial Trust (Now the Rowntree Foundation) has highlighted this issue. The basic assumption for this project was that amongst the YTS cohort there were bound to be a number of young people who had the capacity to cope with higher education, but made no effort to do so for all the well-rehearsed socio-economic reasons. It is all part of the failure to increase participation rates from the Registrar General's groups 4 and 5. If, so the reasoning went, some could be helped to realise their own capacity as learners they might lift their horizons and be encouraged to progress towards studying at that level. The project demonstrated that this could be done. Using APEL techniques and following up with a learning agreement, and completed portfolios it showed this had an impact on career and occupational progress. With few and in some cases no 'O' levels or GCSEs, for example, one moved towards an HND, one was accepted for a B.Ed., another for a law degree, one has moved on to a fashion and design course, and another – illustrating the advice and guidance dimension to APEL work claimed that his portfolio helped at a successful job interview.

Simultaneously however, as demography began to tell it was noticeable that employers who had committed themselves to provide access to YTS trainees for the project tended to make increasing use of trainees as employees so that the training side of the programme suffered. As the number of young people available for employment decreases, so this tendency is likely to strengthen. The danger thus posed is that some young people for whom learning beyond school is more or less automatically rejected may be attracted into jobs which turn into cul-de-sacs.

In an attempt to find ways of combating this tendency, the TA introduced some pilot projects for further education colleges on a scheme called Youth Access. The idea of this scheme was to try to devise a

curriculum for 16+ school leavers who would choose full-time employment if they could get it in which work-based learning was the fulcrum to
a range of other forms of learning, all of which would be related to the
content of the work-based learning. The intended participants on Youth
Access are those who have the ability to study in higher education, but
need careful nurturing if they are to feel able to take that path. The scheme
could only work, however, if the work-based learning was assessable. That
meant converting work experience into a programme of intentional and
planned learning. That assessment could only be based on the principles of
the assessment of experiential learning. And that could only work with the
full co-operation of employers. It is too early to comment on the
effectiveness or ineffectiveness of Youth Access as an additional route to
higher education, but it stands as yet another indication of the range of
possible applications of APEL – and of vital importance, the significant
role of employers as educators in the future.

SUMMARY

Where then is APEL being used for the benefit of individuals? The short
answer is in almost every sphere of post-school education, employment
and training provision. The longer answer is to expand the individual
instances cited here. APEL is being used in some polytechnics and colleges and a few universities, further education colleges, adult institutes, in
major companies and some government departments, with the Youth
Training Scheme, both for trainees and supervisors, and in the new unified
training scheme for the unemployed. Being used in institutions does not
imply that it is in general mainstream use, nor that APEL is to be found
wherever there is a polytechnic or a Youth Training Scheme. It does imply
wide acceptance of APEL as a thoroughly professional addition to the
repertoire of education and training college opportunities available.

And as if to signal the significance of that at the end of the first decade
in Britain when the assessment of experiential learning has been taken
seriously together with its assessment and accreditation, the first university
postgraduate diploma in experiential learning began its life in Goldsmiths'
College in the University of London. Recruited were a group of students
drawn from social work, nursing, company training, as well as further and
higher education.

Running through all these applications of APEL there is the same
sequence of mental tasks for individuals: getting psychologically tuned to
the APEL business; systematic reflection on experience to identify significant learning; the expression of significant learning in concise statements
as formal claims to certain knowledge and skills; the collation and

organisation of evidence to support those claims in forms which can facilitate assessment. And for each individual the process of these stages and their product can become either a component of education, guidance and counselling, and orientation and access to further study, or a route towards advanced academic professional study, and academic credit towards a formal qualification.

In practice this means that there are three strands to the use of APEL in mainstream activity. It can serve as a diagnostic form of self-assessment. It can be used as a short-circuit system of gaining a qualification or a credential. Or it can serve as a programme of learning, valuable and valid in its own right. Challenge examinations, test papers, performance observation, artefacts, viva voces, all the assessment techniques can be used to produce a quick response to claims made to possess certain knowledge and skills where the individual's prime interest lies, which is getting a qualification as quickly as possible. Considered and systematic reflection on experience can serve that purpose, but it takes longer as a mode of learning because it is a deliberate way of providing time and space for individuals to take stock of a current state as learners, creating opportunities for them to plot their future learning with far more information about what they are best suited for than they had before.

Both approaches result in individuals learning as they tackle APEL. But there is no doubt that the second produces the far richer crop of learning. It has a particularly important significance. That significance stems from the fact that all knowledge and skill revealed through APEL is self-generated. No-one else is responsible for having put it there. This means that all that learning is owned by an individual in a way that is qualitatively different from the mastery of topics which comes from formal teaching. In a sense the individual has created it. So the sense of ownership for an individual is powerful. And that powerful sense often enthuses the person so that they have a sense of being more empowered than before to make decisions ranging far wider than the academic ones about future learning.

It would be difficult to dispute that such capacity to make informed decisions was an ultimate purpose of education. Unless that can be denied then it would seem fair to claim that APEL's arrival on the education and training map has added a vital ingredient to the opportunities open to adults for learning. Indeed the claim can go further: that APEL points a way to providing an improved and enhanced education, through helping to promote the debate about improving the systems through institutional change.

Part III

APEL in the future: a two-way street to opportunity

9 Introduction

People react to experiential learning experientially; they experience it. The simple idea that most people are learning most of the time in one way or another speaks of their humanity. No-one needs telling that a child learns. Adults enjoy watching children learning. The three-year-old playing with a pile of bricks, trying again and again to make the pile stand up is, for many adults, a fascinating demonstration of experiment, of the determined attempt to complete something successfully – a delicate balancing act – and if it works, a sense of achievement. But part of that fascination comes from recognition and affinity. The child will become an adult. The adult was a child. Both learn – they have to, to cope with their respective worlds. To be human is to learn.

In the adult world most adults forget all this. All the learning to do this, not do that, mastering something new, gets overlaid with the effort that goes into those experiences so that it is always taken for granted. Taken for granted means of no account. The friends, the lovers, the relatives who feel taken for granted are complaining that there is no recognition of their true worth. They do not matter. It is the same with experiential learning. Because it is taken for granted it does not matter. It is not recognised for its true worth. It is of no account. So when the truth of the simple idea of learning from experience actually dawns on grown people, a sense of recognition can follow. For some individuals it is perhaps something more; a sense of filling a gap left by the feeling of being taken for granted; in which case it can get close to rehabilitation.

Any sense of having accomplished something tends to make people feel more self-confident. And a greater confidence spills over into every aspect of life. So for individuals APEL can be a highly significant experience, and not by any means always for formal educational purposes. For many people gaining a better sense of their own value is sufficient unto itself. Many then are so strongly motivated from recognising what they have accomplished already that they do indeed go on to study more in some way or other. But it is the self-assessment which comes first which is the prime benefit for individuals from APEL.

The relationship between APEL and education institutions is obvious. And this is particularly true for teachers of adults. (It is also true, of course, for teachers of children, but that is not the focus of this book.) For a member of staff in a university, polytechnic or college, or in further education or in adult education, or in basic adult literacy, to stand back from the student and solemnly recite silently, internally, 'All of these people are learners. They are learners without me anyway. What they have brought with them may be as significant as what I can teach them. So my task is to help them learn more of what they know already', can be to transform perceptions of adult students. And it is among teachers that reacting to experiential learning experientially is so important. The realignment that notions about experiential learning can offer employers is important enough. But for teachers whose specific responsibility is to help people learn more, it can be of dramatic importance. It reasserts the individual humanity of learners, something which many adult learners frequently complain is just what does not happen to them. But more important it reminds all concerned implicitly that recognition of worth and accomplishment is the foundation on which the entire educational enterprise rests.

In employment there are increasing benefits as well. For anyone responsible for other people, it can articulate what is known, can sharpen perceptions. Bosses who know that their secretaries are more competent than they are in some respects will change their views of them if all that efficiency which results from a mixture of personal characteristics, on-the-job learning and of formal study is set in terms of knowledge and skills already acquired. Beyond that, views may change of employees in general. If that is the case for a secretary, why not for the janitor, the office junior, the middle manager, the foreman? Maybe bosses could reflect that these people are all undervalued. Maybe they are more valuable to them than they realised. Something of all this applies to all those who work with other people and have any responsibility for them. It is not easy to think of any occupational area where this is not likely to be true. And that includes the home. It is not usually a paid occupational area, but there is no doubt about its occupational significance, and so its potential as a source of learning.

So for individuals, educational institutions and employment, APEL holds out opportunities for moving towards a truly learning society in the twenty-first century via a two-way street to opportunity. Internal reflection to get a better compass reading on the present position as a preparation for external perception of what might be most appropriate in the future – learning from experience as a basis for further experience and learning.

For government agencies there are also rich possibilities in formulating policies which put APEL to work generally and effectively. They alone have the power and indeed the responsibility to do the necessary jungle clearance work of regulations, so that individuals, institutions and employers are able to take their share of responsibility in realising the potential offered through the two-way street to opportunity.

10 Some tensions

There are, however, some underlying tensions. Some concern people as individuals. Some relate to academic institutions and their modes of study. And some relate to the current preoccupations with occupational skills and the introduction of competence as the organising concept for skill acquisition and testing.

The tension for individuals is easily stated but will always remain sensitive and problematic. It is quite simply that the whole premise of APEL is that people have inside them undisclosed knowledge and skill which if disclosed and publicly available for scrutiny might well merit some form of certification. An attempt at such disclosures can easily cause considerable tension for a man or woman. To make public what has been private is rarely easy. And however strongly people may want to gain formal recognition for the informal learning they believe they have acquired, when it comes to assessment there can be the risk that disappointing results can cause dismay, discouragement and at worst create some feeling of failure. And because any such feelings of failure can connect only with aspects of their personal lives – there is no tutor to blame, there is no question of not having learned the content of a course, there is no examination which was 'unfair' – this tension needs handling with the greatest care to ensure that the entire procedure is positive and not negative.

Then there is the tension between cognitive and affective learning. Experiential learning asserts the significance of human qualities. Systematic reflection on experience which is the basis of any assessment of experiential learning almost always reveals a range of personal qualities as well as a range of knowledge and skills which fit into the assumptions of formal education. People learn and develop from experience, from affective as well as cognitive behaviours. They may well learn all kinds of factual information, ways of handling it, interpreting it, applying it to unfamiliar circumstances, – the standard diet of academic study. But they also learn how to get on with people, how to get things done, maybe how to lead, to combine with others. Those capabilities are all based on a set of values which imply respect for individuals. These are capacities which may be learned in classrooms, but they most certainly do not feature prominently in formal assessment of what has been learned in classrooms. So this tension raises fundamental questions about the nature, purpose and methodology of assessment.

That leads into the point about tension with the academic world. By definition, since any prior experiential learning people acquire they gain without any reference to academic institutions, it is unlikely that it will all fit neatly into the course syllabuses which the institution uses to organise its academic life. So there is always the possibility that the evidence on which that assessment of experiential learning is made will reveal both level and quantity of knowledge and skill which is clearly at the attainment level required, but either equates to part of a course, or overlaps two courses, or indeed is in no course at all for the particular discipline. That can prove a tricky question for individuals and academic institutions alike.

There is another tension which is perhaps of particular significance at this particular time, and that relates to vocational qualifications and the tremendous drive there is to produce a national system covering all occupations in the interest of trying to correct the chronic skill shortages which all agree bedevil our economy. Those affective behaviours frequently feature in training and staff development programmes for middle and senior managers, but are only rarely seen as content for learning and development for everyone. The market-place view of what people need to be able to do to make money, does not have a great deal of room for getting on with people as a quality to be valued in terms of qualifications.

Currently there seems to be a tendency for the assessment of experiential learning to be harnessed instrumentally to the market-place view of learning as concerned primarily with vocational and occupational competence. This is because the world of employment and government is waking up to the fact that there are masses of people around who are working way below their capacities. This is becoming an urgent preoccupation as demographic trends are beginning to create problems not only of recruitment, but also of retention for employers. Hence, to use their experiential learning as a building block for future learning and so increase their capabilities makes economic sense. When this is the case it tends to get assimilated in to the language of marketing, targeting, inputs, outputs, strategies, goods, standards and delivery. If APEL does not watch out it becomes a mere part of training.

The importance of that is that the underlying principles of APEL extend far beyond economic benefits of learning as a contribution to the gross national product and the Treasury. A British Standard's seal of approval on a saucepan is useful but it gives limited information. It is the same with competences defined by industry lead bodies and kite-marked as National Vocational Qualifications by the National Council for Vocational Qualifications: useful but of limited utility. So the tension needs sustaining not blurring.

Fundamentally this tension comes from a disagreement about questions of values and attitudes – and properly so. Whilst there can be agreement about what constitutes the technical skills and knowledge a maintenance engineer requires to do the job effectively to set standards, there can be no agreement about the system of values he carries with him however he acquired them, nor about his attitudes. Some may tolerate a grumpy somewhat surly maintenance engineer as the price of having efficiency. Others may dislike those attitudes so much that they prefer to risk being without that efficiency or look elsewhere. And if it comes to an argument there is no particular reason why the maintenance engineer should accept or share the values of a manager, however desirable that might be either way. Since APEL is capable of revealing both technical capabilities and values and attitudes the possibility of tension is obvious.

That tension needs sustaining in the midst of accreditation. Accreditation and its cousin accumulation are the mechanisms which facilitate progression. Knowledge and skill which are accredited mean that an individual is recorded as having achieved whatever is the level and quantity of the credit assigned to the knowledge and skills which have been assessed. Accumulation means simply that what has been accredited is 'banked' in a personal record of achievement which can be added to as more achievements have been accredited or as a means of a person moving progressively to a particular qualification if that is what is sought. Combined, accreditation and accumulation provide for student-paced progression. That is vital as a means of enabling older learners to continue as learners, particularly if they are in employment. The principles of accreditation and accumulation are now being applied to the National Vocational Qualifications established by NCVQ, as well as degree studies at graduate and postgraduate levels. And their significance is obvious for the enhancement of skills and knowledge of people in employment in relation to the performance of individual businesses and industrial concerns and a national economy in general. So these tensions are inevitable and necessary. Just as APEL has significance for individuals, education, employment and government alike, so do tensions need recognising by each of those four constituents of society in their own appropriate ways.

LEARNING OUTCOMES :
CERTIFICATION AND ACCREDITATION

There is one common denominator which can act as a raft to keep the tension afloat and balanced; it is learning outcomes. This means no more and no less than the 'teacher' working out quite clearly what it is pupils/learners/students/trainees are supposed to know and be able to do as a result of studying a particular course, learning programme or assignment, and making it available publicly to the students as an accompaniment to the syllabus or as the syllabus itself. For academic courses this has the huge advantage that if the learning outcomes are clear to that academic, they could be equally clear to the student learners.

Contrast that with what is so often the case. The syllabus for a particular course goes from A to Z. Near examination time the lecturer in philosophy of social work and administration advises students to concentrate their revision time on topics covered broadly by C to E, L to Q, and XYZ, dropping heavy hints that by reading earlier examination papers within those areas it would not be unreasonable to assume that examination questions might thus be spotted. Students are grateful for those helpful remarks, but remain largely in the dark about what they actually mean. Say L to Q covers child abuse in social work and administration. Is it the origins, prevention, treatment, consequences, psychological, managerial or administrative, legal, professional training which is likely to pop up in an examination question? Any one is a thesis in itself, let alone one question out of four in one examination paper out of six. It is all a bit fuzzy. But if that course in child abuse had spelt out clearly what kind of knowledge and what skills the student was expected to have mastered then the fuzziness dissolves into a certain clarity. Mysteries are removed. Nothing undisclosed is up anyone's sleeve. The tutor's particular academic interest in say the legal problems arising from the growing public concern of evidence of the incidence of child abuse, an interest students are well aware of and will tend to meet in their examination answers, if they have their wits about them, will be balanced by all the other learning intentions which have been set out. In other words, something of the flukiness of learning and assessment is removed. This means, not only has the tutor given himself a clearer brief for his teaching, the students have a clearer brief for their learning.

All that relates to formal academic courses. Exactly the same principles underline NCVQ's approach to competences. By setting out descriptions of competences in clear statements, their various component units, performance standards attached to them, and the criteria used for making assessments, in the field of vocational knowledge and skill derived from occupational standards defined by industry lead bodies, NCVQ has set about producing a national system of vocational qualifications. All that information is available through a computerised data bank and is accessible to individuals, employers and education bodies alike.

For example, the Training Agency's booklet on standards of performances for administration, business and commercial staff sets out a 'Unit of Accreditation for Administrative Support', with the competence as:

Arrange meetings involving three or more people.

Performance criteria are set out as follows:

- Availability of participants and facilities always checked;
- Arrangements for meeting made and confirmed;
- Participants informed of arrangements;
- All necessary papers despatched in advance and/or provided at meeting as directed;
- Procedures for security/confidentiality of information always maintained;

The activities, skills/knowledge associated with this competence appear as follows:

Activities:
- Contact participants to confirm availability;
- Liaise with colleagues;
- Book venue and any necessary equipment;
- Order refreshments/make catering arrangements if appropriate;
- Arrange for preparation of meeting papers as directed;
- Issue necessary papers to participants as directed;
- Check meeting room is prepared;

Skills:
- Communicate effectively;
- Use telephone;
- Complete forms/records;
- Estimate/calculate requirements and costs;

Knowledge:
- Structure, location and responsibilities of people in organisation;
- Organisation of meetings;
- Directories and reference books;
- Information sources (eg timetable, hotels);
- Local caterers;
- Procedures for booking meeting rooms;

Another unit of accreditation is 'Financial Record Keeping'. The competence is expressed as

Calculate and record wages and salaries

The performance criteria activities, skills and knowledge are set out as follows:

Performance criteria:
- Gross pay calculated correctly from appropriate documentation with required deadlines;
- Statutory and voluntary deduction calculated correctly using standard tables and reference books within required deadlines;
- Statutory records and returns maintained accurately;
- Procedures for security/confidentiality of information always maintained;
- Pay slips correctly prepared within required deadlines;
- All records up to date, legible and accurate.

The activities, skills/knowledge associated with this competence appear as follows:

Activities:
- Calculate payment hours from clock cards, timesheets or other attendance records;
- Calculate gross pay including bonuses, base and overtime payments;
- Calculate statutory and voluntary deductions using standard tables and reference books;
- Calculate net pay;
- Record details in wages book, on individual tax cards (P11) and other appropriate records;
- Prepare pay advice slips and payslip booklet;
- Deal with pay queries;
- Collect and prepare information for statutory returns;
- Collect and prepare information for employees (e.g. P60);

Skills:
- Read and interpret tables and reference books;
- Use a calculator;
- Financial calculations;
- Complete forms/records;
- Use tact and courtesy in handling pay queries;
- Use a computerised wage/salary package;
- Plan and organise work within deadlines.

Knowledge:

- Tax tables, NI tables and other reference documents;
- Statutory and voluntary deductions;
- Banking/Building Society procedures e.g. BACS;
- Procedures and documentation used in organisation;
- Rates of pay, bonuses, commissions, allowances, pension scheme, holiday pay of organisation;
- Attachment of earnings procedures;
- Statutory sickness pay and its recording/maternity pay;
- Year-end procedures and other statutory returns.

Another example for Financial Services (Building Societies), Level 2 is given in NCVQ's Brief Guide, published in October 1990.

NVQ Title		Financial Services (Building Societies), Level II
Unit	1	Provide information and advice and promote products and services to customers
Element	1.1	Inform customers about products and services on request.

Range of Variables to which the element applies
Products

- Investment – instant access, higher rate, notice account, regular savings;
- Lending – mortgages, further advances, personal secured loans, unsecured loans, credit cards;
- Insurance – property, personal, travel;
- Services – foreign currency, travellers cheques, credit card, share dealing;
- Customers – minors, teenagers, 16+, middle-aged, pensioners, professional contacts, companies, non-resident groups.

Performance Criteria

- Features, advantages and benefits of services sufficient to the customer's request are described clearly and accurately;
- Example calculations are correct;
- Appropriate information is accessed from available resources (including Viewdata);
- Information requests outside the responsibility of the job holder are passed on to an appropriate authority promptly and treated politely;

- customers are acknowledged promptly and treated politely;
- customers are treated in a manner which promotes goodwill

Element of competence achieved	
Assessor	Noted
Endorsement	by candidate

With all the requirements set out like that, whatever is to be assessed becomes absolutely clear. Correspondingly what has to be learned becomes clear. All that remains is to settle the kinds of evidence which can be cited for the assessor to draw on to make the assessment. For the competences given in those examples, the evidence could be a performance observation at the specific task, papers prepared as part of day-to-day work and so on.

In this way the competences, or learning requirements, or learning outcomes seem to de-mystify both learning and assessing. With all that stated publicly, the significance of NCVQ separating learning from assessing becomes obvious. All that NCVQ is interested in is whether or not a man or woman either has or has not a competence as set out. How that competence was acquired is of no significance for NCVQ.

Those NVQ competences are fairly obvious 'can do' or 'can't do' issues. It all gets more complicated when competences relate to dealing with people. Here are a couple of examples of the way attempts are being made in social care to do the same thing. The first is fairly straightforward. The competence is:

'Keep records and reports in relation to service users'.

There are a series of related elements to that unit of competence. The keeping of records, the writing of reports, reporting verbally in response to informal or formal enquiries about service users. Beyond that there are two other related elements: helping to implement various plans, and monitoring and evaluating the way those plans are put into operation.

For each one of those related units there are then performance criteria. For example, for keeping records there needs to be evidence that record-keeping systems are identified and placed within work settings, that the individual's responsibilities in respect of record-keeping systems are observed and kept up to date and that the agency policy with respect to access to records is observed faithfully. In similar ways the units on writing of reports and reporting verbally are separated into different items. So, for example, when it is a question of the unit being reported verbally one of the performance criteria is to see that enquiries are dealt with courteously and that users' wishes with regard to the confidentiality in conversations are adhered to.

There is a further section in this draft which attempts to express the competence with its subsidiary units and their performance criteria for keeping records. It sets out the knowledge and understanding that is required to achieve this competence. Here an individual must know and understand the agency's policy in relation to record keeping; in relation to access to those records; has to understand the significance of different ways of keeping record systems; and how those relate to different purposes. And a very important trio concerning the principle of limits to confidentiality, the difference between fact and opinion, and writing comprehensively.

In the field of social care that may be fairly straightforward and in many ways there would not be significant differences between that competence in record keeping for social care and many other occupational areas. The keeping of records accurately and up-to-date is an essential part of day-to-day activity in many occupations, not only to ensure that the work goes smoothly but also to pay due regard to the legal implications which may arise from different parts of the occupation.

All that, however, is much more difficult when the competence set out is:

'Assist service users with coping with critical periods in life'.

Now the description of that competence includes the importance of individuals being able to demonstrate that they can recognise people's needs in situations of change or crisis and provide appropriate assistance. So the related elements for this particular competence as set out in the draft appear as being able to assist users at critical development stages of their lives, assist them in coping with crises and major changes in their lives and assist them to rehabilitate themselves in their lives.

The performance criteria for assisting users at critical developmental stages are analysed in a fourfold division. To begin with the social care worker needs to be able to anticipate whatever may be the developmental stages in working with a particular client group, such as child, middle-aged or geriatric. Then the client's hopes, concerns and anxieties about the future need to be elicited by the social care worker. Beyond that it is necessary to be able to work out and agree preparations with other agencies, if necessary, and of course the support and encouragement that can be given, and appropriately ended.

When it comes to trying to identify the range of knowledge and understanding required for this particular competence inevitably the range is extensive. For example, it is not possible to anticipate what may be the client's hopes, concerns and anxieties unless the social care worker has a firm grasp of the stages in human development, understands the normal responses to human crises and change and indeed responses to those which fall outside the normal range. Furthermore, there are many different facets to a sense of loss and its many effects, such as normal grieving processes, which are important, and indeed the routes to a sense of identity. Beyond that, if the support and encouragement is to be 'ended appropriately' then the social care worker clearly needs an understanding of the possible network systems for support and encouragement of individuals.

As with the NVQ examples, laying out requirements in this way clarifies for both learner and assessor what it is that has to be learned, what topics are going to be taken into account when assessing. But as with the earlier three examples the question of evidence to be used becomes of paramount importance. For record keeping there will be plenty of performance observation and also documentary evidence which with a short conversation ought to be sufficient for the assessor to make a judgement as to whether or not an individual does or does not have that competence. When it is a question of assisting service users coping with their life crises, however, both the performance criteria cited and the knowledge which is part and parcel of that competence, do not appear to lend themselves as readily to 'can do' or 'can't do' style assessments. But whatever maybe the difficulties of that, there can be no doubt at all that expressing learning requirements for assessment in these terms is a great help to learner and assessor and teacher, if indeed there is any formal instruction, and to an individual who feels able to meet any requirements specified and wishes to be assessed.

So learning outcomes or criterion-referenced assessment can be seen as a common denominator between those who wish to talk about education as opposed to training – and so can competences. They can be a common denominator – but not necessarily. It all depends on the way learning outcome or competence statements are written and how far criterion-referencing is pushed for assessment. Whatever the niceties of that debate, however, it becomes clear that for APEL some such statements of learning intentions and learning outcomes become an important tool both for trying to sort out the uncertificated learning men and women have and which may merit assessment, and for conducting the assessment itself.

COMPETENCES IN AMERICAN HIGHER EDUCATION

In higher education in the USA there are variations on this theme of learning and assessment by competences. At the College of Public and Community Service (CPCS) in the University of Massachusetts at Boston, an entire four-year degree programme is constructed on competences.

'Accounting Practices'

is set out in the student handbook like this:

RATIONALE: Having an adequate financial recording and control system is essential to the smooth functioning of any organisation. For many non-profit organisations the correct functioning of accounting systems and financial controls is even more crucial, due to the constant scrutiny from outside agencies and individuals who are asked to contribute grants or other funds. This competency requires students to demonstrate knowledge and skill in completing tasks in the basic accounting cycle and in establishing adequate financial records and controls.

COMPETENCY: Can understand the accounting cycle and prepare basic financial records for a non-profit organisation utilizing standard accounting practices.

CRITERIA:
1 Describe the steps of the accounting cycle from original entries through the post-closing trial balance.
2 Describe the purpose of a balance sheet and define these terms:
 • Assets
 • Liabilities
 • Fixed assets
 • Restricted funds
 • Fund accounting
 • Fund balance

Determine from a balance sheet the financial position of an organisation by analysing the figures and describing the financial strengths and weaknesses.

3 Describe the purpose of the statement of income and expenses and the statement of changes in the fund balance and analyse these statements from an actual organization by describing the major expenses and income and the direction of change of the organisation's financial status.
4 Describe the difference between accrual and cash accounting and discuss which method is recommended for most organizations and why.
5 Describe the basic purpose of and make proper entries using the following:
 • general journal
 • special journals (i.e. cash receipts, cash disbursements, accounts receivable,accounts payable)
 • Ledgers
 • Trial balance and post-closing trial balance
 • Adjusting entries

- Correcting entries
- Closing entries

6 Describe how to prepare each of the following:
- Cash budget
- Payroll
- Bank reconciliation

Carry out at least one of these tasks from beginning to end using actual figures.

7 Describe basic financial controls for an organization using the following concepts:
- Separation of function
- Purchase order and purchasing systems
- Budget review
- Use of financial statements
- Handling of cash and petty cash
- Equipment/inventory control

STANDARDS:
1 Definitions must be referenced as to source.
2 Entries may be prepared either on traditional accounting forms or using a computer.
3 The financial records used to demonstrate Criteria 1 and 2 may be obtained from the Center or from the student's own experience if approved by the evaluating faculty member.
4 Entries and work on Criterion 5 must be mathematically correct.

METHODS OF EVALUATION (examples):
1 Complete exercises or an exam for a CPCS course addressing this competency.
2 Present a valid transcript of a post-high school accounting course worth three credit hours in which a grade of 'C' or better or the equivalent was earned.
3 Present written documentation of financial records and systems you have developed for a community agency which meet the basic requirements of standard accounting practices from original entry through post-closing trial balances.

In the CPCS Degree there is a competence called

Substantive law

RATIONALE: The legal profession categorizes legal knowledge into 'substantive areas'. To analyse and resolve a legal problem a law worker must find, interpret, and apply the substantive law. Each student must demonstrate a working knowledge of one such area (for example, housing law, privacy law, employment rights, welfare law, health law, consumer law, contracts, juvenile law, workman's compensation, criminal defendant's rights, environmental law, torts, etc.).

COMPETENCY: Can describe the major sources of law and rulings from an area of substantive law: to analyse the outcome of legal problems based on the application of that law to fact patterns typical to that area.

CRITERIA:
Using an area of substantive law agreed upon by the evaluation team:

1 Identify the major statutory sources and describe the statutory scheme for the area 1 the relationship of all the statutes and regulations in the area to each other.

2 Identify and analyse three leading cases in the area 2 cases which are currently the highest source of authority on the issue.

3 Identify three frontier problems in the area 3 significant problems where new law is in the process of being made.

4 Describe three fact situations which commonly arise and which are governed by settled law in the area, describe the governing law, apply it to each of the three situations and analyse the possible outcomes.

STANDARDS:

1 For each statute identified be sure to state:
   a the full legal citation;
   b the purpose of the statute in a few sentences;
   c the citation(s) of regulations, promulgated under the authority of the statute;
   d the relationship, if any, between various statutes and regulations (for example, in AFDC aid to families with dependent children law there is an important relationship between various state statutes).

2 For each leading case:
   a summarize the most significant facts on which the ruling is based;
   b summarize the reasoning of the court in reaching its holding;
   c restate the holding of the case;
   d state why the case is a leading case;
   e state the importance and probable impact of the case as a precedent for the resolution of future cases in the area.

3 For each frontier problem:
  a describe the questions that are left unanswered by the state of the law or open to significantly different interpretations;
  b describe at least two different possibilities of how the current law could be applied to result in different outcomes to a problem.
4 For each of the three fact situations to which you apply the law:
  a identify the sources of law by citation including section numbers where appropriate;
  b where there is more than one possible outcome for the problem based on the situation and the appropriate law, be sure to identify various alternative outcomes.

METHODS OF EVALUATION (example):
For one area of public assistance law, write a paper covering the standards and criteria above.
NOTE: Students may do **three** competencies in Substantive Law by working on different substantive areas (such as one in Health Law and one in Labour Law).

Another competence is called:

Moral argument

RATIONALE: No one doubts that moral questions are among the most important there are. Yet many people despair of ever answering them definitively. Moral concepts ('good', 'bad', 'right' or 'wrong', 'ought' etc.) present certain special problems for the making and evaluation of arguments. For one thing, they are hard to define. For another, the arguments in which they appear sometimes seem irresolvable by the means we are accustomed to. They raise knotty questions about objectivity and knowledge in the moral realm. But despite these complexities, you can become skilled in employing moral concepts in constructing and judging arguments. Familiarity with portions of the literature of ethical theory helps develop this skill. So does practice in the critical study of moral argument.

COMPETENCY: Can critically assess moral arguments.

CRITERIA:
To demonstrate this competency, you must:
1 Identify a particular moral issue and at least two fundamental, contrasting ethical perspectives which attempt to resolve it.
2 Given a statement of each position, you
  a Distinguish its factual claims from its value claims. If there are places where the distinction is unclear, explain why.

    b Give an account in your own words of each author's position about what is ethical. This should include the reasons given for each position.

3 Give an account of the differences between the two positions.

4 EITHER resolve the disagreement between the authors on the issue in question, giving reasons for your judgement in terms of the arguments advanced by the authors; OR

If you find you cannot resolve the issue, explain why not. If appropriate, describe the considerations that would make a resolution possible, e.g. considerations of fact, of clarification of key terms, etc.

STANDARDS:

1 Be sure your fundamental ethical perspective gives a general, systematic answer to the question 'How ought a person to live?' or 'What is the good life?' or 'How should society function?'

2 To state a position, a secondary source is acceptable, so long as it gives a full description and one which the original theorist would accept.

3 Your presentation, whether oral or written, should be clear enough that evaluators do not have to ask about the meaning of key terms you use.

4 Your own arguments (Criterion 4) should be valid and the premises supported by appropriate evidence. The arguments should be in your own words, not quoted or paraphrased from some other source. If you refer to others' arguments you should make clear your own view of those arguments and support it with reasons.

5 All sources must be properly cited.

METHODS OF EVALUATION (examples):

You might examine the issue of experimentation on human subjects using the perspectives of J.S.Mill and I.Kant.

You might examine the issue of obedience to authority using the perspectives of Gandhi and Lenin.

Your might examine different views of the justice of imprisonment, including arguments advanced by those who see imprisonment as just retribution, as deterrence, as means of correction or rehabilitation, or as oppression.

These three examples taken from this College in the University of Massachusetts indicate the extent to which CPCS has used competence as an approach to learning and assessment on a wide-ranging curriculum.

    One of the characteristics of this academic programme is that students can present themselves for assessment of their competences whenever they feel ready. In other words, the programme is student-paced. Since the assessment of prior experiential learning is included as a facility in this degree programme it means that although the degree is expressed as a four-year course, it is possible for people to complete their degree course in two years, and indeed there was one example of somebody who completed in one year. This is because of the student-paced characteristic where completion of the degree programme depends on having demonstrated that the requisite number of competences has been mastered. And because these competences can be acquired either through attending a course or sitting an examination or through experiential learning as set out under the heading methods of evaluation, not only is the academic programme student-paced but to a considerable extent students are able to choose their own way of tackling the learning programme.

At Alverno College (a Roman Catholic women's college) in Milwaukee, Illinois the programme works somewhat differently, but there is the same characteristic of setting out learning requirements in terms of learning outcomes. It describes itself as follows.

Alverno College in Milwaukee, Wisconsin, USA, is a liberal arts college offering degrees in professional areas like management and education as well as in traditional subjects like psychology and music. Besides the familiar model of full-time undergraduate studies, they offer a whole range from a 3 session career counselling relationship (one of many short-term workshops and series) to varied certificate and associate's programs, as well as an intensified baccalaureate curriculum in a week-end time-frame for working learners. More than 70% of their 1,500 degree and certificate students are over twenty-two, and their more than 2,000 non-degree learners range across the life span.

Alverno has developed an approach to undergraduate education that attempts to reconcile the requirements of academic rigor with an increasing delegation of responsibility to the learner. One of its explicit goals is to produce life-long learners.

In order to make learning more accessible to the learner, the faculty have worked to be equally explicit about the goal toward which the learner works – self-directed learning – and about the environment and the services they as educators will provide. They have done this by agreeing on college-wide definitions of the abilities they seek to help the learner develop, and by entering into three levels of contract with each learner.

At the first level, the 'college contract', they specify the college-wide abilities and the various kinds of learning experiences they will 'deliver' to help them. The learner accepts these goals and their services by enrolling in the college.

At the second level, the 'program contract', learner and educator work regularly (for instance, each semester) to negotiate the learner's particular program, selecting courses and other learning experiences to help develop the particular abilities relevant to the learner's career goals as well as those required by the college for general education purposes.

At the third level, the 'course contract', learners decide which of the abilities offered in a particular course of learning experience they will each agree to focus on. At this level as well, each educator specifies the learning opportunities that will be used to help develop an ability or competence as well as the criteria by which its achievement will be judged.

At the heart of this learning process is a method of performance assessment by which learners demonstrate abilities in the context of their field of study, and by which they become proficient self-assessors. These abilities include communication, analysis, problem solving, valuing, social interaction, responsibility for the global environment, effective citizenship, and aesthetic response.

The program is built on the following assumptions:

1 Adult learners need varied approaches to learning.
2 Learning involves developing knowledge and the ability to use it.
3 Educators can keep adapting to the needs of the adult learners if they keep analyzing the experience of the learner and developing theory from that analysis.
4 A complete learning cycle involves experience, reflection, conceptualization, and experimentation.

The eight abilities are set out as follows:

Communication:
The competent communicator habitually makes connections between herself and her audience, with and without the aid of graphics, electronic media and computers.

Social Interaction:
The competent interactor knows how to get things done in committees, task forces, team projects and other group efforts. She elicits the views of others and helps reach conclusions promptly.

Analysis:
The competent analyzer is a clear thinker and a critical thinker. She fuses experience, reason and training into considered judgement.

Responsibility for the Global Environment:
The environmentally responsible person acts with an understanding of and respect for the economic, social and biological interdependence of global life.

Problem Solving:
The competent problem solver gets done what needs to be done. The ability overlaps with and uses all other abilities.

Effective Citizenship:
The involved person meets the responsibilities of freedom with effective citizenship. She acts with an informed awareness of contemporary issues and their historical context.

Valuing:
The competent valuer recognizes different value systems while holding strongly to her own other-directed ethic. She habitually seeks to understand the moral dimensions of her decisions and accepts moral responsibility for the consequences of actions taken in all facets of her life.

Aesthetic Response:
The aesthetically responsive person appreciates that some truths are best expressed through the written and performed arts. She appreciates the various forms of art and responds to their symbolism and message.

One of the opportunities offered to students for learning and being assessed in this way is Alverno's, 'Off-Campus Experiential Learning (OCEL) Program'. A College pamphlet set this out as follows:

How OCEL Works
On the job, the student's role is carefully planned between the employer and the college to make sure it will meet a real need and can be directly related to the student's learning goals.

Using the OCEL experience as a learning base, the student and her faculty mentor also design a course of study for her or integrate the experience with an existing course.

The program's unusual structure provides in-depth support for the employer. Campus personnel, recognized nationally for their experience in field education, meet weekly with OCEL students in intensive seminars to monitor each student's achievement of the goals and tasks she has set and refine her skills and strategies as needed to improve her effectiveness.

At the completion of the project the on-site supervisor and faculty mentor cooperate in a final assessment and evaluation of the student's performance.

What the Student Brings to OCEL
Each OCEL student has had at least two years of successful experience in the Alverno learning process, a unique college education that

develops not just what she knows but *what she knows how to do*.

This is not her first exposure to making what she has learned work in practice. All her college learning has been tested in action – not just on paper – in assessments where she had handled real problems in real and simulated settings. She gets credit only when she can put her learning into action. She is used to taking complex, difficult assignments and analyzing what needs to be done, then going and doing it. She has proven that she can communicate effectively and work well with others to find feasible solutions and carry them out.

For her, OCEL is a chance to put all these demonstrated abilities together in the 'real world'. For her OCEL employer, she is more than just a student – she is a practical learner and problem solver ready to make a real contribution.

The essential point about these examples is that those courses produce graduates who are highly thought of by employers. Alverno is almost besieged by employers wishing to employ their graduates. Employers are so impressed with what the college does that they contribute generously financially, offer more placements than the college can use and serve on college committees to advance its development. All this is based in a Roman Catholic Women's College which was threatened with closure in the early 1970s. Its success stems from the way it adopted learning outcomes and notions of competence in the context of a liberal arts college. Whilst adhering to the sense of purpose of a liberal education, it incorporated these other dimensions to learning and demonstrated that vocational preparation and general education can not only be offered simultaneously, but each enhances the other.

The very foundation of the formulation of the competences which constitutes the degree in CPCS make the same point. That is its success. In downtown Boston it set out to serve men and women in the lower socio-economic groups in generally low-status employment or on some form of state welfare, the kind of people who would not go near a normal state university. It recruits strongly. It is more successful in enrolling members of ethnic minorities than any of the other constituent parts of the University of Massachusetts. But most telling of all the proportion of CPCS graduates going on to master's is higher than that of other parts of the University of Massachusetts and they are sought after by the graduate schools. Put that alongside the career advancement which many CPCS graduates achieve, often while they are still studying as students for their degree, and the story is convincing.

Once again it all depends on the way competences are construed. It seems the more narrowly they are confined the greater the risk that they will turn out to be marginal within the sum total of another person's human capabilities. In other words occupational competences are helpful where jobs and performance criteria can be precisely described. But whilst the intellectual attractions may be strong of trying to press precise descriptions of competence to every level of occupational activity and learning it is not very intelligent to do so. The full range of occupational competence alone is not susceptible to neat definitions and analysis. The range of human learning similarly is not susceptible to a step-by-step series of precise definitions. The sum total of human activity cannot be parcelled into discrete bits each capable of being assessed on a yes/no basis. So the kind of broad competences worked out by Alverno and CPCS offer helpful ways of thinking about improving programmes of learning and their assessment in ways which enable employers to employ the kinds of people they need. Tensions are both contained and sustained.

CREDENTIALS

These examples show how learning outcomes can become the handmaid of APEL, that is where assessment is concerned and with it accreditation.

Accreditation and certification now matter more to more people. Both serve increasingly as passports for entering employment and changing employment. The notion of employment-defined occupational standards which is the mainspring of NCVQ is part of a deliberate attempt to create a hierarchy of occupational competences based on those standards which are nationally defined and applied. The implication is that gradually more and more men and women in employment will have a permanent and accumulating personal record of the competences they have acquired. To accomplish that, more and more employers are going to be involved heavily in on-site assessment of those competences. So at every level within the world of employment, accreditation and certification are going to be part of the day-to-day thinking for all concerned. Employers have long said that what educational qualifications produce is often not what they want. Industry lead bodies and NCVQ are requiring them to say what they want and a vital point, be involved in delivering it. Any delivery system will need to include APEL.

The same goes for further education colleges. Quite how it is all going to work out in practice is not yet clear. What is quite clear is that the certification procedures which have been standard practice for them for the Business and Technician Education Council, the City and Guilds of London Institute, the Royal Society of Arts, the Pitman Institute and so on, will get extended to a far larger sphere and will be conducted in rather different ways. Remember the disaggregation of learning from the assessment of competences which is the fundamental principle on which NCVQ is working. Higher education and the professions are rather different, but there are moves towards mandatory continuing professional development which will edge further towards accreditation and certification.

Not only, then, are we living in a learning society. That society is becoming increasingly a credentialing society. Accreditation is here to stay awhile. It can only be fully effective if what is certified and accredited comprehends all learning and not just whatever is thought to be vocational at any particular time. The tensions must be sustained.

11 Post-industrial learning

The tension described in chapter 10 can be more apparent than real when couched in terms of conflict between education and training. This has always been one of those more futile academic debates, reflected in government and institutional policies. It is best left on one side to concentrate on talking about learning. It is a legacy of the industrial model on which compulsory education was first established. And it is that legacy that makes it so hard to make arrangements for learning appropriate to the twenty-first century rather than the nineteenth.

Learning to acquire a skill is not more or less significant a kind of learning than learning about the historical evolution of those skills. The world is too full of people with skills who do not have very good ideas on how to use them – genetic scientists at one end and plumbers at the other. Serious public discourse goes on about the phenomenal skills of genetic scientists in penetrating the mysteries of life, so that technically, it is conceivable that the discredited attempts at manpower planning could be replaced by human planning on a global scale, while the other side of the debate argues the unsuitability of genetic scientists to be entrusted with any such power. They have the knowledge and skills; they do not know what to do with them, so the argument goes. Equally, serious discourse goes on about plumbers, usually in private though sometimes publicly when the bills arrive. Plumbers are very skilful at connecting pipes, maintaining heating systems and installing new equipment. Frequently, they are very unskilful at positioning the pipes, seeming to do the job for the plumber's convenience rather than for the aesthetic sensibilities of the customer, to say nothing of subsequent good maintenance. In each case it is the same. Pronounced skills of one kind; inadequate skills of another. So both the genetic scientist and the plumber may turn out to be half-learned. And the point is that learning is indivisible.

At one level this is generally recognised. It is what employers talk about when they complain that newly-qualified graduates can be extremely competent at solving problems provided they can take their time and do not have to collaborate with other people. Require those problems to be solved under the pressure of tight deadlines – time is money for an employer – and in concert with other people, and many of them are not very effective. It is what government was concerned about in passing the Education Reform Act of 1988, key elements of which are to introduce a core curriculum buttressed with a series of age-related tests. What is the point of spending tax-payers' money, so the argument goes, if young people do not begin paid employment equipped with the basic tools of learning, reading, writing and arithmetic, replaced as it tends to be now by the three Cs: computing, communication and competence. In each case, the central issue is the curriculum. Government thinks it has answers, though whether the answers are adequate only time will tell.

In their different ways, employers and government are pointing an accusing finger at the education offered by the formal education system and are trying to improve it. The Technical and Vocational Education Initiative (TVEI) was introduced into secondary schools to give greater emphasis to the preparation for work after school as part of the school curriculum. The GCSE was introduced to replace both the Certificate of Education and the Certificate of Secondary Education and serve as a vehicle for a more active role for pupils in their own learning. Problem solving, project work, group work and course work were prescribed for examination assessments to correct the predominantly passive form of learning which had ended in the traditional formal examinations. But also, these were ways of learning which, it was claimed, were better preparation for the lifelong learning style of work which would be pupils' lifelong experience. Government and employers alike are busy encouraging school teachers to take periods of work experience on secondment in industry and commerce as another way of exercising a pincer movement on school education. If teachers know more of the world of work, they will be better equipped to prepare their pupils to work. The Enterprise in Higher Education initiative of the Training Agency is merely a device to try to get changes of emphasis for a student's learning in higher education. A different balance between the academic and the vocational is the Enterprise initiative's target. The new funding arrangements for higher education being produced by the Universities' Funding Council and the Public Sector Funding Council established by the 1988 Education Reform Act in part have the same intention.

One way or another all these various initiatives are asserting the indivisibility of learning. In the earning world of work the need is obvious – and it is general. It is not enough these days for the office worker to use a microcomputer according to the program provided. Heavy investment in the hardware equipment is properly exploited only when that office worker exploits the potential of the computer by devising new programs to meet the new needs as part of their daily work. The push-button operator in an automated production system is relatively useless if not downright dangerous in many cases these days. System controllers are now the human side of automated systems. They need to understand what the system is doing, how it is doing it, so that they are able to deal with faults that inevitably occur. And that machinery is far too expensive to be used passively. It is the ingenuity of the system controller that governs the company's profitability. This kind of skill enhancement is increasingly important for employers and hence their employees. But who can tell whether the operator's ingenuity is the result of attending formal classes, reading instruction manuals carefully or some sudden flash of thought whilst working in the garden? And as well as thinking how best to exploit the possibilities of that system, the man or woman in the garden may have been reflecting on the best way to persuade a difficult colleague and co-worker to try out the bright idea. The affective as well as the cognitive comes into play. Learning is indivisible, if it is to be deployed effectively.

This is where experiential learning has such an important part to play. Learning by doing is far and away the best way of learning for the majority of people and it is an important factor for all people. Most certainly it is not the only way of learning or the best way of learning all things for all people. Outright instruction is as necessary. But due attention to experiential learning is an effective way of getting some sense of balance which, and this is the central issue, makes sense to the learner. It is only when the learner is engaged that there is any hope of an individual acquiring both skills and the knowledge about how to use them. In other words, designing the curriculum is what matters. Its design and implementation dictate what is learned. And both the affective and cognitive need recognition. The industrial pattern had little room for these approaches. Now it must be left behind.

THE CONTEXT

Before considering what this means, making use of the indivisibility of learning, and how APEL fits it, the issue needs putting in context. What Britain is grappling with, is the consequences of a century of formal education which has divided learning into two separate parts, and then tried to find ways of combining them again. Those consequences now explain in part why there is such concern, verging on panic, at serious skill shortages which bring into question the capacity of the country to maintain its economic strength in relation to other countries, but more profoundly with its questions about its future role and position in the European Community after 1992.

The bitter truth is that after a century of compulsory education, after nearly half a century of secondary education for all, after all the initiatives referred to, at least 50 per cent of the population is convinced that after leaving school at sixteen learning is not for them. A large part of the reason for that is that so much of what they are expected to learn before they reach sixteen does not coincide either with the way they can learn best or with the world as they perceive it. Right through the story of secondary schooling since 1944 there has been a continual tension between an extension of the academic grammar school curriculum related to the requirements of progression to higher education and the proliferation of attempts to provide a general, technical, and more recently vocational style of education related to the needs of the majority. Whether it was the tripartite system of the 1944 Education Act of grammar, technical and secondary modern schools, or the Eccles White Papers on technical education, or the Newsom Report, or the introduction of comprehensive schools, or the Curriculum for Personal and Vocational Education and TVEI initiatives, the tension has never been resolved satisfactorily. Hundreds of thousands of boys and girls, men and women have been fed a diet of learning which is not really suitable. This has nothing to do with their capacity for learning; it has everything to do with taking them seriously. It was sufficient to look after the so-called 'academic', bound for universities, polytechnics and colleges, the rest could find jobs and if they needed additional knowledge and skill there were evening classes, night school and part-time study.

This engrained set of attitudes bears on two major contemporary problems. Employers with notable exceptions have not accepted as a prime responsibility the development of their own employees. If they wanted employees with more knowledge and skill, they assumed they could recruit them direct. The country at large simply does not support education as a central national concern. Taken together these two matters amount to a cultural stance which is inimical to the speed and extent of employee development so desperately needed. All the rhetoric in the world about the need for employers to assume greater responsibility for education and training and pay for it will not produce action unless they are convinced that they must for their own survival and profitability. Nor will rhetoric convince individuals unless the need is obvious. Demography now means that need is beginning to be obvious and will become starkly so. It may be, therefore, that we are entering a period of our national story where these external forces may produce the range of changes that all the efforts of the last forty-five years have failed to do. Maybe they are the beginnings of a cultural change. But this will only create the opportunities for effecting change; it will not achieve it. This is why things have to be thought out anew in terms of how people learn best and what best they can learn.

It may be no comfort, but it is worth noting that the Americans face similar problems. The *New York Times* ran three long articles on successive days in September 1989, to coincide with a meeting arranged for President Bush to meet governors from the fifty states to talk about education and what needed to be done about it. The titles of the articles were: 'Impending US Jobs "Disaster": work force unqualified to work'; 'Companies step in where Schools Fail' and 'Schools are trying to Link Good Jobs and Skills'. When the Chairman of Xerox says 'the makings of a disaster' and the former Chairman of Procter & Gamble refers to 'a third world within our own country' and the Chief Executive of Johnson & Johnson says 'the American dream turning into a nightmare' it is no wonder that the *New York Times* gave the story front page prominence. The general line taken was 'America is fast developing into a nation of education haves and have-nots who are fast becoming employment haves and have-nots'. The Johnson & Johnson Chief Executive said 'If we continue to let children who are born in poverty fail to get the kind of education that will allow them to participate in our economy and society productively, then sometime in the twenty-first century this nation will cease to be a peaceful, prosperous democracy.' Some of the pieces documented the evidence for those views with a daunting catalogue of unfilled jobs and drop-out rates from high school. To deal with all this the Chairman of R.J.R. Nabisco Inc. said that if present trends continue 'American business will have to spend twenty-five billion dollars a year providing elementary education instruction to one million workers before they can even begin training them to handle modern equipment'. As for solutions there are variations on the theme of compacts but, and this is where similarities with Britain are so striking, 'to these young people already struggling with the system, the insistent pleas by education and business people to stay in school in the hope that it will prepare them for good jobs, often seems badly out of sync with the gritty reality of their daily lives'.

The President of a community college is so disturbed by the low level of attainment of some ethnic minorities, especially American blacks, that he has invented something called a 2 + 2 + 2 programme. Using group work and a mentoring approach, college staff will work in the high school for the last two years of the course to help these young people reach a level which will enable them to cope with community college courses in a college which is literally open access. The second two years will be in the community college itself with the last two years being spent in what the Americans call a four-year school, leading to a baccalaureate degree. It all sounds unhappily familiar. And the 2 + 2 + 2 is one search among many for a connected curriculum.

CONNECTED CURRICULA FOR YOUNG PEOPLE

Nowhere does this show up more clearly than in the succession of efforts to provide adequate education and training for the 16+. The Youth Opportunities Programme, the one-year Youth Training Scheme, the two-year Youth Training Scheme, the three-part programme which runs throughout all were and are an admirable design. Work experience, on-the-job training and off-the-job training could not be bettered as a design. However, there are five serious flaws which have prevented that design being as successful as it deserved to be. The schemes were introduced to cope with youth unemployment rather than introduced because of their intrinsic merit. Considering the young people who were recruited on to the schemes, to begin them on the three-part programme after leaving school instead of integrating their three-part programme with the school curriculum before they left was simply too late to get the young people as enthusiastic joiners. That after-school provision underlined that the scheme was a second-best set of opportunities whilst the best opportunities were on full-time further and higher education. The design of the three-part curriculum was never turned into an operational reality on a systematic basis, partly because no programme was given sufficient time to establish itself firmly without being changed at the whim of political pressures and inadequate steps were taken to ensure that employers were equipped to play their part fully. Running through each of these five flaws is the failure to recognise the power of experiential learning for motivation, for encouragement, for recognition.

Exploring those flaws in YTS schemes points to some of the directions APEL could take in the future. One way or another the argument will rest on the assertion that experiential education is superior education, for many, probably a majority. It will make connections with the consistent failure of Britain to ensure an adequate number of skilled technicians, as well as the failure to engage in post-secondary school study significant numbers of young people in the Registrar General's social groups 4 and 5.

It all goes back to the cultural problem within Britain about the way learning is seen in contemporary society. The figures are beginning to climb for the numbers who remain in full-time education, but by international standards they remain notably low. It is true that increasingly numbers of people in employment are finding not only that they need further study as part of continuing employment, but that it is rewarding in its own right. And the numbers of so-called mature students who enrol in higher education courses as full-time students, show that people who were not interested in moving from school to post-secondary education, later, for whatever reason, decide formal academic study is what they want. But however encouraging those developments may be, it does not alter the fact that at age 16+, the platform for further learning for a majority is not only very shaky, it has nearly collapsed.

TVEI, CPVE, GCSE are all attempts to strengthen that platform. How far the National Curriculum and tests at the ages of 7, 11, 14 and 16 will succeed in also strengthening that platform, time alone can tell. The intention can be saluted. But there is little point in strengthening the platform unless what comes after is intended to appeal to young people and hold them in the learning business. One of the problems about this is the tendency for CPVE and TVEI, which in many ways are restatements of the Newsom Report in 1963, to be seen as fit for the average and below average and not for the brightest and best pupils. This kind of sheep and goats separation within schools simply gets projected into after-school life, so that seen by many secondary school boy and girl pupils anything that is not higher education is second-best, and much more serious, that they are only fitted for the second-best. The one obvious answer is to ensure that the style content, say, of TVEI is a compulsory requirement for all secondary school pupils. The National Curriculum is a move in that direction. But that will take years to work its way into the system. Maybe boys and girls aged 11 in 1990 will have that experience by the time they reach 16 in 1995. Some will, some will not. But the school curriculum is not the principal concern here. What happens afterwards is. What happens afterwards confronts the national problem. In British society, for a majority, leaving school, getting a job and having a wage packet is a rite of passage; adulthood is in sight. For those young people leaving school, not taking a job and going into something which feels like an extension of school is not an appealing substitute. So the fundamental problem is to design and offer learning programmes to those young people which somehow combine a sense of the rite of passage with programmes with positive learning which does not feel like school extended.

There are some good examples. Fullemploy's programmes of training for young people work successfully because they achieve that combination of a rite of passage and learning. The disciplines of the workplace provide a supportive structure so that the young trainees know where they are, but they also give the young people the sense of doing a proper job, not being at school or college. Being on time for the beginning of the day's work, being dressed properly, having regular tea/lunch breaks, above all being in the presence of and taught by men and women who act and talk as experienced efficient workplace supervisors, rather than school teachers or college lecturers, runs very successful training programmes. Amarc runs a number of extremely successful programmes in many parts of the country. Staff were puzzled, however, that one well-designed course in the North of

England did not seem to engage the trainees so that erratic attendance threatened the entire programme. Asked about all this, one young man said 'There's no 'ooter.' It was not real work, although it was entirely work-based learning. Adults went to work when the hooter began and ended the shift – real work – a rite of passage.

At best those kinds of education and training begin by taking seriously the characteristics of the young people for whom they are intended. Generalising, their views about formal education are utterly negative and at best relatively negative, views which are reinforced powerfully by the cultural influences at work and in particular confirmed by those from their own peer group. Moreover, whilst they can have a low self-esteem generally, their prime interest is in earning money through work. They have a scant sense of 'deferred gratification' as the sociologists would put it, so that distant targets for achievement and success simply pass them by. Turning all that round and thinking about the motivation of these young people, it is clear that a learning course which works to a normal employee's routine is almost a condition of success. So is a learning and training programme which they experience as on-the-job learning or work-based learning. And because these young people are anything but stupid, education and training courses need to be self-evidently preparing them for occupations and jobs which seem a realistic possibility.

Launching and promoting such programmes through the existing formal education provision poses teasing problems. If work-based learning means what it says then it implies work being planned intentionally to achieve learning. This is quite a different matter from providing work experience. Everyone knows that experience is no guarantee of learning anything. It all depends on how the experience is approached. So work-based learning means a considerable amount of planning on the part of all the various participants. Clearly that means beginning with the young trainees/learners. If they are part of the planning then they are much more likely to stay with the programme. If that is pitching things too high, then there is no substitute for all those who are concerned with the design of work-based learning for young people doing some systematic planning themselves. And because further education colleges cannot overnight turn themselves into Fullemploy-style institutions then it means close collaboration between college staff and the employers who are going to provide the places for work-based learning. Obviously that makes high demands on college lecturers and employers' work-placed supervisors alike. It implies a change of attitude and an acceptance of a significantly different role for many college lecturers. Just as significantly, it implies the acceptance by an employer of an additional role which goes beyond inducting a young person into the world of adult work and makes the employer a frontline teacher as well.

All that is only the beginning of it. Assuming that in technical terms an appropriate curriculum has been designed which takes account of the characteristics of the intended learners, the interests of the employers and those of formal education, the whole question of recruitment is a key issue. Looking on the experience of YTS it simply is leaving things too late to talk about the possibilities of a training programme such as this at the point when young people are thinking of leaving school. It needs offering to them as a thoroughly acceptable additional possibility for them when they are aged 16. And that means probably beginning to talk about these possibilities from the fourth year onwards in secondary schools. Clearly then that poses problems for the schools. Just as there are 'boundary' difficulties to be overcome as between further education and employers in any such scheme, so to take discussion down towards the age of 14 immediately points to the possible boundary questions arising for the schools. Given TVEI and GCSE this should not be such a serious problem as it was previously. But offering this sort of possibility to 14-year-olds necessarily leads to questions about an appropriate curriculum for them within the secondary school itself.

Without the commitment of schools, including the Careers Service, further education and employers, there is little hope of securing the commitment of the young people.

The basis for any such learning programme is quite obviously experiential learning. On-the-job learning, work-based learning simply means learning from doing. But by itself that is not enough. To be effective, learning by doing needs supporting and accompanying by opportunities for trying to articulate what was learned from the doing. In other words, a work-based learning programme needs to be paralleled by a thinking-based programme. There is nothing very mysterious about this. There are thousands of good teachers in schools and lecturers in colleges who use this as a standard way of teaching. It would be reassuring to be able to say that approach was the norm. Unfortunately it is not. But it is all part of the argument for trying to rethink both ways of learning and what is to be learned, in the present cultural context to say that a 'debriefing' approach to work-based learning needs to become the norm for the 50 per cent or more of school leavers who at present turn their backs on formal provision of further learning.

Even that is not enough. The think-based learning must include positive instruction and outright teaching. Young people will not learn all they need to know from on-the-job or work-based learning. What they learn in that way needs supplementing and informing by formal study which is related to it. That is the key. Study which is related to some activities which feel like real work appeals to young people in ways in which formal study disconnected from work-based learning simply does not. Once again, this makes high demands on teaching staff and employers alike. Fullemploy often has a clue. In no small measure, its success stems from the fact that its instructors are experienced work-based supervisors. There is no general rule then which says that staff from educational institutions are necessarily the best ones to provide formal study which is related to work-based learning. Once again this talks of the possibility of a change of role for people who work both in education and in employment in the private or public sector.

It also talks about experiential learning as a matter of learning style. Taking the characteristics of the trainees on any Youth Training programme is simply a way of trying to answer the question; what is the best way for them to learn?

CONNECTED CURRICULA FOR ADULTS

The same question ought to be asked about older learners. After all many of them had the same characteristics as the trainees when they were younger. Growing up, being in employment, getting married, having children, with an ever-expanding range of domestic and family responsibilities may or may not have overlaid those characteristics or replaced them with others. Taking an interest in their children's primary and secondary schools often changes parents' views of education and indeed of learning. Having to take a quasi-parental role in relation to ageing parents can easily lead to adults sensing that they need to learn more for their own satisfaction. Finding that acquiring skills and knowledge strengthens the possibilities for career advancement can whet the appetite for further study. Any of those factors can create a readiness for learning which was absent when they were younger. However, readiness is one thing; being fully engaged in learning is another. And that is where people's learning styles are so important.

There are many ways of talking about learning styles from an academic psychological point of view to commonsense observation. For the purpose of the argument here, there are two dimensions worth paying attention to. The first is indeed psychological and the second is the overlay of life experience which can shift the psychological account. David Kolb has combined the two and has produced an account of learning which goes through a learning cycle.

As he sets it out in *Experiential learning* (Prentice Hall, 1984) it moves from concrete experience through to observations and reflections, on to the formulation of abstract concepts and generalisations, through to testing the implications of concepts in new situations and back again to concrete experience. Diagrammatically he expresses this as follows:

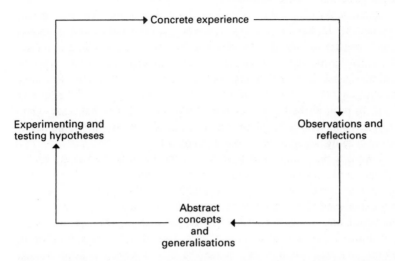

Now the point about that learning cycle is that different people join it at different stages. Some find doing (concrete experience) is the best way of learning. Others find reading, thinking and writing (formulation of abstract concepts and generalisations) their best way of learning. Some learn best through experimenting (testing implications of concepts in new situations). But none learn most effectively unless they reflect on what they have learned already. And Kolb's point is that most people go through this four-stage cycle whether primarily through physical actions or mental activity, but to omit the reflective stage is to lose out on some learning.

Life experiences in succession may well change the point in the cycle where any person joins it. The complex range of factors which bear on an adult at any one time make this obvious. A thirty-year-old woman may be watching anxiously over one child in a primary school and another in a secondary school. She may take the larger share of running the family home with all the organisation of cleaning, cooking, washing, ironing which has to be done however many electrical appliances she may have. Shopping may have become a family outing to the supermarket, but the responsibility is likely to remain hers in seeing that the house is well stocked with food. She may sing in a choir, belong to a local women's group, be a committee member of some society or parents' association, or just help out as a volunteer if she is not too exhausted, because she is also likely to have a part-time or full-time job. And throughout, she can be worried that her husband may be made redundant, and that potential threat to the family income means that family plans for holidays or buying clothes, or redecorating the house are up in the air, and it puts a greater pressure on her to earn what she can.

Redundancy or simply uncertainty about employment continuing may threaten her husband differently. It is not just the possible loss of money which matters to him; it is the threat to his status and standing as a man. So whilst he has been a very active sportsman and spends time with his children in the local swimming pool and does his best to attend parents' meetings at school and take on some of the domestic workload, he finds he needs to push himself to the limit at work to feel that he has done everything possible to hold his place. And often he is so weary that all he can do in the evening is goggle at the box and nod off.

Take out the fear of redundancy and the multi-layered range of liabilities and responsibilities, and pressures remain. Whatever the level of income, whatever the kind of job, something like this pattern is the day-to-day experience of the majority of the population. And it is that majority of the population which has turned its back on learning through the formal education system which is a central concern if the country is to have the progressive acquisition of knowledge and skill necessary to keep industry and the public services going. As with Youth Training, so with adults' learning, experiential learning is a key. This is for the simple reason that if men and women who think of themselves as ordinary, as people who are indifferent as learners, can be given the opportunity to recognise for themselves what they have learned from their life and work experience without realising it, then they may be encouraged and motivated to set about using their ability to learn to greater purpose.

There is one particular aspect to consider about ways of learning which usually gets scant attention: women's ways of learning. Beginning with demography again, all the evidence suggests that in the next decade and more, greater numbers of women will be in part-time or full-time employment. Some of them will be women returners, who previously were in paid work and/or had continued some kind of study after leaving school. Others will be either newcomers to the world of paid employment or 'second chancers' if they join in the formal education system. All the national problems of skill shortages, updating and retraining will be reflected in what these women and their employers will face. For many of them, joining or rejoining paid employment will mean developing themselves as learners.

The difficulties experienced by women in employment are well rehearsed, many of them arising either intentionally or unintentionally through structures of employment within organisations being based predominantly on male patterns of hierarchy. The Equal Opportunities Commission continually draws attention to these issues. Government has a minister of state with a brief to try to improve opportunities for women in the Civil Service. Numerous women's groups act as pressure groups. Assertiveness training is now a commonplace course offered for women. But perhaps more important than any of this, employers know that increasingly they have to assume that women offer one answer to their recruitment and retention problems.

In much of this, little attention is paid to women's ways of learning systematically. Many courses offered in further education for women are designed specifically with their interests in mind. Access courses of all kinds usually go out of their way to ensure that their content and organisation are suitable for women. However, the issue goes way beyond this and highlights the possible benefits of APEL.

As soon as some women are given the opportunity of reflecting on their experience, some of the tendencies which differentiate female from male ways of learning appear. Most obviously, women will more readily lay claim to having learned all kinds of affective behaviours. They will deduce a range of knowledge and skills in dealing with people, supporting, managing, caring for others which often is truly humbling for a tutor. Less obviously, however, the hierarchical pattern of organisation in colleges can be more offputting to women than to men. And the extension of those hierarchies into subject areas and disciplines is perceived by some women differently from the perceptions of men.

So if women are to be given equal opportunities for learning, these factors ought to be taken into account and APEL offers a particular way of doing just this. It is all of a piece with using APEL to enable people to recognise their own preferred ways of learning. And that is the essential prerequisite for using readiness for learning as a launching pad for active additional learning.

In *Forms of Intellectual and Ethical Development in the College Years*[1] (1970) William Perry developed an account of what he considered to be the way in which students moved from being dependent to independent learners, learning to move from first of all accepting authority towards questioning that authority and finally accepting the personal responsibility for becoming authoritative in their opinions and judgements themselves. According to William Perry, the student learns that he has to work towards 'a privilege having (his) ideas respected'. This is peak point of intellectual development, reached at the end of an undergraduate course. After demonstrating the ability to think in complex conceptual ways, the young man has arrived.

He has proved himself as a thinker, and so graduation admits him to the ranks of his superiors. Perry's research was conducted predominantly with male students. And according to other American scholars this account is unsatisfactory as a description of some women's intellectual development.

According to *Women's Ways of Knowing* – (1986)[2] 'this scenario (Perry's) may capture the "natural" course of men's development in traditional hierarchical institutions but it does not work for women.' The book quotes a typical story which makes the point nicely.

'Welcome to the community of scholars' the President announces at Harvard commencement (graduation). 'That sure sounded weird to me' said a woman graduate, 'He says welcome and then shows us the door.' For the authors of *Women's Ways of Knowing* this is precisely the point. They say 'for women, confirmation and community are prerequisites rather than the consequences of development'.

The book goes on to cite several characteristics of women's learning which are almost identical to evidence drawn from the uses of experiential learning in Great Britain. There is the question of authority and the way women so often feel put down. One woman interviewed for *Women's Ways of Knowing* described how she had telephoned a doctor to ask about her son's attack of projectile vomiting. She reports the doctor's response as 'don't worry about it'. But she went on 'I wasn't asking for the complete history of projectile vomiting. I just really wanted an explanation, simple, something like you would give a child if they asked you a question like where do babies come from.' She was tangling with the expert's way of learning, whereas what she was asking for was her own way of learning. The book goes on 'What these women needed perhaps more clearly, consistently and sincerely ... was confirmation that they could be trusted to know and learn'. Relating that to higher education, examples show that once women are confirmed that not only could they be trusted to know and to learn 'but that they did indeed learn something already' then 'I'm accepted for what I am, the ability to be me. I came here and discovered that I am not a shell. I've got a lot of stuff in me.'

Making Experience Count (MEC), the course at Goldsmiths' College, always recruits a significant number of women. One woman who was moving from paid work to full-time study said 'I'm convinced that MEC was a stepping stone for me to do something that I've wanted to do for years, but never felt able. The MEC course made me realise that I had lots of valuable experience which gave me confidence to apply for the course I am now on.' Another woman said 'Without attending MEC I would never have known the opportunity for study was open to me at my age.' Yet the common feature MEC offered for women such as those was confirmation that they had already learned a good deal from their life and work experience, despite the fact that there was no formal recognition for it. And further that they were quite capable as learners. Both of these realisations came partially through the support that they found in other members of the group, as they all tried to review their experience and document what they had learned from it. 'Confirmation and unity are prerequisites rather than the consequences of development.' It is the same story, apparently on both sides of the Atlantic.

For those who are serious about developing the opportunities for learning for adults, the message is clear. Beginning with learners and asking the question how best can they learn is the foundation for their subsequent learning. Finding appropriate ways for women to learn requires particular attention given demography and needs of employment in the future, quite apart from the intrinsic ethical questions of equal opportunities. Finding appropriate ways for men and women to learn then is a bit like recognising that in any class or student group all are not at the same starting point, and that individual starting points are where individual students need to begin. This becomes a sophisticated issue, if women's ways of learning are to be taken as seriously as those for men are. But the matter ends there, clear to be confronted and only the ill-informed or myopic can ignore it.

This extends into questions of structure, choice and freedom. Again the impressions gained from Making Experience Count as well as *Women's Ways of Knowing* are consistent. A sure structure for a formal learning programme is something most women value. Many do not relish being thrown on their own devices whatever the level of tutorial support. But within that structure choice is essential. This bumps up against the authority question already mentioned. So being able to select courses of study rather than having them all prescribed in advance is an important feature in adequate provision for women as learners. And within that structure and those choices freedom to work at an appropriate pace without feeling pressured into working against what appear to be arbitrary schedules for completion again is consistent with many women's requirements. Many of these factors are, of course, equally important for men. Many institutions are working to meet these requirements as they modularise their academic programmes and move towards student-paced curricular arrangements. But again the points are important to register as the general argument evolves.

APEL can have additional significance for women in these times when clarion cries go up for more to undertake paid employment because there remains the danger that women will be short-changed. What kind of work is it that women are to join, because that is an essential question. If it is predominantly part-time, with pressure to become self-employed, or short-term contracts, or work attached to any other device for paying as little as possible it would be a sad disaster story all over again when women are being treated as second-class employees. And all the efforts to implement equal opportunities programme practices so far show the difficulties of combating these obstacles to women having an equal range of opportunities to those open for men. One of the prime benefits for individuals of APEL is a revaluation of self-value. As evidence of accomplishments already completed emerge from systematic reflection on experience and comes from nowhere else but from within, self-confidence can increase and with it a different set of attitudes toward any next step whether opportunities for learning or for employment. So whether in any education provision or within employment, APEL can act as a strong motivator for individuals to seek due recognition of their capabilities which have been revealed and reported by solid evidence. For women in contemporary society when they are being urged to join the ranks of the employed this could be particularly important.

To summarise this part of the argument, there is little point in setting out to create a better educated population, unless the characteristics of the potential learners are the basis for any curricular design. Nothing could appear more obvious. Unfortunately it is precisely what is not done for the majority of people. It is more often attempted than it was in further and higher education. But the attempts are patchy and need to become more widespread if the fundamental national anxiety is to be quietened: that more people need to learn more for longer during their earthbound years. Lifelong education, in a word. It is a nice idea which will only mean something in individual lives, if as a prerequisite, their characteristics as learners are taken seriously, rather than talking about people with learning difficulties after the event. This goes for every stage and aspect of formal education, and employment be it said. But what is to be explored here is what that has to say about post-secondary school learning.

WHO NEEDS CONNECTING?

So who are these individuals? How does this all apply to them?

Young people, older men and women in work and out of it, they have been discussed before. There is one more thing to say about them to put them in context before turning to possible applications of APEL. For a start, they all live somewhere, usually at home. But simply to think about everything that happens in a home is quickly to recognise that it may well be a place of significant learning. For women this is obvious. There is no need to dwell on that. But the same goes for young people and men. The new baby is born. These days many fathers and adolescent brothers and sisters pick up a good deal of knowledge about child rearing, infant growth and development from the conversations which follow from pre and post-natal clinics, health visitors' routine calls, doctors maybe, not to speak of all the material which peppers magazines, radio and television programmes, as well as the advertisers' junk mail urging the benefits of this or that baby food. Or DIY – how many hundreds of thousands of men, women and their children have learned the rudiments of construction, installing central heating, and house maintenance, the niceties of nurturing seeds and tending growing plants – just think of the proliferation of garden centres – and the intricacies of photography, still and moving. Or computers – the home pc is fast becoming a normal piece of equipment in many households and increasingly there is more than one.

Then consider leisure, entertainment and holidays. The amazing collection of advertisements in every imaginable newspaper and magazine and on television is simply a reflection of the millions of British people who take their holidays abroad. And not all of them are people simply sunning themselves, complaining that the food is not like good old fish and chips and loading up the car or luggage with duty-free for the return journey. Nor is it like that at home. The millions of families who visit famous country houses and gardens, or who walk the national parks or heritage coastal paths are doing things which many a school calls educational visits as part of the history, English or art curriculum, whatever it may be. And at home itself – television and radio programmes about the environment, the animal world, geology, archaeology, books and literature, not to mention political and economic affairs, are not all watched or heard by people who have already studied these things. Many older and younger people pay attention to these programmes because they find them interesting. They get something from them.

Or paid and unpaid employment – now of course a lot of employment is dull and boring with only two good things about it. It stops at five o'clock and for holidays, and it produces money. But not all is like that. Certainly not all unpaid employment is like that. Why else would people volunteer for the Citizens' Advice Bureaux, the National Trust, community groups, the parish and district councils and so on. And increasingly the everyday experience of those in work is that they are having to learn. New procedures, new systems, new production methods, whether in the boardroom or on the shop-floor, in the manager's or the general office, whatever was followed last year can well be changed this year. Moreover occupations change. Job descriptions alter. New roles have to be mastered. And all the time people are learning.

At checkout counters in supermarkets the combination of automatic price recording mechanisms, payment by cash, cheque, voucher, credit card or company charge card put a premium on dexterity, accuracy and quick thinking, since the idea behind it all is to increase the company's profits through customer satisfaction through not having to wait in long queues as well as providing information about sales and therefore computerising restocking requirements and getting more work from the employee. And since breakdowns are continual on these alleged labour-saving devices, a certain ability to be unruffled and good tempered is also at a premium. Or think of education and law – heads of schools, school teachers, vice-chancellors at universities, directors at polytechnics and their lecturing and administrative staff all having to master new ways of doing things, whether academically, administratively or financially. Solicitors are having to handle an almost impossible task of keeping up to date. As for those who work in education, the flow of statutory law and administrative ordinance which governs the way they do their jobs threatens to become almost overwhelming. It is so much easier to enact legislation than carry it out.

A most important part of learning at work, of course, is through company-provided in-house courses. The kind of provision made by flagship companies such as IBM, ICI, Jaguar Cars and Marks & Spencer is well known. Maybe the excellent training facilities used by the TSB and Tesco, Barclays and others are far less well known. So is the provision made for in-service training for teachers. But social work too has staff training officers in every employing authority and agency. What is not so well recognised or known is the extent to which trade unions make provision for their members to learn more. The EEPTU has two colleges of its own, one dealing with the technical side of the electrical business and the other for the supervisory and managerial side of things. Many other trade unions have similar facilities.

So no matter what kind of work, many people are learning while doing it. But as well as living somewhere, enjoying some kind of leisure, being in some kind of employment, an increasing number of people learn formally through one kind of education or another. It may be anywhere in the entire range of possibilities from adult basic education through to studying for a doctorate. The courses of study leading to formal qualifications are important here in terms of access to them, and credit toward them. For that it is the multifarious range of possibilities which do not lead directly to qualifications which is so important. A long tradition of university extra-mural boards often teaching in association with the WEA, has long been paralleled in further education colleges. Polytechnics and colleges of higher education have built on these traditions and have developed their own versions of opportunities for older men and women to learn what they want to learn without any necessary interest in seeking qualifications. Voluntary organisations provide a whole range of opportunities for their volunteers to learn to be better at the job. Citizens' Advice Bureaux, Women's Institutes, the National Trust, the National Council for Voluntary Organisations, Relate (formerly the Marriage Guidance Council), the National Association for School Governors and

Managers to name but a few, all devote considerable resources to helping their members learn more. Then there are organisations like the Industrial Society and the Education Committee of Business in the Community whose purposes are entirely to advance education and training of those in work.

For the argument being developed in this book there is one other category of formal learning which is potentially of the greatest importance and which is usually overlooked. This is all the knowledge and skill acquired by thousands of young men and women who entered higher education courses at degree level and withdrew either during or at the end of the first year of the course. By definition all these people were judged competent to study for degrees. What has happened to them? When they withdrew, almost certainly, they thought that what had been learned was wasted in qualification terms, that because they had withdrawn there was nothing they could do with that one-year study in using it towards obtaining the qualification which they had turned their back on for whatever reason. It is the burden of this book that it is not necessarily so. But seen from a national perspective of the need to make better use of this country's brain power, then this becomes an important issue.

So when the national cry goes up that there is a desperate need for more people to learn more for the sake of our economic survival, one central issue is how to get a sensible articulation and recognition for all this learning which is going on anyhow. And essentially that is what this book is about: finding ways of giving formal recognition and where appropriate accreditation to what people have learned already.

But that articulation has to be such that it has some chance of reaching the 50 per cent of the population who have the capacity to learn, but do not believe learning is anything much to do with them despite the fact that in reality they may have learned a good deal.

12 Access: a two-way street

It all comes down to access. Now access can be interpreted in many ways. Currently there is great emphasis on access to higher education. There needs to be far greater emphasis on access to further education. But access can just as easily mean access to upward social and occupational mobility. As a result it can be access to higher incomes. More important, it can refer to the social and economic factors which prevent people using access routes which are open to them. This is especially significant when the emphasis as here is on access to opportunities for learning.

Access implies a means of entry. Sometimes it is risky. A street sign which says 'buses only' decoded means that it is closed to all vehicles but that the intention is that buses only should go down this lane. It is not unknown for trucks, cars and motorbikes to interpret that sign as meaning that they can drive down it if they can get away with it. Perhaps a car gets stopped. A policeman may ticket a truck for a fine. Magistrates might not like the sound of it. It is access with risks. The access being explored here is access by right to opportunities for learning, not by some other's permission, except within the necessary conditions attached to being able to study for whatever course or programme is in question. And for these purposes access needs to be seen as a two-way business. Access for people to what they have learned already, a sort of internal recognition. And access externally to pursue whatever it is they both wish to turn to and have the ability and qualities to tackle – private access and public access.

Two-way access requires a gateway. If one direction for access is internal, trying to establish what an individual has accomplished already as a learner, then the route has to be through that individual's mind. And almost by definition many individuals are going to need help in exploring what is in the mind. Remember who the rhetoric of access is aimed at – those who do not at present join in learning opportunities open to them. But the other direction for access is outward. Outward then means the range of opportunities open. This poses a similar range of problems to those for the internal access route. And equally important, it may well be that individuals need some help. So in either direction of this two-way flow of access an intermediary facility looks like being an essential servicing agency.

This can be expressed as a pattern diagrammatically. It is like a transport system. Major airlines have hubs. Flight routes come in; flight routes go out. The hub acts as a passenger exchange and direction-finding system. Main roads often converge on roundabouts. You drive along one, select the one to leave on, but you have gone round a hub. Now if the hub is seen as a broker receiving from one direction and despatching in another, and transpose that inanimate system into an animate system for dealing with people instead of aeroplanes, cars or trucks there appears the idea of some personal brokerage arrangement. If some people need help in plotting where they have come from, their learning routes so far with its accomplishments signed like milestones, and then could do with some help in plotting which route to take towards any future, what a personal brokerage service needs to provide is information to deal with approach and departure routes, together with an understanding of the essential features of those routes and what happens to people who take them. And just as APEL in general can connect with individuals, education, employment and government, so does this interpretation of access as a two-way street have serious implications for each of those four categories within society.

PEOPLE AND TWO-WAY ACCESS

Inside the person lies a heterogeneous collection of knowledge and skills, accumulated from anywhere and everywhere. Outside that person lies an increasingly heterogeneous array of learning opportunities. That inside knowledge and skill have to come from the sum total of a person's life and work experience. Outside learning opportunities range from the full-time formal classes with the entire bureaucratic apparatus of application, registration, attendance and examination, to every possible combination of part-time, periodic, occasional, distance learning, and individualised learning agreements and now at bachelor's and master's degree levels, credit accumulation as an individual right and student-paced. Somehow if the two-way version of access is to work then both the internal and external factors need to be explored.

It is worth emphasising that talking about APEL and individuals is not the same as assuming that everyone's central interest lies in qualifications which relate to employment or qualifications at all. We may be living in times when more and more people need qualifications to get employment, stay in employment and get promotion, but not everyone is caught up in that hierarchy of requirement and for the health of everyone, that is just as well. Many adults continue in the best traditions of adult education of simply wanting to study to know more about some topic for the sheer satisfaction of it. For them APEL can sometimes become a beckoning hand to do just that. This is where the tension referred to pulls in the non-vocation direction. But for those who are concerned with formal qualifications the two-way street version of access can be a most telling factor, with some brokerage service at the point where the two streets meet. Outside each person lies a world of bewildering opportunities. Inside there is a private world, most of it taken for granted. Internal and external access then becomes the means of a person creating the best personal life.

Given the need for more people to know more, be able to do more, this two-way access becomes a vital factor for the world of personal learning. Many people can use this two-way access route for themselves without any assistance from any formal service. Their own educational story can have enabled them to develop the principal mental traits required for access to their own accomplishments, make informal decisions about the way they relate to some future purposes. These are the people on the inside track. They know how systems work, whether education, employment and internal personal systems, so that they can use all three as they set out to achieve some new goal. They know how to get the information they need by using libraries, catalogues, etc. and telephoning or writing their enquiries. Usually they have friends and relatives who act as an informal information service. And they know how to make sense of the information they obtain, extracting from it what they need and discarding the rest. And if they need direct personal help from people in careers offices or in educational institutions, they know how to seek out somebody who can give that help and they can simply get on with it.

In later sections this book has something to say which applies to those people. But here the focus of the discussion on the two-way access is those people who are not well equipped to move confidently down either route. And the case being argued is that APEL can be of profound significance for many people in developing the confidence necessary to move effectively in each direction. Now, obviously it is usually helpful to know how one arrives at a particular place as a means of moving somewhere else; using a map, in other words. The approach to APEL has been explored generally. There is also an increasing range of related facilities available to individuals to plot where they are on a personal map.

Advice services for adults

The Unit for the Development of Adult Continuing Education (UDACE) listed seven different activities concerned with offering educational guidance to adults in its publication *The Challenge of Change: Developing Educational Guidance for Adults*. This is how they set them out:

Informing

Providing information about learning opportunities and related support facilities available, without any discussion of the relative merits of options for particular clients. Since most published educational information is produced for promotional purposes 'pure' information is rare.

Advising

Helping clients to interpret information and choose the most appropriate option. To benefit from advice clients must already have a fairly clear idea of what their needs are.

Counselling

Working with clients to help them to discover, clarify, assess and understand their learning needs and the various ways of meeting them. Clients requiring counselling are likely to be unclear about their needs and require time to explore their feelings about the options, and counselling is therefore more likely to involve a series of contacts with a single client.

Assessing

Helping clients, by formal or informal means to obtain an adequate understanding of their personal, educational and vocational development, in order to enable them to make sound judgements about the appropriateness of particular learning opportunities.

Enabling

Supporting the client in dealing with the agencies providing education or training, or in meeting the demands of particular courses. This may involve simple advice on completing application forms, advice on ways of negotiating changes in course content or arrangements, or assistance to independent learners. A further kind of enabling is provided through 'Access' and 'Wider Opportunities' courses which may offer both group guidance and the teaching of study skills.

Advocating

Negotiating directly with institutions or agencies on behalf of individuals or groups for whom there may be additional barriers to access or to learning. (e.g. negotiating exceptional entry arrangements or modifications to courses.)

Feeding back

Gathering and collating information on unmet, or inappropriately met, needs, and encouraging providers of learning opportunities to respond by developing their provision. This may involve practical changes (e.g. changing the presentation of course information or changing timetables) or curricular ones (e.g. designing new courses for new client groups, or changing the way in which existing courses are taught to make them more appropriate for adult learners).

In practice the seven activities are closely interrelated. Thus, for example, the choice of what information to present to a client, and how to do so, itself involves an 'assessment' of that client, whether or not this is consciously done. In the same way, the confidence-building role of the 'enabler' often depends upon counselling skills.

Without an adequate base of information none of the activities are possible, but a service which seeks only to provide information cannot, in any adequate way, meet the guidance needs of its clients.

Implicitly APEL as a theme runs right through that list.

If that is the ideal there are a variety of services which according to their lights have tried to meet it. However, it cannot be said that they do so. There are services on offer by public libraries. There are the database systems offered by the Educational Counselling, Credit Transfer and Information Services (ECCTIS) and the Training Access Points (TAP) and the Materials and Resources Information Services (MARIS). There are several national bodies; the National Institute of Adult Continuing Education (NIACE) and the Educational Guidance and Assistance Service and more recently the Credit Accumulation and Transfer Registry (CATS) at the Council for National Academic Awards. There are specialist services offered for the students by the National Union of Students and for women by the National Advisory Centre on Careers for Women. There are specialist services offered in careers through a variety of offices run by local education authorities and of course, the private sector. Most of this provision is concentrated heavily on offering information. Public libraries are the biggest providers but their effectiveness depends on library staff's personal commitment to this aspect of library work. Citizens Advice Bureaux are in the same category. ECCTIS provides a comprehensive public information service on the provision of higher education throughout the UK. TAP provides a detailed information service about training opportunities for individuals, in particular localities. The National Bureau goes beyond providing information where possible and extends into referral and some advice. MARIS provides a computer-based information service on open learning materials.

Then there are the advisory interviews which tutors in further and higher education have provided so generously for so many years. Many-so called 'mature' students have drawn great benefits and often comfort from the sympathetic hearing they have had as they have worked their way through their own story of educational qualifications, of what they have done since getting them, either in work or out of it, and possible courses they might study. Similarly courses like 'Fresh Horizons' or 'New Opportunities for Women' or the weekend courses offered in a college like Hillcroft have as one of their prime objectives the kind of two-way access referred to. So do the drop-in centres at some further education colleges. And of course Making Experience Count and its imitators take the two-way access point as the curriculum itself.

The problem remains however of encouraging more people to use all these facilities, and what encouragement colleges, polytechnics and universities can offer. That leads on to a discussion of institutions' stance. Talk to most tutors in further and higher education about the way in which their institution tries to encourage greater participation and they will reel off a whole series of opportunities for individuals to find out what the place has to offer from its publicity efforts and its success in extending recruitment. If hard pressed to assess all those efforts as effective ways of reaching the lower socio-economic groups which are the principal concern at this stage of the discussion, then many tend to falter – and this is the problem. Conscientious, often devoted academic and registry staff do their level best. They recognise the problem. They make honest attempts to deal with it. But rarely do they deal with it effectively. This is because even when a college or polytechnic or university has made its most imaginative efforts for these men and women, the institution remains rather daunting, forbidding, complicated and an unwelcoming place. Teenage experience of education is not forgotten easily. And for men and women who have little confidence in their own capacity as learners, making the first move towards a formal educational institution can often take a great deal of moral courage and personal effort. So the institutional question is how to take account of those factors as part of its access policy. And institutions here means employer and government as well as education.

EDUCATION INSTITUTIONS AND TWO-WAY ACCESS

One way of thinking about this issue is to transpose the two-way access idea from an individual to an institution. For the individual the mind was the receiving and dispatching marshalling yard. For an institution, a student services centre could be conceived of in the same way. The receiving arm could work from the outer periphery in all forms of out-reach activity and advertising efforts into personal advisory and consultancy services while the dispatching arm would move into whatever education provision was offered by the institution. So instead of the individual's mind it is a student services centre which acts as the marshalling yard.

Picture two triangles one standing on top of the other, balanced and joined point to point. The lower triangle represents the increasingly varied heterogeneous and, we hope, growing number of potential learners who either wish or need to use opportunities for learning offered by institutions. The upper triangle represents the increasingly complicated array of learning opportunities offered by institutions: courses in small units; facilities for studying with attendance patterns ranging from, say, two hours a week to full-time; remedial classes; 'top-up' facilities for getting NVQs; distance learning materials; independent study, maybe on negotiated learning agreements; credit for APEL; credit for company in-house education and training; and any combination of them. All this can baffle members of academic staff. It can be, and often is, bewildering for applicants and students. So putting a circle round the points where the triangles meet fixes both the positon and role of a student services centre. It stands as the broker between the potential learner looking into the institution and the institution looking outwards towards the applicants. Its task is to get the best possible fit between what is best for the student and what the institution has to offer.

The core to such a student services centre should be a diagnostic and assessment service with the emphasis on self-assessment. Equipped with ECCTIS, TAP and MARIS, and the NCVQ database when it is available, and staffed by people well versed in the techniques of APEL the service would start where it mattered most – dealing with individual men and women.

Ideally a student services centre would have its headquarters in its institution, but with the capability of operating as a dispersed service. Wherever outreach activities suggested that there was a group of people who would use the services then the services would go to them rather than attempting to persuade them to come to the institution itself. The analogy with distance learning is obvious. If the best way to encourage some people in further learning is to enable them to study without attending formal institutions then it makes sense to take information and advice services to them as well. Of course, this is precisely the case for developing computerised databases and putting them in places like public libraries. But just making information available in those ways, does not begin to touch the problem of attracting those who do not already think of using them. Personal attention is essential. So whilst the full range of computerised databases needs to be available within the institution, outreach activities can manage without them because personal attention is the essential prerequisite for getting them engaged in searching for information in mediated services.

So prior learning assessment opportunities need to be provided both as part of the outreach activities placed away from the institution wherever they are, as well as within the student services centre. It would be really like turning the facilities of the course Making Experience Count into an institutional provision. With this difference – not everyone who might be encouraged to approach either an outreach base or student services would need the helpful canopy of a provided course like Making Experience Count. But all ought to have the opportunity of a fairly rapid systematic and reliable means of coming to an understanding of their own status and standing as learners as the first step towards trying to work out what learning programme makes best sense for the future. As now, some people would need practically no help at all. Others would need very extensive help. But the essential point is that if everyone who was not absolutely clear about the course they were seeking was required to go through these moves, as a formal requirement, in student services either in outreach or within the institution then they would be much more likely to make best possible use of what the institution had to offer. It could well be that the best way of seeing the outreach provision is simply a section of the student services centre working away from the institution in parallel to whatever student services offered within the institution. There would be no need for people to make use of both.

Once a man or a woman was ready to enrol with the college, polytechnic or university then the other services of the student services centre would come into full play. These are essentially of two kinds. First there is advice and help in composing what seems to be the most appropriate learning programme drawing on all the opportunities the institution has to offer. And second, adequate support for students whilst following their chosen course of study. Both are demanding activities for the institution to undertake.

Composing appropriate learning programmes has become a great deal more complicated just as the opportunities are more extensive, even richer. Accreditation and accumulation become the essential watchwords. The task would be for each individual to get an accurate picture of the learning achievements which they brought with them, and then work out an individual learning programme which was the best possible extension of what had been achieved already. This programme might easily contain nothing but a selection of the courses taught within the institution. Alternatively it might contain some of those courses together with an individually negotiated learning programme which could be undertaken away from the institution. An individually negotiated programme might be closely related to the person's employment or to leisure pursuits, or it might be a project connected with a formally-taught course, but taking a direction which the course itself did not include. In a higher education institution which had its own credit accumulation and transfer scheme or which was making use of the CNAA Credit Accumulation and Transfer Scheme, individuals might go and study courses in other institutions or the Open University with the results of those courses being accredited on an accumulation system in the place where they were enrolled.

But there is a further implication of seeing student services operating in this way, almost like an academic registry, and that relates to the curriculum. The amount of information which a service like this would collect on the basis of its experience of working with individuals could serve as a professional intelligence unit for the benefit of the institution as a whole. Academics working in student services like this would acquire a shrewd understanding of how far the institution's curriculum was tuned to the wishes and needs of the men and women making use of its services. In other words, student services seen in these terms could become a ready-reckoner for the institution's curriculum. Since student services to be effective would need organic connections with all the academic faculties, schools or departments of the institution at the point of enrolment – student services in no sense can be seen as a self-standing independent facility in the institution – then the lines of communication would be open for this intelligence service.

The academic implications of exploiting this intelligence service could be far-reaching. It could be the key to enabling institutions to be responsive to the needs of potential students living as they do in a rapidly changing society. The 'top-up' learning opportunities which the institutions especially will need to make once the assessment of competence for NVQs becomes a significant part of their activities is a case in point. If those possibilities do not exist already, they will need to be provided. That means being able to change in a relatively short time from what is already on offer to what needs to be provided. At the higher education level it implies both being able to supply tailor-made learning programmes, negotiated individually, and being able to change the emphasis on some existing courses and replacing others as the need suggests. Again there is nothing new in any of this. Most institutions are acutely aware of their need to keep their courses under review. It is simply that seeing students services as a curriculum intelligence service could enable an institution as a whole to conduct curriculum review and revision on a systematic basis.

The student support service facilities on offer in such a student services centre would then be an amalgam of what is often called the pastoral tutor system and educational advice as students move through their learning programme. One of the vital matters to take into account is the possibility that some students would wish to change the composition of their learning programme once they had begun it. Naturally the rules and regulations governing the work of an institution would provide the framework for any such renegotiation, but the need is obvious and will have to be met.

If that sort of support is a necessary facility to enable students to make the best that they can of what an institution has to offer then it needs to extend into helping students moving on from the institution to whatever lies next. In this sense the careers advice service to be found in most institutions then would become part of the student services centre.

Seeing student services in this way is largely talking about ways of rearranging many of the facilities and services on offer in most institutions as a matter of course. It is more the organisation and management of the services which need to be reformulated to take into account the needs of the increasing number of people it needs to attract. This is a matter of regrouping and reconstituting; it is not a matter of inventing anything entirely new, introducing some alien ideas.

What is different is seeking to install APEL facilities as a regular part of mainstream activities in an institution. One of the reasons for establishing an APEL service within students services is to make it as economical as possible and to serve the institution as well as the individuals. The alternative to having APEL as an institution service is to see APEL working within admission arrangements for separate courses. That implies multiplying the number of academic staff who would need to be familiar with the techniques involved. By having an institutional APEL service, tutors responsible for accepting students on to courses would be receiving the evidence of learning produced by applicants instead of having to help students produce it from the start. That way their academic judgement remains the essential feature of APEL since they would be considering APEL results in the same way as they considered those with formal educational qualifications. The evidence would be different. Their function and responsibility is unchanged. In institutional terms this is sticking to the threefold academic role which is one of the principles of good practice for APEL. The initial support and help is provided by staff in the students services unit. As necessary they call in expert academic advice to help applicants organise and prepare their evidence for assessment. Assessment falls to course tutors and admission officers. The implication is that admission is initially to the institution. Which courses would then constitute a programme of learning, gets decided by the academics responsible.

Seeing APEL as an institutional service to itself as well as to individuals, is bound up with the overall issue of institutional funding. One of the most difficult questions raised, since APEL first appeared as a possibility for higher and further education, has been cost. At the simplest level it raises the question in higher education that if APEL is not a taught course within a degree programme where it is financed like any other course, it must be self-financing either through fees or through some priming arrangements from TEED or a local education authority. In further education APEL provision could usually be brought within a college budget by juggling the numbers of hours allocated to different departments. But all this is being overlaid by the financial changes brought about by the establishment of the Universities Funding Council, the Polytechnic and Colleges Funding Council and local finance/management for further education under provisions of the Education Reform Act 1988 and their unknown consequences. Corporate status for polytechnics and colleges of higher education and governing bodies for all non-university institutions with heavy representation from employers is intended to introduce a market economy style of financial management. Trying to answer the question how provision is to be paid for has been a central one for heads of institutions and their governing bodies for decades. But the question revolved around the permitted levels of staff–student ratio. Now all kinds of other ratios and cost centres will come into the reckoning. However, one thing is absolutely clear: the numbers of students enrolled representing income will be the starting point for balancing the books for expenditure which has to be met. Whether full-time, part-time, occasional, sometime, short-term, long-term, open learning, distance learning, any student in any mode will count.

This is where a curriculum intelligence unit offered by APEL within student services could become so important. Institutions which can respond to change in student demand are likely to be stronger and more healthy than those which cannot. As pointed out before, this will now apply to many higher and further education colleges, polytechnics and universities. Some will continue to do what they have been doing for the simple reason that they are good at it and that people want it. But for those who both need to become more responsive and wish to do so, there has to be some means of coping with changes in ways which preserve the academic integrity of the institution. One of the fears of a market economy version of post-secondary education where responsiveness looks like talking about a naked customer service is that it all leads to a supermarket style provision which trivialises everything. In other words the brave new world of financial self-management could be where the price of everything is financially calculated and the value of everything becomes irrelevant. Quality could be at a discount. So to have academic decisions about curriculum, courses, learning programmes and student provision based on a flow of intelligence could be a bastion to protect quality.

There are some examples of institutions developing down these lines with varying degrees of coverage. Wolverhampton Polytechnic has an 'Education Shop' placed right at the main crossroads in the town which serves mainly as an information centre about what the Polytechnic has to offer to potential students, but that is where any APEL considerations begin. From the shop people are referred to the appropriate faculty where academic assessment and degree planning takes place. And because Wolverhampton has developed its own version of credit accumulation, the full range of possibilities of gaining academic credit exist from previous study, work-based learning especially through companies' in-house training provision, and prior experiential learning, its Education Shop is where all these goods are put on full display to any enquirer, either casual or determined. For years Thames Polytechnic has had the beginnings of this kind of service in its Education Shop under a continuing education banner. Newcastle upon Tyne Polytechnic does more or less the same through its Associate Student Scheme. Based in the Centre for Continuing Education APEL and degree planning facilities are there. Links with academic departments ensure that academic standards are maintained and appropriate courses of study are planned. But again the full range of possible sources of academic credit is available, which means that it is well down the road of developing a student services centre. The Polytechnic of North London has done something of the same kind through its Evening Degree Scheme for some years. Hull, Liverpool, Sheffield City, Polytechnic of Central London, Portsmouth Polytechnic are all in some way or other developing these kinds of facilities with a special interest in older students. For universities, Sheffield seems the front-runner in this regard, with the prospect of turning its degree courses into a modular organisation with credit accumulation built in from the start.

So there is nothing new in the idea of combining a range of different services in a coherently organised student services unit. Including APEL is one new factor, and that is hardly new any more. What would be a genuinely new factor would be the exploiting of student services with APEL as a component as an institutional intelligence and research unit. Apart from the kind of surveys conducted as a sort of market research exercise to support applications for developing new courses in the past, most institutions of further and higher education had no policies for collecting student data which would give them a comprehensive story of how they had developed and some reliable basis for making predictions about what their most appropriate forms of future development might be.

Bunker Hill Community College in Boston, Massachusetts is an instructive example of what this kind of research can do for an institution. At the flick of a page on a printout or the touch of a button it can look up an analysis of its total enrolments over a number of years, divide them into the various categories of age, sex, racial background, occupational background, geographical distribution within its overall catchment area, the results of the entry testing, the courses taken, their success rate, the amount of academic credit brought with students into the College subdivided into APEL, other certificated learning, companies' in-house training and so on. This enabled the college to spot early on that its efforts to recruit ethnic minority students were not working, to refine them until now it is the most successful college in the area. Similarly it saw from the records of admissions testing and the courses taken that it needed to put on more preparatory courses in some disciplines as a form of remediation, and to move from that to a college requirement that satisfactory performance in English and maths was a condition for being allowed to proceed to a full associate degree programme. The Dean of Development was providing the College with information which enabled it to make effective curricular changes, alter its advertising and recruiting strategies, and as a result boost its enrolments at a time when demographic trends could have meant declining student rolls.

All this works in Bunker Hill because the admissions office is a one-stop shop for all the pre-entry information required, the registrar's office holds all information about courses taken and results, and the learning centre administers all entry testing and passes those results through to the registrar's office.

There is nothing necessarily new in any of that for British institutions. What makes the data collection at Bunker Hill such a powerful institutional tool is the existence of a Dean of Development with the responsibility of co-ordinating all the collection of information, developing ways of using computer programs to facilitate both collection and retrieval, and for making policy suggestions based on the trends of development which printouts reveal.

Of course it is not cheap to develop or run. But then neither are empty classrooms cheap to keep empty. It is a question of deploying existing resources for the best possible return. Given the fine tuning of expenditure and income which will be increasingly the concern of institutions, this kind of information could be well worth its price. And this goes for further education just as for polytechnics and colleges of higher education and some universities. As with APEL itself there is no suggestion that this kind of approach needs to be adopted by all institutions. Some will have no need of it at all. The point is simply that for those institutions who are wishing to take serious account of their recruitment because of demographic changes, then using APEL as part of a service agency for the institution as a whole is an additional factor to bear in mind.

In the new regime of institutional accounting, on-course experiential learning could become very important. This is not referring to sandwich courses. It is looking to the provision of practical and work experience by colleges, polytechnics and universities as learning programmes generating academic credit within three-year degrees which are not necessarily explicitly vocational. This would offer a mixture of learning through doing and formal academic study to those who do not choose sandwich courses. As an option this could appeal to many young people for whom three years straight academic study is not really suitable, an appeal strengthened through offering a period of introduction to the world of work without any vocational commitment. For example, students studying in the humanities could take a term working in a museum, library, art gallery, an office or in manufacturing, social services, local government department, when the work was planned on a negotiated learning agreement which would be supervised and assessed within the same academic standards as applied to learning in classrooms, lecture halls and laboratories. The principles of the assessment of experiential learning can ensure that. Work internships for academic credit within first degrees could become another version of two-way access. It would offer access to the needs of many students to use different learning styles harnessed to the same objective of getting a degree. For the institution they could offer opportunities for both recruiting and engaging students who do not choose sandwich courses, not being sure how they want to earn their living and who equally are not sure that three years' full-time study is suitable for them. Assessment of experiential learning would become an instrument for curriculum development expanding the range of learning opportunities on offer. At best this could turn out to be a way of making greater headway in attracting into higher education young people from lower socio-economic groups, one of the central issues in an attempt to raise the participation rates. Furthermore, if work internships of this kind were incorporated in facilities for mixed modes of learning, moving from full-time to part-time study as the need arose, then the attractions might be considerable.

Work internships of this kind could also offer additional opportunities to older men and women needing part-time study since it could generate academic credit for them on the basis of their current employment. Applying the assessment of experiential learning to their work experience with a view to awarding academic credit could become a powerful encouragement to older men and women to join or rejoin formal study for qualifications. It could just as well interest their employers. Given credit accumulation facilities with the implications for student-paced learning, this could be an attractive proposition for those with domestic responsibilities to discharge as well as those holding down full-time employment.

Seeing APEL in this way as part of an institutional service which provides for the two-way access routing simultaneously for individuals and the institution itself, is of course providing a mechanism for dealing with the tensions referred to earlier. It could also become the institutional centre for coping with a distance-learning version of APEL. The best example of this so far is the provision now available in the province of British Columbia in Canada.

Somewhere there is room for another facility which could cope with other tensions as well. And it needs to be national. In theory outreach activities can remove much of tension for people who are hesitant or not confident about approaching a formal education institution and yet want what it can provide. Or they can enable people to use facilities which their home and work circumstances make it impossible for them to get from the institution itself. There have been plenty of examples of distance-learning initiatives to meet this need. The Open University is a shining example of how this can be done successfully, but never again is it likely that such an institution will be established with such generous start-up funding for planning and curriculum development to ensure the very highest quality of learning materials, to lay the foundations for that very success. For training and updating the Open Tech launched in 1982 was an attempt to promote an open and distance-learning scheme nationally in the occupational field. At sub-degree level the Open College which began its work in 1987 is another such initiative. Far longer than any of them, the National Extension College has provided an invaluable range of learning opportunities at the access to further study level, explicitly through its flexi-study arrangements with colleges of further education. Since 1986, the Credit Accumulation and Transfer Registry at the Council for National Academic Awards has offered a national service for those wishing to work for bachelor's or master's degrees without being confined to the regulations of any one university, polytechnic or college. The latest service of this kind is the Open College of the Arts, yet another inspired initiative from the ever-fertile mind of Michael Young. But this time unlike his blueprint for the Open University as a state-supported enterprise, it is entirely self-financing with no direct subsidy at all from tax money.

But despite all these many and costly attempts to provide a

comprehensive national service covering all levels of study, there is a patchwork quilt of provision which shows few signs of attracting the broad mass of people who for the most part stop learning systematically beyond the age of 16. Individual institutions are making significant headway in their own areas so that the patchwork pattern gets filled in a bit. The fact remains that there is no convincing national coverage. Given the benefits of APEL, and its articulation as a system of two-way access, APEL could serve as a national integrating tool. If a major obstacle to persuading more people to learn more for longer during their lives, is the belief, which experience of school has induced in them, that they are not much good as learners and that in any case learning more doesn't really matter, some means has to be found of persuading them that they are wrong in that belief. Rhetoric from government down is insufficient. Whatever may prove to be the effectiveness of Training Enterprise Councils as a means of beefing up training in local areas through the involvement of employers as central players in the business, they have a long hard job trying to change this cultural characteristic.

The case here is that APEL could begin to do just that. A properly promoted national service of APEL could make a powerful contribution to changing this prevalent attitude to learning. An APEL kit could be available on a distance-learning mode. Advisors could be recruited from universities, polytechnics and colleges through the land. Teams of assessors could be appointed. Results could be recorded in a credit bank. Certificates of credit could be issued to individuals who asked for them. Those certificates could be presented to institutions at which individuals wished to further their study. Institutions would have no need to worry about the validity of those certificates of credit because they were issued by duly appointed assessors responsible to a national board. Cost would be the only serious issue.

Maybe this is something the Open Polytechnic could undertake. There are many objections to such a proposal. The most serious is that it could relieve institutions of the responsibility for developing these facilities themselves. Implicitly it would add another strand to the battery of qualifications and for many there is too much of that already. In any case, institutions would decide themselves whether to accept any such recommendations for credit. But on balance it may be an idea worth exploring.

The province of British Columbia in Canada offers an interesting set of pointers for the establishment of such a service. There in 1986, the provincial government decided that some new initiative had to be taken to cope with the need to lift the education standards of its population. It had to be an initiative which took account of people living away from easy reach of existing institutions as well as those living near them. It could not be an initiative which created sufficient institutions to serve people where they lived. And so the provincial government decided to create a new institution to serve the entire province on a distance-learning basis. APEL was their chosen tool.

Now there is no insuperable problem in instigating the same kind of provision in Great Britain. What with the Open University, CATS, the Open College, the National Extension College, all capable of being serviced by ECCTIS, TAP and when it comes the national database of the National Council for Vocational Qualifications, adding another service to what is already available should not be too difficult provided there was some determination somewhere to provide it. And of course sensible arrangements for dealing with the cost. At that stage the focus shifts to goverment and its departments.

EMPLOYMENT AND TWO-WAY ACCESS

The pair of triangles joined at the apex, looking like one pyramid balanced on another, can be just as appropriate an image applied to employers and employment as for individuals and educational institutions. The two-way access is every bit as significant to employers concerned as they are about recruitment, retention and retraining – getting employees, keeping them and keeping them up-to-date – as it is for men and women thoughtful about their own futures and institutions which have accepted the role of a responsive agency to assist people's development as learners.

For employers it was not always so. Until fairly recently, much of heavy industry could rely on a steady recruitment to its workforce from families who had a tradition of working with it. Sons followed fathers. Daughters often went into clerical work in the same firm. What training there was, was part and parcel of employment. The decline and reduction of so-called smoke-stacked style industries, especially in the early 1980s made a dramatic change to the even rhythm of things. So did the rapid development of the so-called service industries, based on food, travel and finance. Technological changes in production intensified the changes. High tech with its rapid incorporation of microelectronics accelerated those changes. Demographic trends introduced an unfamiliar factor through its implications of smaller numbers of young potential employees with the corresponding increasing importance of older employees. And more than that, demographic trends directed the attention of employers to sections of the older population not already in work, but who could be seen as potential employees. Essentially that meant women and ethnic minority groups. When all that is put against the continual need for more and more employers to have employees who are competent learners, then the notion of two-way access can become a serious proposition.

An example for a company concerned about recruitment of young employees illustrates the point. The application form used by Rover Group conveyed the impression to 16-year-old potential employees that their formal education record was the only thing the company recruiters took seriously. Since by definition many of those potential employees have not shone at secondary schools, those application forms set the scene for an essentially limited consideration by company staff of the young people who offered themselves for consideration. Having become interested in the principles and practice of APEL, the Personnel and Training Manager of Rover Group considered that the limitation imposed by this traditional approach on both the company and the young people themselves was doing positive damage all round. So the procedures for recruiting people were extended to include what is best described as a questionnaire concerning everything that they have done outside formal education. The idea was to give them the opportunity of displaying a whole range of capacities, skills and competences which they could have acquired through part-time work, voluntary activities and outright leisure activities. A young man with a slender record of formal education attainment who was extremely good at organising table tennis competitions in his youth club will present himself differently to a prospective employer if he has been invited to think about all that and put it on paper and send it in before an interview, than if he approached an interview with the leaden recognition that his formal school record was not much to shout about. Similarly the prospective employer will see that young man with very different eyes, if the educational record is complemented by an account of what he would interpret as administrative and organising skills. The net result could be the young man getting a job instead of being rejected and the employer getting an employee he might have lost. The same is true for young women. An adolescent girl, who in effect is running a home while still at school because both her parents are out at work, could well be developing a range of managing and organising skills which would not show up at all if application form and interview concentrated heavily on formal educational records. This is two-way access at work. The young people are being given access to their own accomplishments – interest in and personal recognition of what they have done already – and so giving employers access to them as well, whilst both are being given access to a future which otherwise might not exist.

There is a significant extension to this development at Rover, and as with so many instances of the development of APEL it came from a combination of two different but related ideas. In this case it was the YTS into HE project on the one hand and on the other, government pressure for employers to provide work experience places for secondary school pupils. With the support of the Department of Trade and Industry and the Department of Education and Science, Rover had the idea of running a national competition for schools offering work experience programmes for their pupils. Government had been urging schools to incorporate work experience components for young people before they left school. Some firms were being bombarded with requests for work experience placements. Surely, reasoned the Manager, Young People, Resourcing and Development, at Rover, some steps could be taken to attempt to introduce notions of quality into all these arrangements. So a pamphlet was published and issued to every secondary school in the country on the criteria to be met by schools submitting entries for what was called The Rover Award for Quality in Work Experience. They were set out as follows:

Principal Criteria
The responsibilities and obligations of the parties involved to be clearly defined, ensuring that each knows what to expect from the other.
A clear statement of the planned educational objectives and how the placement of pupils is designed to help in achieving these.
Equal opportunity access to work experience placements and positive action to overcome sex-stereotyping.
Systematic and effective preparation for work experience, appropriate to pupils' needs.
Appropriate means by which progress and achievement in work experience can be reviewed and recorded, with the active involvement of as many of the parties as possible.
Systematic and effective post-placement follow-up and cross-curricular integration of work experience outcomes.

Additional Criteria
Understood and accepted school policies on work experience providing for cross-curricular integration and a commitment to quality.
Appropriate means by which the effectiveness of work experience provision will be assessed and reported to the parties concerned.
Appropriate in-service training to support 'whole school' commitment to work experience.

That approach to criteria was in part informed by Rover's involvement with APEL in the YTS into HE project. Thinking about ways of attracting more young people into that project the Rover representative suggested that leaving the introduction of the general ideas of APEL to young people until they were sixteen was probably leaving things too late. After all, he pointed out, most of those young men and women were unlikely to have been told at school that learning was not confined to classrooms, that what they did outside school might be just as significant as what they did – or were supposed to – learn at school. When the Rover Award for Quality in Work Experience Competition emerged it found a way of making its point explicitly: that to be of any value work experience had to be seen as work-based learning. Further, it could be a way of introducing the idea to Rover managers that work experience should possibly be seen as a learning experience and by extension a way of Rover taking the initiative over work experience placements for schools. Instead of responding to requests from schools, Rover could say that placements were available on terms designed to ensure that these were placements for learning and not for experience only.

Returning to the theme of possible benefits of APEL for employers, if there is anything in that as an approach to the recruitment of young people, then it is a great deal more significant as an approach to older people in two categories: those already in employment, and those who are not at work. It is difficult to judge which is the more important of the two. Increasingly it looks as if employers have great need of both. Instead of assuming young recruits can replace older workers and those who retire or move on, an employer has to look at the older men and women already on the payroll. And instead of assuming, as many employers have done in the past, that if he needs people with additional skills to those he has already he can recruit them from outside, he is likely to find that that is not so easily done. He has to ensure his present people are kept up to date, retrained, reskilled, skill-enhanced as some of the current jargon will put it, but he is also in danger of having his best people poached from under his nose. So while employers may calculate that fortuitous combinations of poaching and being poached may solve problems of recruitment and retention, one thing stands out above all other. Employers are needing to make the best possible use of the adult employees they actually have.

Several things follow from this. Employers need to know as much as they can about the full range of capabilities contained in their existing workforce. Employers need to convince their employees that they are really interested in that range of capabilities and not merely those which relate to the immediate job and occupation in hand. More than that, employers need to demonstrate their concern to assist employees to develop their capabilities, both, and this is the vital point, for the sake of the employees themselves and for their own proper and necessary concerns as employers. In a phrase, human resource development is moving up the agenda items for more and more businesses rather than being a masthead banner for a few flagship companies.

So in between the two triangles, one on top of the other, apex joined, APEL can act as a two-way access mechanism and can take centre stage for employment under an even stronger, brighter set of floodlights than those for institutions. Without older students in significant numbers, some institutions could well close. Without employees businesses go bankrupt. Bankrupt businesses do not generate the income which in large measure keeps educational institutions alive and functioning. Hence, it may turn out, because of demography, that APEL can do even more for employment than it can for education. In the short run that is. In the longer run, APEL will serve education to assist it to service industry better.

As with other ways of using APEL, what the Americans have developed with employers over the past nine years offers some useful pointers. This all began in 1982 when the Ford Motor Company and the United Automobile Workers labour union did a deal as part of their collective bargaining. For each blue collar worker the company paid 5 cents an hour into a fund to be administered jointly by Ford and UAW through the National Development and Training Center to be used for education and training by Ford workers, and this is the arresting point for Britain, previously employed Ford workers who had been laid off, but were still on their recall lists, and their spouses. Under that rubric something called the Colleges and Universities Option Programme (CUOP) was developed. The Council for Adult and Experiential Learning was commissioned to put this into effect. It acted as a broker between the various Ford plants across the United States and colleges and universities near to them.

Institutions were given the opportunity of joining in CUOP provided they accepted certain requirements. These were that they would either accept APEL results for academic credit or provide assessment for experiential learning or both, that they would design tailor-made courses to satisfy what Ford workers wanted to study, if those courses were not already in the course catalogue of the institution, that they would provide teaching at the Ford plant if asked, and that they would fit their teaching into the rhythms of shift workers' time off from work. To enable Ford workers to prepare themselves for taking advantage of those facilities, counsellors were trained to work in the Ford plants and 'Returning to Learning Workshops' were specially designed by CAEL and staff trained to conduct them. Steadily the amount of money paid into the joint fund increased through further collective bargaining negotiations from the first 5 cents an hour to 10 cents an hour. Simultaneously the participation rate of the Ford programme rose sharply.

That was a pioneering effort. Now General Motors and Chrysler have the same kinds of arrangements with the UAW. CAEL has worked with different independent companies of the former Bell Telephone company to introduce and administer flourishing programmes of a similar kind arranged with the Communications Workers of America union. The Scott Paper company introduced its own programme for its workers with CAEL as its agent for development. In the Philadelphia area the United Food and Commercial Workers have commissioned CAEL to design and run a programme for them. Government has got involved directly with CAEL. The Office of Personnel Management of the Federal Government has approved a pilot 'Returning to Learning Workshop for Federal Employees'. It is almost as if a tidal wave of interest is rising in employment generally.

Several characteristics run throughout all these initiatives. All are concerned with APEL. All are concerned with further learning opportunities. And whereas not all offer unlimited choice of topics to be studied, limiting possibilities to occupationally related courses, many do give choice, and all are based on the straightforward acceptance that employees who are learning are better employees than those who are not. The amount employees are able to spend annually on studies varies between $1,200 and $2,000 but it is the employer who is paying. And there is one further characteristic which is particularly telling, and that is prepayment. In other words once it is agreed by all concerned what courses an employee will take at a particular institution, then the employee does not have to pay up first and then get paid back later; the company pays the bills direct.

Unions are keen about programmes like this for a variety of reasons. For a start if they can demonstrate their ability to win benefits for members like this, then it helps their recruitment at a time when union membership has declined. Then opportunities like this help to ensure that their members stay in employment with their company, or if they are made redundant or 'let go' as the American euphemism has it, they have had the chance to prepare themselves for some other job. Employers see these arrangements as ways of ensuring that they have the kind of skilled workforce which they require. And within that they reckon that this kind of provision can the more readily facilitate the kinds of redeployments within their organisations which they know must follow technological advances. And if it comes to 'letting people go' or declaring redundancies, then at least they have done their best to enable those affected to cope with what that means for them as individuals. So whether it is a question of what goes into wage packets and salary cheques, or what goes into company profits, the message seems clear. Money spent on what are called in America 'Joint Venture Programs' is very well spent.

So far there is only one well-publicised example of anything similar in Britain: Ford UK have launched their 'Employee Development and

Assistance Programme' (EDAP). It is too early to comment on its results since it was only started in July 1989. But many of the thrusts are similar to its American parent: prepayment of tuition; wide choice of topics; jointly administered through local Ford plants; involvement of local colleges and so on. And they all rest on similar interests on the part of both unions and company: job security and employment opportunities on the one hand; an up-to-date alert and engaged workforce on the other for the company. There could hardly be a more sensible pair of reasons. Underlying both, APEL is wanting to make itself heard. Each set of reasons is all about wanting to enable individuals to make the best of themselves. There are different motives of course. But all motives are mixed so the fact of some common interest can be more important than the different interests at play. For the central point about Joint Ventures in the USA and any development such as in Ford UK is agreement between employers and unions of the importance of men and women continuing to think of themselves as learners and acting so as to demonstrate it.

In terms of APEL and two-way access potentially schemes like Ford's EDAP go a great deal further. A local 'plant committee' is composed of equal numbers of hourly-paid and salaried management staff who elect their own Chairman. The committee is responsible for administering a tuition budget and handling applications for funds from anyone who works in the plant – it is bound to become tacitly a form of adult education. For some men and women the experience of that kind of co-operative activity could well change their perceptions of the Ford Motor Company itself and the area where they live. If they are part of making decisions in one important part of their lives they may want to become more involved in decisions which affect other parts of their lives. Given the numbers of plants run by a major company like Ford, this could be a not inconsiderable factor – beyond those plant committee members, however, the message from a scheme like EDAP to all Ford employees is strong and clear: please participate. And as with Plant Committees their experience of participating will not stop at the gates of EDAP. It is quite obvious that all these possible consequences of EDAP-like schemes whether intended or not can raise significant issues for the management of companies at every level. Worker participation remains more fiction than fact and often stuck in controversies about representation on committees and boards. Schemes like EDAP could produce a lively worker participation of an entirely different kind. If anything comes of any of these possible developments a great deal of additional learning is going to be acquired at work.

There is a more recent development which fits into this general theme. It is an extension of the credit rating of companies' in-house in-service provision for their own employees. Some companies have reacted so enthusiastically to the possibilities opened through having some of their own education and training schemes recognised as carrying academic credit towards either the bachelor's or master's degrees. They are seeking collaboration with academic institutions or CNAA to have their entire internal in-service provision assessed academically, with the possibility in view of becoming accredited institutions in their own right, on a par with a college, polytechnic or university within the bounds of the areas of teaching and learning that they offer. This has been a standard practice in the United States for many years so that companies such as Xerox and 3M are licensed to award their own degrees under the same regional accrediting arrangements as colleges and universities. But in Britain as a relatively new development it serves to strengthen the general case about the capacity of employment to contribute significantly to promoting the cause of learning for all.

The case here is that APEL in employment can be the handmaiden for these kinds of developments. And nowhere does this appear more compelling than in the two-way version of access. On the internal route, APEL can offer the chance for individuals to reveal a range of interests and capacities to employers which most probably neither individual nor employer recognised. Redeployment, retraining, updating and all the rest can become more effective, more purposeful, more intelligible when based on the fullest information than when relying on the evidence of work performance and hunch which is usually the case. And on the external route there are better chances of matching people to updating and retraining courses. A finance clerk who was a volunteer in the Red Cross or St John Ambulance Brigade might turn out to be a better candidate for training as a health facility manager than for retraining to cope with the latest financial recording systems. APEL can reveal that sort of thing systematically instead of the chancy business of relying on gossipy exchanges.

This suggests that rather like educational institutions having some sort of student services centre with APEL as its core, employers could do with APEL being installed at the heart of their personnel function. Putting together the Rover Group views on recruitment, and the joint venture approach to employee development, APEL begins to look like a usable common denominator. As with educational institutions there is nothing especially new about any of this. Many companies have highly sophisticated procedures for dealing with recruitment and promotion at managerial levels. And more recently many have employed external consultants for the same purposes and especially for helping those made redundant to plan for different futures. Most of that is at considerable expense. So all that is being suggested here is that something of the same kind of considerations should be given to employees at all levels.

So for student services, read personal and employee development as the broker of two-way access. For recruitment, think of the internal route of two-way access as a means of enabling applicant and recruiter to have the fullest account of the range of capabilities, knowledge and skill which the applicant could bring to the company. For the external route, possible lines of occupational development as well as the particular jobs on offer would be laid out. Job applications then become more of a mutual exploration between applicant and recruiter than a suppliant deferring to a patron. A two-way street with two-way traffic. But again this is precisely what happens with a large number of jobs, just as many education institutions take all this trouble with their admissions procedures. But it cannot be claimed to be applied either systematically for all levels of employment within most companies, nor can it be held as the general practice throughout the majority of British employment.

Two immediate difficulties arise which can rapidly become solid objections. The first is cost. There is no doubt that working along these lines mops up resources. But that budget line of expenditure would need to be seen against the more tricky costs involved in calculating the pluses and minuses of recruitment and retention in the present context of demography and economy generally. And there is no easy answer to that. It is rather like trying to work out a balance between preventive and curative medicine. Software programs and spreadsheets so far cannot provide answers. So it is a matter of deciding which is the most useful way of using existing resources to achieve what is required. Just as education institutions are finding, under their new financial arrangements, choices are hard. Businessmen spend their lives trying to deal with those hard choices. Recruitment and retention simply introduces another set of choices which have to be faced. The case here is simply that viewing APEL and its possibilities as something which can be put to the service of a company, is one way of looking at those issues.

Another is to say that the more companies move towards having their in-house education and training provision recognised academically, the more they are taking on some of the characteristics of academic institutions. If it makes sense for the latter to think of a student services unit being a necessary part of their way of discharging their prime purpose, the development of learners who are employable, then perhaps it suggests that a personnel and employee development unit in a company is a helpful way of thinking about companies discharging their prime task of being profitable through ensuring that their employees' effectiveness is enhanced through employees as learners. Two-way access is a working environment.

VOLUNTARY ORGANISATIONS AND TWO-WAY ACCESS

In all the current debate about access and the need to increase participation rates in all forms of further and higher education, there is little reference to voluntary agencies and organisations. This is odd. It can only be an omission but it is odd nevertheless. There are hundreds and thousands of men and women engaged in one form of voluntary work or another. Given the panicky anxieties about skill shortages, labour shortages and the need for more women to enter the workforce it is reasonable to suppose that these volunteers could be a rich source of recruitment. Putting alongside the statement that 600,000 more women will be needed in employment over the next few years and the preponderance of women amongst volunteers this could be very important indeed. We know for example from the General Household Survey of 1985 that 1.5 million of the 6 million providing voluntary care services are working at it for more than 20 hours a week. We know that the National Federation of Women's Institutes provides annually for some 4,000 of its 300,000 members to have some form of management training to bolster their work as volunteers in the organisation. Moreover the NFWI is forging links with the Royal Society of Arts' Advanced Diploma in the Organisation of Community Groups with the prospect that diploma holders maybe awarded National Vocational Qualifications by the National Council for Vocational Qualifications. Citizens Advice Bureaux have approximately 23,000 volunteers. All go through some form of training courses to help them do their volunteer job better. And this could go on endlessly. Youth and community work, local government, trade unions, once the question is asked where are people engaged in voluntary work from which they may have learned something, the maps of communities get peppered with entries.

Two-way access and APEL could be deployed through voluntary organisations for the benefit of individual volunteers, their parent voluntary organisations and some educational institutions. For a start any course offered by a voluntary agency which can command recognition from NCVQ for NVQs offers an obvious bonus to all three. Individuals receive a formal qualification. Voluntary organisation acquires the status of offering courses which become part and parcel of a national system of qualifications. And educational institutions benefit either through being involved as assessors or through offering 'top-up' facilities to complement the competences accredited through those courses, and/or using those facilities to recruit additional students. Once the result of assessments of prior experiential learning were added to individuals' score cards then, as in so many other spheres, individuals could achieve significant recognition for the learning that they had acquired informally.

For individual men and women there could be a good deal more to gain which has nothing to do with NVQs – and this is of particular importance to women. Among the scores of thousands who work for voluntary agencies there are many who have fallen into the category of folk who have a low opinion of themselves as learners. The education system has sent them that message. Their organisation, however, takes no notice of that message and values them for what they can do. But everyone loses because they live and do their volunteering under a cloud because they do not have formal qualifications. This is but a segment of the general problem encapsulated in the concept of equal opportunities. If voluntary agencies could be encouraged to think of their own education and training provision and what their volunteers learn from their volunteering as a contribution to the national jigsaw pattern of learning opportunities, offered alongside those provided by employers and formal education with the same range of articulated relationships between employment and education, then once again everybody would win and no-one would lose.

There is a further possible benefit. Voluntary agencies could contribute to changing the general culture climate which influences the ideas of lifelong learning with further study and progression in learning. They could be missionaries carrying the message to their own constituents that opportunities for progression through further study, and in occupations, are not restricted to those with formal educational qualifications nowadays, rather that opportunities now exist for people to capitalise on their learning from experience. This could stand as a part of the traditional purpose of voluntary organisations: to pioneer. If they were successful in carrying this message then perhaps statutory bodies such as the civil service and local government could follow suit.

GOVERNMENT AND TWO-WAY ACCESS

Respect of persons, recognition of accomplishment is the thread which stitches together individuals, educational institutions, and employment. It is recognition that lies at the heart of APEL. Hence the argument being put forward. It is impossible to imagine anybody, man, woman or child who does not respond to being appreciated by another. Often there is no outward sign of this. Sometimes personal hurt results in frozen emotions and an inability to respond; then appreciation can be like drops of warm water that in time melt all the ice. Sometimes people have been without appreciation for so long that they cannot quite believe it when it is offered. But generally when appreciation of another's actions is offered genuinely, some response will come. A sense of being recognised and valued is part and parcel of a sense of wellbeing. Behind that of course, is a complicated set of issues concerning self-recognition and even understanding of personal value; the ego strength that psychologists refer to. This is the two-way street again.

Human resource development (HRD) is this writ large. HRD is simply a version of what Robert Owen tried to achieve with his employees in the early nineteenth century, dressed up in clothes of contemporary methods of production and the nature of employment that goes with them. So often commentators on some serious industrial dispute which leads to strike action will explain patiently that although the point at issue appears to be money or what sort of wage increase, deeper down there is a sense of frustration, so that wages are a symptom rather than principal cause of the row. Numbers of hours at work each week, numbers of weeks of holiday, changes in production systems, may be involved. But often far more significantly the frustrations stem from the feeling of not being consulted, and about alterations to existing practices, of being a pawn moved around at will by others. In other words not being fully recognised as a person. So HRD and APEL are cousins.

And that takes the discussion to government. The pattern of a couple of pyramids, one upside down on top of the other, can fit here. Put all the men, women and children who make up our population in the lower of the two pyramids. The upper then contains all the varieties of institution which all those people belong to which constitute society. Families, schools and all of the post-secondary education institutions, business, industry and commerce, all forms of employment, and all the thousands of clubs, associations and voluntary activities that people belong to because they want to are all there in that upper pyramid. Government then stands as the broker between the two, with the principal task of facilitating people's progression into whichever of those institutions within society suits them best. Facilitating not directing – two-way access. Only by enabling people to recognise their own capacities, abilities and talents can they move into a kind of institution which suits them best whether in employment, education or any other activity. And since the health of any society depends on as many people as possible doing just that, government's role in encouraging it all to happen in every conceivable sphere becomes of commanding importance.

Another way of putting it is to speak of social policy. Members of parliament are elected, whatever the alleged deficiencies of the present first-past-the-post system, as representatives of the population. Government then acts as the executive arm of the people. Party politics determine what kind of a government. Its social policy is a consequence of the dominant political party. Very quickly that gets into a debate about what sort of democracy exists and how it may develop in the future. Hence the importance in the late twentieth century of education.

There is no doubt that education and, in government's view, its partner training have moved near to the top of its political agenda. It is not part of the purpose of this book to debate the pros and cons of what government has done. It is central to the argument though to say that whilst there have been some attempts to free universities, polytechnics and colleges from some of the dead weight of bureaucracy alongside government's clarion calls for higher participation rates for all levels of post-secondary institutions, nothing of any significance has been done to pay attention to the other side of participation – potential students. In the long run the movement towards enabling institutions to charge full-cost fees as a means of their recruiting greater numbers may or may not prove successful. Tinkering with the present student support and maintenance systems and the introduction of student loans for higher education does not begin to tackle the central question – what kind of financial support for all kinds of students ought to be established which is equitable and affordable and calculated to produce the highest numbers of lifetime learners which is the core to policy for post-secondary education? Equity demands that no category of student should be penalised for not being in another category. That means first, that part-time students should be entitled to the same level of financial support proportionately to full-time students. Second, it means that proportionate to the costs and fees involved the same entitlement should apply to a student studying say, a BTEC National Diploma aged 18, as a first-year undergraduate reading archaeology. And third, it means that low income groups should receive greater financial support than higher income groups.

There does not seem anything very controversial about those three criteria for a student support system, except that it needs to apply to the entire population and not merely to full-time higher education and certain categories of higher and further education as at present. And the implication of that is either that the total bill to be met by the Treasury goes up, or that an entitlement for the adult population means that each individual gets less than those who at present receive grants. Or a mixture of the two.

So what can be afforded nationally has to be answered before policies for learning can be worked out. It is now generally accepted that the tax-payer alone cannot finance all the post-secondary education which is necessary. Complicated calculations about student loans, employer sponsorship, employer purchase, which is different, private savings then come into the reckoning. But what has been missing so far is any positive incentive for individuals to use their own money. Tax rebates or deductions is an obvious answer. But the affordability issue should not be concerned only with what the Treasury considers the annual budget enacted through parliament can stand. Affordability concerns the cost of saying what cannot be afforded. Statisticians are not much help for that calculation. The political will of government is what matters for that calculation. But if all the various attempts to raise the general standard of education in the country have either not resulted in convincing results so far, or in the case of the national curriculum promise results many years away, then more immediate steps need to be taken. In other words, in the matter of financial support and incentive for adults to study more and for longer during their lives, government has the responsibility of putting some substance into its rhetoric, matching it with action. Only then can there be any reasonable expectation that participation rates will rise to any satisfactory level in, and this is the vital point, all forms of post-secondary education and not just the higher education levels. The standing danger in these kinds of discussions is to assume that it is only higher education that matters. For too long that has been the tendency and this is why some equitable form of an adult learning entitlement is so necessary together with incentives attached to find and spend the money on learning which the state says it cannot afford.

On this theme of two-way access that is one route which government alone can clear. A national APEL service as referred to in the last section is a route which government could open up to increase the traffic flow in both directions. All that is needed is priming funding to get such a service established and running. Thereafter it would be funded under the same umbrella arrangements as all other provision. The same mixture of state funds through an adult learning entitlement, loans, sponsorship and private money and savings could keep the service running.

If a 'student' chose to pay for the service privately all well and good. If the 'student' preferred to have the charges for the service deducted from the adult learning entitlement, it would be an open choice. Employers might pay the fees themselves. So might grandparents for their burgeoning grandchildren. And since tax deductions and rebates would apply as well, there is no knowing what resources might be forthcoming.

There is, however, another way of thinking about the resources which are yet largely untapped. But this requires going behind speculations about the curricula for learning, modes of delivery and the problems these pose for educational institutions, employers and government and reflecting on the characteristics of what can now be called a learning society. Running through this book there is the assertion that schools, colleges, polytechnics and universities are now only one source of learning for hundreds of thousands of people of all ages. Formal institutions have an important role, a unique role, but second in importance and sometimes of primary importance is what is learned at work. So the resource question is essentially to do with finding ways of capitalising on both to avoid duplication and so avoid wasting money. Many examples have been given of how and when this is the case and how effective collaboration can provide the economical use of the related systems. Now if those examples are convincing, there would appear to be no particular reason why in principle they cannot be used as pointers to a way forward.

What all these examples are showing – the validation of companies', in-house provision, learning agreements for employees, APEL for employees, YTS supervisors and trainees, for credit towards a qualification or latterly a National Vocational Qualification – are in one form or another variations of institutional ways of working. They are in effect small scale instances of de-institutionalising institutional practices so as to re-institutionalise them in ways which are more appropriate to the contemporary world. They are all piecemeal attempts to demonstrate that those approaches can work effectively, produce evidence of the whys, wherefores and means that have appeared to work, and then hope that through equally piecemeal efforts at dissemination, the ideas will be more widely adopted. Implicitly each initiative has asked the questions; what is it that an individual can do best, what is it that an employer does best, what is it that an educational institution can do best, and has formulated action on the basis of the three sets of answers.

If the examples of actions are convincing, then some means should be found of converting the piecemeal into the general. That requires a nationally promoted initiative. And that means government. It is splendid to announce a target of increasing dramatically numbers in higher education which has good public appeal and raises the adrenalin level in the staff of the institutions who would have to achieve those greater numbers. It is an unnecessary blight on good intentions to dither about incentives for institutions who have to execute that policy instead of accompanying the policy announcement by a clear commitment to financial incentives. Government's view of the market economy ought to have a ready sense of the value of financial rewards for effective performance. It seems unprepared to apply its principles to education.

So the simple point is that if financial rewards could be offered to institutions who did ask those three questions – what is it that individuals can do best, what can employers and educational institutions do best – and deliver their answers in terms of more students becoming more skilled in a shorter time and costing less, then there could be a set of tactics related to the overall strategy which would attract widespread and enthusiastic support. Rapidly that could set up a ripple effect of consequences which would begin to affect further and higher education as a whole. That is for policy.

The effectiveness of any such policy would be based on the assumption that employers as well as education would react favourably to what would be essentially an explicit sharing of an educational role. Enough has been said about education. There is another thing to say about employers. Currently, all government rhetoric about further training and education, whatever the policy, is based on the proposition that individuals and employers ought to pay more and that taxation revenue funds should pay less. By playing on the money card so single-mindedly it may be that a vital trick is being missed.

In Philadelphia, Pennsylvania, USA things look different. There the Philadelphia Center of the Great Lakes Colleges Association runs a programme for undergraduates during which students spend four days a week for a semester of fifteen weeks in full-time work in a wide variety of places of employment. The students are at that work to learn. A learning agreement is negotiated between a field supervisor at the place of work, an academic tutor from the Philadelphia Center and the student. The learning agreement sets out what is to be learned, how it is to be learned and how the learning acquired is to be assessed. The fieldwork supervisor, the employer, undertakes day-to-day supervision of the student, working alongside the student to ensure that the learning agreement is adhered to, and if necessary, renegotiates it. On average, employers working in that way reckon to spend about ten hours a week directly with the student.

The critical question is why should busy people, highly paid, with heavy responsibilities to their companies devote that kind of time? What is it that makes people such as the Senior Vice-President for Investment of Prudential Bache Securities, the Creative Services Director of the *Philadelphia Magazine*, the Chief Economist for Conrail, the Assistant Vice-President of the Provident National Bank, the head of the education department of the Philadelphia Museum of Art, eager to undertake this assignment? No money changes hands. The students are not paid by the employer. They are simply on full-time tuition arrangements as if they were in their own colleges. Employers are paid nothing by the Philadelphia Center. Yet employers love it.

Why do you do it? That was the question put to all those very same employers. Separately they produced strikingly similar answers. Of course an extra pair of hands, a bright lively well-motivated young man or woman was a welcome addition to the staff. It meant that some tasks could be accomplished which otherwise got put to one side under the pressure of business. However, there were three other significant comments. First the fact that the students were paid nothing by the employer established a relationship which was essentially as between mentor/teacher and student learner. Since there was no money cost to the employer, in a way this was paying for the students' services with the currency of the employer's time. But it went beyond that. Each employer using different words said that they took positive pleasure in inducting the next generation into the world of employment. There was no question of the Senior Vice-President for Investment implying he was training stockbrokers. That was not his reason at all. He was keen to use the opportunity of helping young people understand more of the world of work so they could make better decisions about their intended chosen career. And his was a representative view. The other intriguing answer to the question – why do it? – was the employers' view that the arrangement was a contribution to their own staff development. Having a student as an unpaid assistant with prescribed tasks to undertake – and they were significant assignments; no xeroxing, stapling and paper shuffling but research projects dealing with customers, preparing copy for the printer – prompted them to consider again the way they handled their regular team of employees, dividing up the jobs, trying to bring them on to the next stage.

The question arises, if in Philadelphia why not in Plymouth, Pontypool or Preston; if the USA why not Great Britain? Whatever the cultural differences between the two countries there are enough characteristics in common to suggest that given similar opportunities, perhaps numbers of business people and professionals would react similarly. And maybe this is the missing trick. If business and industry could feel that they were significant actors in the education and training scene instead of feeling continually billed to pay for the production and glossy programme note, then there might a more purposeful move down the road towards answering those three questions and getting them answered in terms of what would make better use of the sum total of resources already committed to education and training. What is it that individuals can do about their learning better than either employers or educational institutions? What is it that employers can do to promote learning which they can do better than education? And what then can education do to develop individuals as learners better either than employers or individuals themselves?

None of this can be accomplished without some commitment to some version of human resource development, the best reason overall. None can afford to ignore the significance of experiential learning and its potential importance when assessed. Many are doing much about these things – more need to do more. Government needs to devise schemes for encouraging, stimulating, and rewarding all those who strive to do more.

There is one other thing that government can do, which no-one else can do: provide a national advertising campaign. One of the major problems of increasing participation rates is connecting with the groups of people from whom the larger numbers have to come. There are three such groups and it is a reasonable assumption that very few in those groups know of the arrangements that now make it easier and indeed more attractive for them to join in. First there are the scores of thousands of men and women who began higher education courses and withdrew either during or at the end of the first year. Most of them are unlikely to know of the credit accumulation and transfer schemes which mean that they can now expect to get some academic credit for that study. When they left higher education they believed it was worth nothing and in straightforward higher education terms, they were right. Now that is not the case, but it is unlikely that they know it. The second group covers the older men and women who similarly will have little idea of the flexible study arrangements available to them in higher education, nor will they understand what the NCVQ can do for them in having their competences recognised and recorded through further education. The last group are the able young people in the lower socio-economic groups who are convinced that education is not for them.

Now the one thing we can be sure of about each of those groups is that they look at the television screen and absorb great quantities of information which influence what they do with their time and money. So if the task of raising participation rates is taken seriously, a series of television adverts which lay out the opportunities which now exist is one obvious way of trying to connect with them. This in no way underestimates the efforts made by individual institutions. It is simply pointing out that their very best efforts on restricted budgets do not make it possible for them to mount television adverts of the quality required and even if they did have those resources in a country of this size with its population of fifty-five million the waste would be phenomenal through duplication.

The analogy is with nurses, employment training and the Youth Training Scheme. So if government means what it says about skills shortages and the need for a more educated workforce, then government agencies should do what was done for employment training and the Youth Training Scheme and by the Department of Health: spend money on trying to persuade people to enrol by using TV advertising time. There is little point in institutions putting the huge efforts required into changing the way they do things to fit the changed circumstances of those they exist to serve and relying on words in pamphlets, brochures, adverts and stories in local newspapers, when everyone knows that the television screen is the most effective way of conveying information. Of course, it is not that simple. No advertising programme can be screened unless institutions are ready to respond. But where there is a crisis, needs must find a solution.

Increasing awareness of opportunities is the first step to getting those opportunities used. And these days television is the most powerful way of doing it as politicians and governments know very well. Perhaps this could be high on the agenda for a government education and training overlord.

13 Restructuring, reorganising, redeploying

The case being argued – that APEL within two-way access can be a powerful stimulus for trying to achieve the levels of education and training which all agree the country needs – comes at the end of a decade of developments in this very field. Following on from the many initiatives referred to throughout the book, APEL does now stand as a valid, reliable and acceptable way of enabling individual men and women to make best use of their uncertificated knowledge and skills for their personal growth, their education and their occupational development. Many higher and further education institutions and open college federations and networks have incorporated APEL in their regular arrangements. Combined with the CNAA CATS provision and the increasing number of universities, polytechnics and colleges which are developing their own CATS schemes, and NCVQ, APEL is contributing to significant institutional developments designed to improve access services for potential students. Some employers are making use of APEL procedures alongside learning agreements and the validation of in-house courses to enhance the skill acquisition and capacity of their employees in the context of problems of recruitment and retention. Government agencies have taken a number of important initiatives each of which is intended to lift the level of general education in the population and cope with the skill gap which has such alarming implications. So there is a climatic change in the weather conditions for education, training and learning. But there are a number of further steps to take before there can be any solid evidence that any of these developments are succeeding in their overall intention – to produce a better-educated, more skilled and efficient, self-reliant population. There is no shortage of prestigious statements about what needs to be done. Every one of these suggestions implies some restructuring, reorganising, redeploying. And since to be effective each depends on persuading, encouraging and enticing more individuals to be more active learners, the first additional step must concern them.

Learner-centred, student-centred learning is beginning to acquire a new partner – learner-centred finance. Either implicitly – in discussion about top-up loans and full-cost fees in higher education or corporate status and local financial management for colleges or employers' contributions to training – or explicitly, as in the CBI's Task Force Report, recommending training allowances for individuals; and in ministers' reactions to them, or in the views being expounded by some vice-chancellors and directors – the debate about individual participation is moving towards the idea of money following learners, of students taking money with them when they enrol for any learning programme provided by any institution. That approach can only result in the higher participation rates being sought at all levels if it is generalised into some form of adult learning entitlement. Whether such an entitlement should be means-tested, accompanied by tax deductions or dependent on matching funds from other sources involves technical details which are not explored here. The simple point is that unless the financial barriers at present facing all except full-time higher education students are removed, there is little hope of increasing the participation rates to anything like the numbers required. There is no point in preaching sermons about the need for more people to become better educated and more skilled to the increasing number of adults who are among the 85 per cent who did not go into higher education, if they are going to be penalised financially when they respond. So if government is serious in its rhetoric then it must pay attention to incentives to individuals as its top priority. It means restructuring, reorganising and redeploying all forms of student financial aid. Tinkering at the margins raises heated debates which actually divert attention from the central issue.

For many institutions this is likely to mean that the key factor will be its public stance and declared policies. If individual men and women as potential learners have the fee money to take with them, they will be able to choose a learning programme which they consider suits them best, or if it is their employer who is part-financing them then what suits the company best. An institution's public stance then becomes the external sign of its internal arrangements. For most further education colleges and many higher education institutions, that public stance needs to be one which invites admission and offers help in selecting from what it has to offer whatever is most suitable to meet an individual's needs. Such a posture implies that admission policies and procedures, academic organisation and management and student support services are all harnessed to the purposes set out in the declared institutional policy. In an ideal world, everyone from receptionists at telephone switchboards or in enquiry offices, cleaners and janitors to the director would show a smiling face and open arms and have been trained to convey a welcoming responsiveness. In the workaday world, institutions need the nearest they can get to a sunny friendliness. Higher participation rates depend on engaging sections of the population which at present are not engaged in systematic learning. They will only become engaged if an institution sets out to engage them. That means tackling head on the reasons that they are not engaged at present; recognising their characteristics and working with them. Going with the grain and not against it. And for that the starting point is to recognise and value the knowledge and skill they bring with them. The restructuring, reorganising and redeploying implied is the obvious next step for many institutions.

Employers too are faced with something of the same need for the three-part programme of restructuring, reorganising and redeploying, if they are to take the next step forward towards the kind of learning workforce which many say they must have to survive in the brave new world of international competition, not to speak of 1992 and the European Community. It may not be the same kind of radical treatment required for many educational institutions, but in terms of emphasis it is none the less worth noting. For employers need to convince their employees that they are all in the learning business. Many if not all have convinced themselves. The problem is to establish a commitment to learning as a central concern for the business whether public or private employer, large or small, production or service. As with educational institutions if that commitment is to get translated into day-to-day action, it means taking as the starting point the characteristics of the employees as potential learners. And that means recognising that they are likely to be effective learners in spheres not necessarily confined to the bounds of what they are employed to do. It is all of a piece with the general thesis that most people are reckoned to be worse at learning than they actually are. So some means of enabling employers to recognise and then to value the abilities and capacities of their employees is the cornerstone of what effective employment policies should be. And increasingly that means finding ways of conveying to employees and potential employees that learning is what counts in employment. In a sense it is the same point as the public stance offered by education. How a company or employer is perceived from the outside is a reflection of what goes on inside. Recruitment policies, equal opportunity policies, staff development, career and promotion policies, employee support services all come into the reckoning. In many ways restructuring for employers is the flip side of restructuring education. If education needs to become more businesslike, employers need to become more like employee-centred educators.

For government too there is a two-sided issue concerning money, and a large institutional issue which the 1988 Education Reform Act did not address, both of which call for restructuring, reorganising and redeploying. One side of the money issue goes back to the point about financial barriers to individual students. It is a prime responsibility of government to remove, or at the very least to lower, financial barriers to those potential learners government says it needs to become active learners, if the country is to have anything like a reasonable future. The other side refers to rules invented for different purposes by different government departments which have the effect of producing an arbitrary and contradictory set of consequences. There is something plainly ridiculous in urging people to become more employable through learning more and acquiring additional skills and then throwing up the twenty-one-hour rule (working more than twenty-one hours forfeits eligibility for benefit) for the unemployed which effectively prevents many of them doing just that because they have to present themselves in person to employment offices to prove their availability for employment. It is a variation of the theme of the inequity of giving full maintenance grants for higher education students (albeit means-tested against parental income) but preventing part-time students of the very same age receiving any financial support from tax-payers' money. There must be better ways of guarding against scroungers, for that can be the only rational defence of the twenty-one-hour rule. In any case it is ineffective seen from the other way round. There are plenty of full-time students who work for money in various jobs for twenty-one hours a week, yet no such exclusion rule can apply to them. Anomalies of this kind are not unique to Britain. A study in the USA identified forty-eight regulations which positively inhibited adults from pursuing further learning. That does not make our own less ridiculous. The latest example at the time of writing concerns Ford's EDAP programme. The Inland Revenue has taken a baleful interest. It has ruled that all classes and instruction conducted on Ford's premises are exempt from income tax, as are all courses taken by Ford employees in educational institutions, provided those courses lead to some recognised certification. Everything else undertaken by EDAP participants is liable to personal taxation. One effect of this is that employees working at Ford plants which are too small to offer on-site classes, or where there are no on site facilities available will be taxed, whereas employees working at large plants taking exactly the same classes will be exempt if the classes are on site. This is simply one government department, acting no doubt properly, obstructing the pursuit of public policy of another government department – to encourage more adults to learn more.

That confusion touches the other side of this money issue. Waste of money by government through lack of co-ordination. Behind government rhetoric about need for higher participation rates and increased numbers of adult learners, there is the most dreadful waste of taxpayers' money because there is no rational co-ordination of effort to ensure a common thrust even if there was (and there does not appear to be) a common policy beyond the most plausible generalisations. There is the Department of Education and Science, the Department of Employment and the Department of Trade and Industry, all spending money on trying to increase the amount of learning which goes on in the population, and each making up its own rules in the process. The Department of Health and the Department of Social Security are also spending considerable sums of money to enhance adult learning as a means of improving the services available to the public. There can be considerable waste through overlap or sheer ignorance of what another department is actually doing, but the waste runs further than that. Those who seek funds from those various departments for developments in furthering adult learning within the briefs of those respective departments, can waste an inordinate amount under different headings all to enhance the same cause. When universities, polytechnics and colleges set up departments with the task of writing proposals and soliciting public funds from these different government departments, then it says something important about the complexity of arrangements for which government alone is responsible.

What is now sorely needed – to produce within government the kind of efficiency it sees fit to urge on education – is some kind of a learning overlord with the brief to rationalise all the various spending currently undertaken by different government departments and with the power to introduce measures designed to produce a coherent and rational account of all the funds being allocated. This is a high policy matter, likely to be obstructed by ministers and their senior civil servants in existing departments with all the boundary controversies which afflict uneasy neighbours. It is not a departmental matter. It is a government matter, it requires a Cabinet committee. Furthermore, it should be a parliamentary matter. There is no reason why government should be exempt from the restructuring, reorganising and redeploying it requires of other institutions.

The large institutional issue faces the Department of Education and Science. It concerns the broad institutional division between further and higher education in non-university education, between degree-level studies and studies leading to qualifications at a level which do not overlap with undergraduate work. This is not a straightforward matter, but it affects critically the success of policies intended to increase participation rates and encourage a sense of progression.

In some ways it is like the financial barriers which stand in the way of individuals learning on a part-time or occasional basis: sets of rules invented at different times and for different purposes. Regulations under which further education colleges work are different from those applying to higher education, something which has been intensified by the 1988 Education Reform Act. Historically these different grant regulations were paralleled by patterns of award-bearing courses which separated further education with its Business and Technician Education Council, The Royal Society of Arts and the City and Guilds of London Institute, from higher education with its undergraduate and postgraduate studies. However appropriate or inappropriate that may have been in the past it makes little sense in the present context. In no sense does it mean that all institutions, further education colleges, colleges of higher education and polytechnics should do the same thing. It does mean that what is provided in further education colleges should be a natural stepping stone to what is provided in higher education and that wherever there is overlap between the two in terms of academic attainment, as of right an individual should be able to carry academic credit from further to higher education. This is talking about the unhelpful way in which institutional separation has resulted in inappropriate academic separation.

Participation rates will increase to the extent that pathways to learning are cleared of obstacles and made part of the natural order of things. Progression is an essential concept towards that end because it becomes a powerful motivation for individuals. Adults are no different from children in that they cherish the idea of progressing. Just as children find great satisfaction in being able to progress from a 'baby' reading book to a 'grown-up' one because it means they are becoming more proficient, so adults relish that sense of progression whether it be in gardening, DIY, rock climbing, learning a language or using a wordprocessor. Transposed into the realm of formal adult learning this means that to be able to move steadily from a basic literary class, through all the intermediary stages to undergraduate and postgraduate studies is the most powerful encouragement to individuals next to the removal of financial barriers. In other words higher participation rates depend heavily on a man or woman being able to join in or rejoin the learning business at whatever proves to be the appropriate stage and level and keep going for as long as the individual wants, or has ability to take them.

It is too simple to suggest that widening access to existing courses will produce the desired results. That is the equivalent of tinkering at the margins with student financial support arrangements. All the story of APEL development supports this thesis: that recognition for learning acquired with a facility to move up the hierarchy of formal learning can transform individuals who thought they were hopeless as learners into keen purposeful students.

In some ways this is an area in which America organises these matters better. Community colleges, often called two-year institutions, award associate degrees. In some states it is a mandatory requirement for four-year schools, universities offering baccalaureate degrees after four years' study or its equivalent, to award two years' academic credit towards a BA degree to an individual having an associate degree. Naturally there are the necessary caveats about academic matching. A business studies associate degree is not going to count half a degree for a pre-medical student. The principle is clear: study in one institution, academic credit in another. And until similar arrangements exist for adult students in British institutions, the higher participation sought will not be achieved. Government's role in effecting this development is clear although of course it is complex.

Grant regulations for the further education system need reformulating to ensure that academic progression is standard practice; that would go a long way to clearing the academic obstacles. However, there is another requirement for removing academic obstacles. The country needs an overarching national validating body to service further education in the way that CNAA has served degree and postgraduate work in higher education. Through the establishment of the National Council of Vocational Qualifications, a great deal has been done to establish a coherent relationship between the respective qualifications offered by BTEC, City and Guilds, the RSA and countless other awarding bodies. Through NCVQ the Government can and does encourage and suggest and exert all kinds of pressure. Indeed the reserve legislative powers are in the statute book to require an articulation between these various awarding bodies should that prove necessary. But, and this is one of the current difficulties, these arrangements apply to vocational qualifications only. If the progression routes are going to be cleared with inviting signposts pointing the way, then equal requirements must apply to non-vocational study. There is no national overarching body with the authority to validate and make awards at sub-degree level in non-vocational study. To some extent this is covered by the GCSE and advanced levels in the General Certificate of Education, but in current circumstances that is too restricting and in any case most other examinations are unsuitable for many adult learners. None of them have the power or indeed the capacity to award any form of academic credit on the basis of APEL, let alone formal study which falls outside prescribed syllabuses unless a new syllabus is written and approved. In some ways this issue is being tackled by the open college federations which have sprung up in recent years. But whilst they can establish local arrangements the only national route for them is through NCVQ and the associated awarding bodies.

With discussions under way about the relationship between CNAA and BTEC and between NVQ and the national curriculum and General

Certificate of Education examinations at GCSE and Advanced levels, there is neither the time nor place for detailed discussion. The essential point is that within all the current initiatives for restructuring, reorganising and redeploying, this particular issue is a Johnny-come-lately. But it is critical. Without an overarching validating body for further education attempts to achieve higher participation rates in all forms of post-secondary education are inhibited when everything possible should be done to facilitate them. Goverment alone can effect the necessary changes.

14 Endpiece

This speculation about restructuring, reorganising and redeploying in the interests of trying to engage more men and women to learn more for longer during their lives is another way of saying that the country needs to move beyond the industrial pattern of education and training devised for the purposes and needs of the nineteenth century and create patterns which are designed to fit the requirements of the twenty-first century. Factories needed people to be trained, however rudimentarily. Children were prepared for factory work and associated clerical skills in schools which looked like factories and for a long time were as regimented. Work and education were organised and managed on strict hierarchical patterns of control. Training fitted into that world as a way of referring to skills required for clearly-defined jobs. But all that speaks of the past. And it is a past when education took its cue from industry.

What seems to be happening now is that education is learning from employment all over again. Flexitime working is increasingly reflected in flexitime study. Team building and devolution of responsibility in production is increasingly matched in education by group responsibility for learning programmes or resources or recruitment and the increased financial responsibility being given both to institutions and through them, on a unit-costs basis, to a number of teachers and academic staff. Human resources development programmes are matched by staff development programmes. If the health of employment depends on these developments so does the health of education itself.

But the matching needs to go further than that. Since it is the case that increasingly employers depend on employees' initiative and ingenuity to get the best value from investment in new equipment and changed procedures, then the way people are encouraged, even taught to learn needs to be a deliberate attempt to develop those qualities of initiative and inventiveness. So all the devices for relating learning opportunities to the needs of individuals, their learning styles, their domestic and work circumstances and personal inclinations become essential, not merely interesting additions to the traditional way of doing things. Learning centres, access to expert tutorial help, mixed modes of learning, interactive computer programs, distance learning, tape/slide programmes, learning agreements, on-the-job learning, all combined with facilities for assessment, need to be provided as well as formal classroom work. They are no more and no less than education facilities to mirror requirements at work and societal developments.

Pre-eminently those requirements are for men and women to accept responsibility for what they do at work. So education needs to provide for people taking responsibility for their own learning. Timetabled classes alone cannot do that. There must be choices in ways of learning which individuals are free to choose. And one of the most important choices for individuals to make about their learning is pace. Student-centred learning, which is the nub of the learning business, is meaningless unless students can control the pace and rhythm of their own learning through choosing appropriate ways of learning. Only then will they develop the qualities employers need to sustain the national economy and society's prosperity.

In its way some industry, business and commerce is grappling with these issues within employment. Education must perforce follow suit – and so must government. Important developments are under way. They need to be pressed more energetically and systematically. That cannot be done without restructuring, reorganising and redeploying. This is the significance of talking about cultural changes, diifferent attitudes to learning throughout society: to mobilise more people to learn, more especially the 50 per cent who currently treat post-secondary education as some form of leprosy.

It all goes back to access. But the key question there is access to what? This gets relatively slight attention so far in the general debate. There is a nasty trap laid in this thicket of discussion: 'we' and 'they'. There is a standing danger of politicians, civil servants and heads of institutions assuming that they are evolving policies to effect these cultural changes which apply to others and not themselves. Although they understand the need for changes they do not necessarily remember that they are not exempt from the need to change. In other words they can tend to forget that they are part of the problem. The question 'Access to what?' can only be answered effectively if the institutions providing education, and government which sets the funding arrangements, really do accept that they are part of the problem. The previous section offered some thoughts about how they might become part of the solution. The overriding approach to the solution must be a thoroughgoing revision of curricula – content, methodology and delivery – taking account of those groups of potential learners who need to be drawn in. And that needs to be done with due regard to the need of upholding standards. Quantity without quality is worse than useless. There must be no hostages to the 'more means worse' brigade. Changing systems must mean making them better, if the effort is to be worthwhile.

And that is the central issue about APEL – quality and quantity combined. Wherever learning from experience takes place, APEL can encourage it, extend it through the motivation which comes from recognition, identify and shape it ready for assessment and accreditation, all because it is simply a way of paying due regard to the facility of human beings as learners. It is that characteristic above all which dignifies men, women and children. APEL merely salutes them. It is a means whereby society, through its formal education and employment, can salute them too. But because APEL as argued here is only worth talking about in terms of learning assessed within valid and reliable methods, it is a means of increasing the quantity of accessible learning while looking to its quality. APEL, the two-way street to opportunity, can attend to both.

Postscript

As E M Forster said of Democracy – two cheers. Perhaps one and a half on reflection. One cheer is deserved for government trying to correct the omission from the 1988 Education Reform Act of further education and post secondary provision, apart from higher education. Corporate status for further education colleges and sixth form centres is bound to release energy, initiative and perhaps even create a greater pride in those institutions through their increased responsibility. Quite what it means for local government is another, more complicated matter. The half cheer is for trying to tackle the vocational/academic divide which bedevils efforts to increase the participation rates of all sections of the population in post secondary education of any kind. (It is only half a cheer because the suggested solutions seem as likely as not to add to the difficulties rather than solve them.) Introducing some general as opposed to occupationally specific NVQs, a couple of diplomas at two different levels on which vocational and academic results can be recorded, and trumpeting that vocational qualifications are to be seen as prestigious as academic qualifications will fool no one, let alone convince them of what ought to be the case – 'And vocational qualifications and colleges are still undervalued. We want to see full equality of status between them and their academic counterparts.' (paragraph 1.2) Only a unified system of qualifications will begin to meet that requirement; and as long as there is dogmatic ideological commitment to 'A' Levels in their present form (despite almost universal opposition to them from people who actually have to work with them and their results), there will be no significant movement towards removing the lower caste stigma attached to most vocational qualifications. They are for those not bright enough to proceed down the academic route – at present, whether it be fact or fiction, that is how they are perceived. And most people believe it. Embossed diplomas will not change it. So half a cheer for government. But the missing cheer is for the absence of signs that government has accepted that learning is a human business and not something related solely to the financial considerations of the market place. The statement that adult education will only attract discretionary funding unless it leads to formal qualifications is simply wrong-headed in terms of what the White Papers are attempting to promote. There is not, and can never be, a neat division into learning which leads to qualifications and that which does not, what is vocational and what is not. It is also mean-spirited, displaying a narrow-minded instrumental view of people. In paragraph 1.7 we read: 'We realise these proposals are ambitious, they require a major cultural change in our attitudes to further education and training.' Indeed we do, but any change in attitudes to further education and training will rest on a wider acceptance by more people that continuing to learn after leaving school is important. That is the really significant cultural change which needs to be effected; and to deny committed funding to adult education save when it leads directly to qualifications is an indication of second order thinking when first order ought to be the hallmark of government proposals to lift the general educational level of the entire population.

And there is proof of this notion which government could have noted given its particular interest in what happens in the corporate world rather than in the world of formal education. Both Ford UK's Employee Development and Assistance Programme and Lucas's Continuing Education and Training programme demonstrate that when formal training in skills required for employment is paralleled with opportunities for employees to learn things which they themselves choose, achievements rise in both categories of learning. In other words, concentrating on the acquisition of formal qualifications is not necessarily the only way of promoting their acquisition. Many people need nurturing in their sometimes very tentative steps into the world of formal learning after leaving school. Small things can lead to greater things. On the evidence of what Ford UK and Lucas have done for their employees far more people than might be expected will follow in the path of small things leading to larger things, when they are given a non-threatening opportunity. There is no news for adult educators, but it points to what appears to be a limited understanding by the authors of the White Paper about what is involved in talking about cultural change. The argument of this book is that APEL can help effect just such a change. So much for adult education.

But whatever their deficiencies in their instrumental way the White Papers send a clear message to further education that APEL is something they had better think hard about. Not that experiential learning is mentioned in the White Papers, but it connects directly with several thrusts of policies being proposed.

The first is payment by results, dignified with reference to funding according to recruitment numbers and the number of vocational qualifications achieved. Everything which has been said earlier applies here about APEL serving as a recruiter for potential students who have not thought of themselves as people who can join in the formal learning business. There is no need to rehearse it, save to say that the message APEL can send to possible learners is likely to be more attractive for many of those who do not come near further education colleges or higher education at present, because of their assumption that without the formal qualifications they did not get at school they are outside the system.

That is rather general. It gets quite specific when the increasingly important role for TECs are considered as a central part of these White Papers. Since TECs are apparently going to be funded largely on the basis of the number of national vocational qualifications they record, and since further education colleges are bound to seek as substantial contractual relations with TECs as they can manage to secure additional funding, and since training credits at £1,000 a time are going to be the entitlement of sixteen-year-old school-leavers, then the significance of APEL stands starkly obvious. Unless colleges are equipped to provide welcoming, unthreatening, walk-in assessment facilities for those who may be seeking national vocational qualifications, with the top-up opportunities implied for completion of those qualifications, then they are bound to miss out on one source of funding which seems likely to be of increasing significance to them.

This appears to apply particularly to young people, but that is only half the issue – back to the one and a half cheers for the White Papers. Adults are going to be just as important in realising the government's hopes, if not more so. In part this goes back to the recruitment aspect of APEL but there are other possibilities related to funding. Any formal provision for adults to go through APEL procedures is just as likely as not to interest them in going forward to attempt some formal qualifications. This in no way denies what has been said repeatedly, that one of the prime benefits for adults is self-assessment. It is to insist as a matter of educational policy it is just as reasonable to produce formal classes for APEL on the grounds that it is a route for them towards formal qualifications as any other reason. On those grounds then formal provision for APEL classes should become a means of extracting direct funding from the soon-to-be-established Colleges Funding Council. And since APEL will bring into the formal arena all kinds of learning experiences which relate to the liberal education tradition of further education colleges, as well as potential to the vocationally orientated courses, then APEL can become a bridge between the two and of particular significance for funding purposes. That tension can be sustained.

So one way of looking at APEL in relation to White Papers, is that it can minister to the inevitable tensions which those papers cause between the liberal adult education which was funded with security in the past, and the apparent dismissiveness of the White Papers of anything which does not come within the description of 'vocational'. By extension, APEL could be represented as a civilizing influence which can be brought to bear on government policy, enunciated as it through the White Papers, but in ways which perhaps had not occurred to it. What is absolutely clear is that APEL can be a very powerful instrument to enable colleges of further education to exploit the opportunities offered to them by this latest set of public policies. That may be of particular importance for the smaller colleges. Critical mass and scale of institutions is plainly something implied by the general thrust of the White Papers; and here the small but beautiful argument can be strengthened for smaller institutions which can find ways of using APEL to enhance their performance according to the criteria which apparently are going to be used to judge their effectiveness as and hence their funding levels.

For higher education the White Paper has only one short statement which relates directly to APEL. Again APEL is not mentioned but the implication is there for those who want to use it. In Higher Education: A New Framework, paragraph 73 proposes to abolish CNAA. In paragraph 74 we read, 'It will also be necessary for the Council to consider with the institutions and the Funding Councils the best future location for the services it currently provides in respect of, for example, credit accumulation and transfer schemes, the promotion of dissemination of good practice, the recognition of access courses and the promotion of debate on matters of current interest.'

The point has been reiterated throughout this book that CATS without APEL is deficient. It has also been asserted that government alone is in a position to facilitate developments leading to a national APEL service as a means of informing the population at large of the possibilities which are open to them, as well as enabling more people to use those facilities as an essential complement to what is already being provided by an increasing number of institutions. What the White Paper leaves out of the list of services which need to be continued is any reference to the after-care needed to support the considerable number of postgraduate students currently registered directly with the CNAA.

All this suggests that the consultations between CNAA, the institutions and the Funding Councils might consider rather more than the location of the services which need to be continued. They could find themselves planning for a National Regent's College. Its purpose would be to provide the nation-wide service for the present CNAA CATS Registry, which includes not only direct service to individuals at both bachelors and masters' levels, but the credit-rating and validation service of companies' in-house provision. As we have seen this can lead eventually to a company such as British Telecom becoming an accredited institution with the delegated authority to teach and award higher education awards. All that includes necessarily APEL.

A National's Regent's College could inherit from CNAA the relevant parts of its existing Charter. It could be constituted under the academic authority of what must surely become a combination of the present University of the present University Committee of Vice-Chancellors and Principals and the Committee of Polytechnic Directors. It would be responsible to and a creature of that body, which would clearly be the pre-eminent higher education authority in the land, thus ensuring the quality of its provision. In liaison with the Open Polytechnic it could provide a national distance-learning service. It could undertake the registration of all the validated credit-ratings of companies' in-house courses, whether completed centrally or through its own procedures or those offered by individual polytechnics or universities. And perhaps most important of all, it could provide the facilities for individuals to negotiate their own personal learning programmes in those cases where a local higher education institution did not suit that individual's purposes, for whatever reason.

In effect, this would solve one of the difficulties which has attended the development of CNAA CAT's scheme from the outset – how to make a reality of the rhetoric about it being a transbinary scheme. Inevitably, universities were not enthusiastic about joining energetically in a scheme which originated in the public sector and was promoted by CNAA. There would be a chance that for some universities some of those susceptibilities would diminish if they were co-owners of a National Regent's College. A National Regent's College could fill in another part of the jigsaw pattern of higher education designed to encourage progression to mass participation, and APEL would have a critical part to play in moving things along.

So, in the light of this latest onset of attempts to enhance the employability and effectiveness of the population when they go to work, it could be that instead of talking about APEL in terms of an idea whose time has come for the late 1980s, for the 1990s it is more a case of APEL as an activity whose time is fast becoming fully operational.

Appendix: study tour participants

June 1981

Colin Griffin, Hillcroft College
Ned Binks, Pro-Rector, Head of College, St Katharine's College, Liverpool Institute of Higher Education

July 1981

Malcolm Brewer, Secretary, Association for Sandwich Education and Training, Sheffield City Polytechnic

October 1982

Colin Titmus, Dean, Adult and Continuing Education, Goldsmiths' College, University of London

Summer 1983

Pamela Linn, Thames Polytechnic
Tony Hendry, Thames Polytechnic
Ginnie Eley, North East London Polytechnic
Richard Gorringe, Further and Higher Curriculum Development Project, Inner London Education Authority

November 1983

Phoebe Lambert, Principal, Hillcroft College
Norbert Singer, Director, Thames Polytechnic
Peter Toyne, Deputy Director, North East London Polytechnic
Anthony Turner, Deputy Course Leader for the Diploma in Higher Education, Middlesex Polytechnic

February 1984

David Fenton, Head of Department, Business Studies, Thames Polytechnic
Neil Dorward, Head of Business School, Polytechnic of North London
Kevan Scholes, Head of Department, Economics and Business Studies, Sheffield City Polytechnic
John Sellars, Chief Executive Business and Technician Education Council

March 1984

Martin Findlay, Joint Vice-Chairman, Whitbread & Company
Stephen O'Brien, Chief Executive, Business in the Community

May 1984

Dr Edwin Kerr, Chief Officer, Council for National Academic Awards
Dr Noel Thompson, Under-Secretary, Department of Education and Science

November 1984

Jim Wiltshire, Assistant Secretary, Manpower Services Commission
G. A. Williams, Assistant Education Officer (Secondary), TVEI
Diane Garrard, Assistant Chief Officer (Continuing Education), Business and Technician Education Council
Dr Penny Childs, Personnel Planning Officer, Legal & General Insurance Company
Dr R. G. Wallace, Hertfordshire Project for the Technical and Vocational Education Initiative

January 1985

Ray Hall, Co-ordinator, Evening Degree Courses, Polytechnic of North London
John Buckle, Principal Lecturer, Sheffield City Polytechnic
Sue Proudfoot, Head of Division of Business Policy and Operational Management, Thames Polytechnic

March 1985

David Burns, Assistant Director for Academic Affairs, City of Birmingham Polytechnic
Brian Gay, Course Tutor for Part-Time Business Studies Degree, Bristol Polytechnic
Judith Hinman, Further and Higher Education Curriculum Development Project, Inner London Education Authority
Roger Mills, Director of the London Region, Open University
Harry Mitchell, Head of Recurrent Education Service, Newcastle upon Tyne Polytechnic
Edgar Wille, Head of Management Development, National Coal Board

May 1985

Peter Ashworth, Principal Lecturer in Psychology, Sheffield City Polytechnic
Richard Lewis, Assistant Chief Officer, Council for National Academic Awards
Professor Michael Romans, Head of School of Building & Surveying, Polytechnic of Central London

October 1985

Joe Collerton, Acting Assistant Director, Newcastle upon Tyne Polytechnic
Stephen McNair, Head of UDACE, National Institute of Adult Continuing Education
David Parkes, Director, Responsive College Programme, Further Education Staff College
Jim Wilson, Head of Department of Mechanical and Production Engineering, Stockport College of Technology

February 1986

Stephen Jones, Staff Inspector, Higher Education, Department of Education and Science
Derek Pollard, Registrar, Credit Accumulation Scheme, Council for National Academic Awards
John Stoddard, Principal, Sheffield City Polytechnic
Peter Knight, Director, City of Birmingham Polytechnic

April 1986

Dr Padraig MacDiarmada, Director, National Council for Educational Awards, Dublin
Denis McGrath, Research and Development, National Council for Educational Awards, Dublin

October 1986

George Burns, Education Advisory Officer, National Association for the Care and Resettlement of Offenders
A. G. Goddard, Co-ordinator, Continuing Education, Lancashire Polytechnic
Neil Moreland, Head of Curriculum Studies, Polytechnic of Wolverhampton
Anne Sofer, Education Spokesman, Social Democratic Party
Tom Meinhard, Meinhard Associates

December 1986

George Chadwick, Acting Dean, Continuing Education, North East London Polytechnic
John Nieto, Advisory Teacher, FHE Curriculum Development Project, Inner London Education Authority
Derek Portwood, Centre for Unemployment Studies, Polytechnic of Wolverhampton
Peter W. G. Wright, Chairman, Communications and Information Committee, Portsmouth Polytechnic

February 1987

Dr Arnold Goldman, Assistant Chief Officer, Council for National Academic Awards
Dr Elizabeth Gerver, Director, Scottish Institute for Adult Education
M. K. Harrison, Director, Polytechnic of Wolverhampton
Dr Christina Townsend, Director, Research, Education and Training, National Health Service Training Authority

September/October 1987

Mike Abramson, Co-ordinator of the Part-Time Combined Studies Programme, Lancashire Polytechnic

John Cooper, Head of Faculty of Computing and Information Technology, Polytechnic of Wolverhampton
Anne Hilton, Co-ordinator, Continuing Education, Essex Institute of Higher Education
John Storan, Professional Associate LET and Lecturer at Goldsmiths' College, University of London

November 1987

Dr K. Jeanette Anderson, Depute Principal, Napier Polytechnic of Edinburgh
Michèle Bailleux, Administrator, Learning From Experience Trust
W. Keith Davies, Youth Programmes Manager, IBM United Kingdom Ltd
John Martin, Director of Standards and Development, Pitmans Examinations Institute
Sue Otter, Project Director, Student Potential Programme, Unit for the Development of Adult Continuing Education.
Freda Tallantyre, Centre for Continuing Education, Newcastle upon Tyne Polytechnic

January 1988

Philip Barnard, Deputy Director, Docklands Skillnet
Gerald Dearden, Deputy Director, Learning From Experience Trust
David Robertson, Head of School of Continuing Education, Liverpool Polytechnic
Paul Sokoloff, Education Advisory Officer, Business and Technician Education Council

April 1988

Linda Butler, Principal Liaison on the Manpower Services Commission Training Access Points (TAP) programme
David Kelso, HM Inspector (Further and Higher Education), Scottish Education Department
Geoffrey Stanton, Chief Officer, Further Education Unit
Robert Graham Wilson, HM Inspector, Scottish Education Department

September 1988

Douglas Cotton, Principal, East Warwickshire College of Further Education

Barry Hobson, Senior Lecturer, Mechanical Engineering, Coventry Polytechnic

Clive Robertson, Principal Lecturer, Hotel and Catering Management, Oxford Polytechnic

Edgar Wilson, Principal Lecturer, Co-ordinator Combined Studies Degree, Crewe and Alsager College of Higher Education

January/February 1989

John Bale, Head of School of the Built Environment, Essex Institute of Higher Education

Martin Johnson, Development Officer (Adult Education & Training) Further Education Unit

Dr Ann Rumpus, Development Officer, Certificate in Continuing Education, Polytechnic of Central London

Liz Stopani, Co-ordinator, Continuing Professional Development, Education Development Group, Croydon College

September/October 1989

Peter Bates, Senior Lecturer, School of Computing and Information Technology, Polytechnic of Wolverhampton

Terry Jeeves, Access Services: Curriculum Development, Liverpool Polytechnic

Iain Marshall, Director of Work-Based Learning Projects, Napier Polytechnic of Edinburgh

Brian Robinson, Head, Centre for Polytechnic Access and Continuing Education, Trent Polytechnic

January/February 1990

Jeff Braham, Professional Associate, LET

Joyce Fogg, Educational Management Consultant

Jeannette Maddox, Director, Tower Hamlets Sixth Form Centre

Ceri Williams, Lecturer, Tower Hamlets College

April 1990

Rob Allen, Director of Education & Training Developments, Thames Polytechnic

Michael Field, Principal, Croydon College

Peter Harrison, Adviser for Curriculum Development in FE, County Hall, Hertford
Michael Sargent, Senior Inspector for Post-16 & Community Education, London Borough of Tower Hamlets

September 1990

Rob Brown, Director of Social Work Courses, Croydon College
Susan Lee, Assistant Education Officer, London Borough of Croydon
Len Moore, Dean of Continuing Education, Polytechnic of Wolverhampton

Notes and references

FOREWORD

1 *Curriculum Opportunity*, Norman Evans, FEU, 1983
2 Established by the Department of Education and Science in 1978 as a focal point for further education matters and as a centre which would make possible a more co-ordinated approach to further education curriculum development.
3 Formerly the Manpower Services Commission, later the Training Commission then the Training Agency – all of the Department of the Employment – and hereafter referred to by its initials, TEED.

CHAPTER 1

1 By then CAEL had become the Council for the Advancement of Experiential Learning and in 1985 became the Council for Adult and Experiential Learning.

CHAPTER 3

1 *A Curriculum Opportunity: a Map of Experiential Learning in Entry Requirements to Higher and Further Education Award Bearing Courses*, Norman Evans, FEU, May 1983.
2 *Access to Higher Education: Non-Standard Entry to CNAA First Degree and DipHE courses*, CNAA Development Services Publication 6, August 1984.
3 *Making Experience Count*, John Storan, The Learning From Experience Trust 1988, £1.75.
4 *Building Your Own Portfolio*, Anne Woodrow, FEU 1987.
5 *Exploiting Experience*, Norman Evans, FEU/PICKUP, November 1984.
6 *Two Urban Stories: the Development of APL in Newham Community College and Sheffield LEA*, LET, January 1991.
7 *Assessing Experiential Learning: a Review of Progress and Practice and Accompanying Case Studies in the Assessment of Prior Learning*, N.Evans, (for the FEU), Longman Resources Unit, 1987.
8 *Continuing Professional Development: A Learner-Centred Strategy*, Anna Garry and John Cowan, Heriot-Watt University, Edinburgh, FEU/PICKUP 1986.
9 *The Assessment of Prior Experiential Learning*, CNAA Development Services Publication No. 17, February 1988.

10 Appendix 1. List of Participants.
11 *Learning at work: Youth Trainees and Youth Trainers*, Jeff Braham and John Storan, LET, 1989.
12 *Learning While Earning: Learning Contracts for Employees*, Gerald Dearden, LET, 1989.
13 Unpaid Work: the developing potential for accreditation, Linda Butler, LET, 1991.

CHAPTER 4

1 *A Learner's Introduction to Building on your Experience*, John Buckle, LET, 1988

CHAPTER 6

1 *Assessing Experiential Learning: a Review of Progress and Practice and Accompanying Case Studies in the Assessment of Experiential Learning*, Norman Evans (for the FEU), Longman Resources Unit, 1987.

CHAPTER 7

1 These variables and guiding principles are based on extracts taken from Development Services Publication No 17, *The Assessment of Prior Experiential Learning*, Council for National Academic Awards, 1988.
2 *Learning While Earning: Learning Contracts for Employees*, Gerald Dearden, LET, 1989.

CHAPTER 11

1 *Forms of Intellectual and Ethical Development in the College Years*, W. G. Perry, Holt, Rinehart & Winston, New York, 1970.
2 *Women's Ways of Knowing*, Mary Field Belenky, Clinchy, Goldberger and Tarule, Basic Books Inc., USA, 1986.

Selected reading list

UK

Boud, D., Keogh, R. and Walker, D. (1985) *Reflection: Turning Experience into Learning*, London: Kogan Page.

Boud, D. and Griffin, V. (eds) (1987) *Effective Teaching and Mentoring*, London: Kogan Page.

Boydell, T. (1976) *Experiential Learning*, Manchester Monographs.

Burke, J. W. (ed.) (1989) *Competency Based Education and Training*, Basingstoke: Falmer Press.

Entwistle, N. (1983) *Learning and Teaching in Universities: the Challenge of the Part-time Student, Part-time First Degrees in Universities*, Conference Report, Goldsmiths' College, University of London.

Entwistle, N. and Ramsden, P. (1983) *Understanding Student Learning*, London: Croom Helm.

Evans, N. (1981) *The Knowledge Revolution*, Grant McIntyre.

Evans, N. (1982) 'The Evaluation of study service: what does the student learn?', in Goodlad, S. (ed.) *Study Served*, Windsor: NFER-Nelson for HE Foundation.

Evans, N. (1983) *Curriculum Opportunity: a Map of Experiential Learning in Entry Requirements to Higher and Further Education* further Education Award Bearing courses, Further Education Unit.

Evans, N. (1984) *Exploiting Experience*, Further Education Unit.

Evans, N. (1984) *Non-standard Entry*, Council for National Academic Awards.

Evans, N. (1985) *Post-Education Society: Recognising Adults as Learners*, London: Croom Helm.

Evans, N. (for the FEU) (1987) *Assessing Experiential Learning: a Review of Progress and Practice and Accompanying Case Studies in the Assessment of Prior Learning*, Harlow Longman Resources Unit.

Evans, N. (1988) *Assessment of Prior Experiential Learning*, CNAA Development Fund.

Hart, M. (ed) ( ) *Adult Education, Work and Everyday Experience*, London: Routledge.

Hartree, A. and Marum, M. (1985) *Valuing Your Experience: a Tutor's Handbook*, Hillcroft College/MSC.

Marsick, V. (ed.) (1987) *Learning in the Workplace*, London: Croom Helm.

Rogers, C. (1983) *Freedom to Learn for the 80s*, Weston, Ontario: Merrill.

Usher, R.S. (1986) 'Adult students and their experience', *Studies in the Education of Adults*, 18 (1).

Weil, S. and McGill, I. (eds) (1989) *Making Sense of Experiential Learning*, Oxford: OU Press.
Winter, R. (1989) *Learning From Experience, Principles and Practice in Action-research*, Falmer Press.

Forthcoming publications

Griffin, C., *An Introduction to Experiential Learning: Issues and Theories*, London: Routledge.

Learning From Experience Trust Publications

Braham, J. and Storan, J. (1989) *Learning at Work: Youth Trainees and Youth Trainers*.
Buckle, J. (1988) *A Learner's Introduction to Building on your Experience*.
Dearden, G. (1989) *Learning While Earning: Learning Contracts for Employees*
Evans, N. (1989) *The Assessment of Prior Experiential Learning and Higher Education, Some Issues: Some Anglo-American Comparisons*.
Gorringe R., in association with County of Avon Education Department (1987) *Handbook for the Assessment of Experiential Learning*.
Gorringe, R., in association with County of Avon Education Department (1987) *Resource Materials for Assessing Experiential Learning*.
Griffin, C. (ed.) (1988) *Report of the LET Conference: Assessing Prior Learning: Progress and Practices*.
Storan, J. (1988) *Making Experience Count*.
Challu, M., Edwards, P., McKelvey C. and Wilson, P. Two Urban Stories: the development of APL in Newham College and Sheffield LEA LET 1991
LET publications can be ordered from:
LET Publications The Learning From Experience Trust, 6 Buckingham Gate, London, Tel: 071-630 0733

USA

Chickering, A. (1977) *Experience and Learning: an Introduction to Experiential Learning*, Change.
Chickering, A. and associates (1981) *The Modern American College*, San Franciso: Jossey-Bass.
Daloz, L.A. (1976) *Effective Teaching and Mentoring*, San Francisco: Jossey-Bass.
Keeton, M. (1976) *Experiential Learning: Characteristics and Assessment*, San Franciso: Jossey-Bass.
Knowles, M. (1987) *Using Learning Contracts*, San Franciso: Jossey-Bass.
Kolb, D. (1984) *Experiential Learning*, Prentice Hall.
Lewis, L.H. (ed.) (1986) *Experiential and Simulation Techniques for Adults*, San Francisco: Jossey-Bass.
Ryder, K.G., J. Wilson, *et al.* Co-operative Education in a New Era, San Francisco: Jossey-Bass.
Schon, D.A. (1983) *The Reflective Practitioner*, New York: Basic Books
Schon, D.A. (1987) *Education the Reflective Practitioner*, San Francisco: Jossey-

Bass.

Council for Adult and Experiential Learning publications

Keeton, M. and Tate, P. (eds) (1978–84) *New Directions in Experiential Learning:*
  No. 1: 'Learning by experience - what, why, how'.
  No. 2: 'Enriching the liberal arts through experiential learning'.
  No. 10: 'Building new alliances: labor unions and higher education'.
  No. 13: 'Business and higher education: towards new alliances'.
  No. 16: 'Building on experiences in adult development'.
Knapp, J. and Sharon, A.T. (1975) *A Compendium of Assessment Techniques.*
Mandel, A. and Michelson, E. (1990) *Portfolio Development and Adult Learning: Purposes and Strategies.*
Simosko, S. (1985) *Earn College Credit for What You Know* (Student Guide), (under revision for reissue by Lois Lamdin).
Whitaker, U. (1989) *Principles of Good Practice in Assessing Experiential Learning.*
CAEL publications can be ordered from:
CAEL publications, 223 West Jackson, Suite 510, Chicago, Illinois 60606, USA, Tel: 312 922 5909
(All these are valuable for insights into different aspects of the assessment of experiential learning, but all are written by Americans for the American context.)

Index

access courses 19,67, 102–96
Access to Higher Education 16
accreditation 62, 66–71, 124–141
adults, *see* older learners
Advisory Council for Adult and
    Continuing Education 37
Alverno College 137
Amarc 149
Anderson, Jeannette 28
'APEL in the Context of Student
    Services' 44
Assessing Experiential Learning 23, 24
assessment 48–50, 66–71, 76, 81–2, 124
assessment of prior experiential
    learning (APEL): and adult
    education 32, 46; and higher
    education 15, 31, 46, 72–102; and
    further education 15, 20, 31,
    103–115, 142; and youth training
    46–7, 112–14; and management
    education 98–9; introduction of to
    UK 9–45; gains national seal of
    approval 38; and progression 40, 62,
    109; and organisational change 42;
    and student fear of failure 32; and
    staff development 48, 94; and
    participation rates 202; and
    admission for advanced standing 19,
    38, 77–8, 85–9; and modular course
    provision 90–2; benefits of to
    teachers 120; self-assessment
    69–71, 79–80, 94, 168; role of
    government in 189–96; need for
    'learning overlord' for 201; in
    British Columbia 176–8; *see also*
    accreditation, assessment, credit

accumulation, Credit Accumulation
    and Transfer Service, portfolios
Assessment of Prior Experiential
    Learning, The 25
Atlantic Richfield 28
Austin, Dr Rita 16,17
Avon Education Authority 20, 21

Bailleux, Michèle 40, 45
Barclays Bank 160
Bell Telephone Co./Communication
    Workers of America scheme 183
Binks, Ned 12, 13
Birkbeck College 37
Birmingham Polytechnic 35
Bosanquet, David 39
Bourne, Richard 23
Braham, Jeffrey 44
Brewer, Malcolm 12, 13

Chemical Industries Association 107
Citizens' Advice Bureaux 159, 160,
    166, 187
City and Guilds 62, 101 107, 108, 109,
    142, 202
Clark, Thomas 31, 34, 35
Cockerell, Janet 12, 13
Coldstream, Patrick 39
College of Public and Community
    Service 6, 7, 35, 131
College of Ripon and York St John 12
Commission for Racial Equality (CRE)
    18, 21; reflections on failure of CRE
    projects 51–2
Community Service Volunteers 31
competences, and NCVQ, 108, 125–6,

128; in American higher education 131–41

Confederation of British Industry 65, 198

Constable, John 98

Construction Industry Training Board 107

continuing professional development 99

Continuing Professional Development: A Learner-centred Strategy 23

'Co-operative Assessment of Experiential Learning, The' 4

Council for the Advancement of Experiential Learning (CAEL) 4, 6, 9, 10, 11, 17, 27, 28, 33, 37, 53, 182

Council for Management Education 99–102

Council for National Academic Awards (CNAA) 5, 16, 22, 24, 25, 35, 36, 102, 203

Cowan, Professor John 23

Cox, Edwin 12

Craft, William 35

credit accumulation 62, 109, 124, see also CATS

Credit Accumulation and Transfer Scheme (CATS) 35, 36, 38, 62, 74–75, 95, 166, 170, 176, 178, 197

Cronin, Jenny 20

Curriculum Opportunity A Map of Experiential Learning, 15, 21, 22, 24, 25, 36

Curriculum for Personal and Vocational Education 146, 149

curriculum intelligence unit, proposals for 172–7

Davies, Alun 20, 21 27

Davies, Keith 28

Dearden, Gerald 25, 44, 45

Delaware Community College 7

demographic changes 63, 64, 88, 94, 110, 113, 146, 154, 178

Department of Education and Science 4, 5, 63, 64, 180, 201

Department of Employment 201

Department of Health 201

Department of Social Security 201

Department of Trade and Industry 180, 201

Thomas Edison State College 7

East Ham Further Education College 22

Eccles White Papers on technical education 146

Education Beyond School 14, 24

Education Act 1944, 46

Education Reform Act 1988, 9, 64, 110, 144, 172, 199, 202

Educational Counselling and Credit Transfer Information Service (ECCTIS) 22, 166, 168, 178

Educational Guidance and Assistance Service 166

Edwards, Paul 22

Electrical, Electronic and Plumbing Trades Union 160

Eley, Ginnie 27

Elser, Dr Arlon 7, 9, 10

employers 51, 65, 178, 199; benefits of APEL for 93–8

Employment Training (ET) 106

'Encore' program 7

Engineering Council 100

Engineering Industry Training Board 107

Enterprise Initiative 142

Exeter University 17

Experienced Manager, The 99

experiential learning: definition *vii;* sponsored 11; unsponsored 11; *see also* APEL, Experiential Learning Network

Experiential Learning 152

Experiential Learning Network 31, 33, 34, 39

Exploiting Experience 21, 22

Ezra, Derek 24

Findlay, Martin 28

fieldwork experience 16–17; see also sandwich courses

Ford Motor Company/United Automobile Workers' College and University Options Program 27, 182–3

Ford UK Employee Development and Assistance Programme 45, 184, 200

Forms of Intellectual and Ethical Development in the College Years 155

Fowler, Gerry 22
Fullemploy 149
further education 15, 20, 31; and APEL
    103–115; and need for national
    validating body 203
Further Education Unit (FEU) 12, 20,
    21, 34, 55, 106

General Motors/UAW scheme 183
Glaxo 44
Goldsmith's College 12, 18, 23, 39, 44,
    114, 156
Goodlad, Sinclair 12
Gorringe, Richard 20, 23, 27, 33
Great Lakes Colleges Association 28,
    193
Griffin, Colin 12, 13
Groombridge, Brian 14
La Guardia Community College 7

Hackney College 21, 23, 24
Hall, Ray 26
Hammersmith College 21
Harrison, Roy 24
Hendry, Tony 18, 27
Henebery, Corinne 45
Heriot-Watt University 23
higher education 15, 31; and APEL
    72–102; and part-time study 90; and
    quality assurance 101–2; students
    who fail to complete 161; transfer
    between institutions 62
Hillcroft College 12, 13, 23, 24, 167
Hinman, Judith 27
Hoggart, Richard 12, 17, 18, 36
Hotel and Catering Training Board 107
Hotel Catering and Institutional
    Management Association 101
Hull Polytechnic 173
human resource development 189

IBA 44
IBM 28, 44, 93, 160
ICL 44
Industrial Society 161
internships 11
Inner London Education Authority
    (ILEA) 20, 21, 27

Jackson, John Hampden 3
Jacques, Frank 3
Jaguar Cars Ltd 44, 95 160
James Report 5
Job Training Scheme for Unemployed
    Adults 64, 106
Joint Matriculation Examination Board
    for the North of England 16
Joint Venture Programs 27, 182–3
Joseph Rowntree Memorial Trust 40,
    113

Keene State College 3
Keeton, Morris *viii,* 7, 9, 10, 12, 35
Kellogg Foundation 6, 7, 8, 12, 13, 14,
    17, 22, 24, 25, 26, 36, 43
Kerr, Dr Edwin 9, 16, 37, 38, 39
Knowledge Revolution, The 14, 15, 23,
    24
Kolb, David 152

learner-centred finance 198
learning cycle 152–4
learning contracts 31, 95–7
learning outcomes 125
'Learning Contracts for Employees' 43,
    44, 95, 99
Learning from Experience Trust 33–6,
    39–45; creation of 33–6; first
    statement of aims 41–2; early focus
    on older learners 42
Leeds Polytechnic 97
Leeds University 13
Legal and General 51
Linn, Pamela 18, 27
local financial management of colleges
    64, 110, 172

'Making Experience Count' (MEC) 18,
    19, 20, 21, 23, 156–7, 167, 169
Making of Managers, The (Handy
    Report) 98
Making of British Managers, The 98
management education and APEL 98–9
Manchester Open College Federation
    107, 111
Mansell, Jack 12, 14, 15, 18, 21, 23
manuals project, reflections on failure
    of 51–2
Marks and Spencer 160

Materials and Resources Information Services (MARIS) 166–7, 168
mathematics and science in HE project 45; reflections on failure of 51, 54–5
McCormack, Roger 98
Middlesex Polytechnic 23, 24, 26, 30
Morley College 21

Nabisco 147
Napier Polytechnic 28, 93
National Advisory Board for Local Government Higher Education 38
National Advisory Centre on Careers for Women 166
National Coal Board 24, 25, 35, 92, 99
National Council for Vocational Qualifications (NCVQ) 45, 47, 50, 55, 63, 99, 103, 107, 108, 109, 110, 111, 125, 128, 141, 168, 178, 187, 197, 203
National Council for Voluntary Organisations 160
National Economic Development Office 98
National Examinations Board for Agriculture, Horticulture and Allied Industries 107
National Extension College 176, 178
National Federation of Women's Institutes 160, 187
National Institute of Adult and Continuing Education 106, 166
National Nursery Examination Board 19
National Trust 159, 160
National Union of Students 166
National Vocational Competences 111; *see also* competences
National Vocational Qualifications (NVQ) 45, 109, 111, 124, 128, 131, 187, 188, 192, 203
Newcastle upon Tyne Polytechnic 25, 44, 173
Newcastle upon Tyne University 74
Newsom Report 146, 149
New York Times 147
New Training Initiative 34
North East London Polytechnic 22, 26, 27
North London Polytechnic 26, 37, 173

Nottingham University 4

O'Brien, Sir Richard 39
O'Brien, Stephen 39
Office of Personnel Management (US) 183
older learners 63, 88, 110, 152–61
'Off-Campus Experiential Learning Programs' 139
open college federations 106, 203; and APEL 50; Manchester Open College Federation 107, 110; Open College 176, 178; Open College of the Arts 176; Open College of the South Bank 20; Sheffield Open College 107; South Yorkshire Open College 111
Open Poly 177
Open Tech 55, 176
Open University 16, 37, 74, 95, 97, 176, 178
'Opportunities for Further Education and Higher Education arising from the EDAP (Ford UK) Programme' 45; *see also* Ford UK

Parker, Sir Peter 24
part-time study in higher education 90
Perry, William 155
Philadelphia Museum of Art 193
Philadelphia Urban Center Program 28
Philadelphia Magazine 193
Pinder, John 39
Pitmans Institute 107, 108, 109, 142
Policy Studies Institute 9, 12, 13, 15, 20, 26, 31, 33, 39, 45
portfolios 10, 18, 19, 21, 31, 70, 86, 94, 103–6; Portfolio Preparation Workshop 104–5
Portsmouth Polytechnic 173
post-experience courses 4
Preliminary Evaluation of the In-Service B.Ed., The 4, 5, 7
Proctor and Gamble 147
Professional and Industrial Commercial Improvement (PICKUP) 99
progression 40, 62, 109
Provident National Bank 193
Prudential Bache Securities 193
Public Sector Funding Council 144
Regent's College 40

Relate 160
REPLAN 106
'Returning to Learning Workshop for Federal Employees' 183
Rockland Community College 31, 34, 35
Ricketts, Ray 36, 37
Rover Group 179–81; Award for Quality in Work Experience 180–1, 185
Royal College of General Practitioners, membership examination 100
Royal Institute of British Architects 101
Royal Society of Arts 62, 107, 108, 109, 142, 187, 202
Ruffitt, Freddie 9
Rutherford, Andrew 39

Sainsbury plc, J., 44, 97
Sainsbury Trusts 27
sandwich courses 28, 66–7, 91–3, 116–17
Scholar Exchange Program 25–31, 35, 36, 43; *see also* study tours
Scott Paper Co. 28, 163
Scottish Education Department 28, 93
Scottish Institute of Adult Education 23
Scottish Vocational Educational Council 23
'Senior Secretaries into Management ' 45
Sheffield City Polytechnic 12, 17, 23, 24, 25, 26, 35, 92, 97, 173
Sheffield Open College 107
Sheffield University 173
Singer, Norbert 18, 22, 37
'Skills Assessment and Vocational Guidance for Unemployed People' 20, 106
Smith, Peter 6
Smith, Vernon 23
South East England Association of Colleges 37
South Yorkshire Open College 111
sponsored experiential learning 10
Storan, John 44
Strange, John 6, 7, 35
student services, proposals for 166–76, 186
study tours 17, 25–31; and staff

development 30; for employers, failure of 27–8; *see also* Scholar Exchange Program

Tate, Pamela 9, 10, 35
Technical and Vocational Education Initiative 144, 146, 149, 151
Tesco 160
Thames Polytechnic 18, 22, 23, 26, 27, 97, 101, 173
3M 185
Times, The 15
Titmus, Colin 12, 13
'To explore the accreditation of Prior Learning (APEL)' 109–10
'To explore the potential of APEL in Universities' 45
Tolley, Dr George 12, 24, 55
Toyne, Peter 17, 22
Training Access Points (TAP) 166, 168, 178
Training Education and Enterprise Department (TEED, formerly MSC, TC, TA) 17, 34, 43, 44, 45, 64, 92, 95, 97, 98, 99, 109, 111, 114, 126; booklet on standards of performance for administration, business and commercial staff 126–8
Training Enterprise Councils 110–11, 177
transfer between higher education institutions 62
'Transitions: a study of possible access to further study for ethnic minorities' 18, 21
Turner, Anthony 24
2+2+2 program 147

Unit for the Development of Adult and Continuing Education 165
United Food and Commercial Workers 183
Universities Funding Council 144, 172
University Grants Committee 38

'Validation of Companies' In-House Provision, The' 45
Vauxhall College 21, 23, 24
Vermont Community College 6, 7
voluntary organisations 187–8

Wates Foundation 17, 20, 21, 43
Wellcome Foundation 51
West Ham Further Education College 22
Whitbread 28
Whiteley, Frank 39
Wolverhampton Polytechnic 98, 173
Workers Educational Association 3, 32, 160
Williams, Shirley 9, 22, 39, 40
Willie, Edgar 24
Wiltshire, Jim 34, 35
Wimpy Foods International 95
women 63, 154–8; returners 32; and NCVQ project 45; and open college federations 50
Womens Ways of Knowing 156–7

Woodrow, Anne 20
Woolwich Equitable Building Society 44, 97
work experience 148

Xerox 147, 185

Young, Michael 176
Youth Access 114
Youth Opportunities Programme 148
youth training and APEL 46–7, 112–14
Youth Training Scheme (YTS) 43, 44, 64, 112, 148, 195
YTS into Higher Education Project 44, 113; reflections on failure of project 51, 53–4